NGO Accountability

NGO Accountability

Politics, Principles and Innovations

Edited by Lisa Jordan and Peter van Tuijl

London • Sterling, VA

First published by Earthscan in the UK and USA in 2006
Reprinted 2007

Copyright © Lisa Jordan and Peter van Tuijl, 2006

ISBN: 978-1-84407-367-2 paperback
ISBN: 978-1-84407-368-9 hardback

Typeset by MapSet Ltd, Gateshead, UK
Printed and bound in the UK by TJ International, Padstow, Cornwall
Cover design by Susanne Harris

For a full list of publications please contact:

Earthscan
8–12 Camden High Street
London, NW1 0JH, UK
Tel: +44 (0)20 7387 8558
Fax: +44 (0)20 7387 8998
Email: earthinfo@earthscan.co.uk
Web: www.earthscan.co.uk

22883 Quicksilver Drive, Sterling, VA 20166-2012, USA

Earthscan is an imprint of James and James (Science Publishers) Ltd and publishes in
association with the International Institute for Environment and Development

A catalogue record for this book is available from the British Library

Library of Congress Cataloging-in-Publication Data:
NGO accountability : politics, principles, and innovations / edited by Lisa Jordan and
Peter van Tuijl.
    p. cm.
Includes bibliographical references.
ISBN-13: 978-1-84407-367-2 (pbk.)
ISBN-10: 1-84407-367-X (pbk.)
ISBN-13: 978-1-84407-368-9 (hardback)
ISBN-10: 1-84407-368-8 (hardback)
1. Non-governmental organizations. I. Jordan, Lisa, 1964- II. Tuijl, Peter van.
JZ4841.N34 2006
352.106—dc22

2006013772

The paper used for this book is FSC-certified and totally
chlorine-free. FSC (the Forest Stewardship Council) is an
international network to promote responsible management
of the world's forests.

Mixed Sources
Product group from well-managed
forests and other controlled sources
www.fsc.org Cert no. SGS-COC-2482
© 1996 Forest Stewardship Council

Contents

SECTION I – KEY QUESTIONS AND CONCEPTS IN THE CURRENT GLOBAL DEBATE

SECTION II – TRADITIONAL APPROACHES: LEGAL ACCOUNTABILITY, CERTIFICATION AND DONOR REGIMES

SECTION III – THE BENEFITS OF EMBRACING ACCOUNTABILITY

SECTION IV – INNOVATIONS: EXPANDING THE ACCOUNTABILITY FRONTIER

Foreword

When the first systematic writings on NGO (non-governmental organization) accountability became available in the mid-1990s, NGOs still occupied a relative backwater in politics, international affairs and academic research. Ten years on, both NGOs in general and the accountability question in particular have moved to centre stage, for some good reasons and some not so good, and this book represents the new cutting edge of thinking and practice in this increasingly important and contentious arena.

Commendably, the editors of this volume have made no attempt to enforce a consensus on the contributors, who disagree with each other on definitions, approaches and priorities, and especially on the degree of external (government or supragovernmental) regulation that may be appropriate for the NGO sector. Context is vital, and there are no universal answers to the dilemmas of NGO accountability, or even universally applicable standards and methodologies. Protecting sufficient 'safe space' for innovation, iteration and experimentation is therefore essential, a theme to which I will return in a moment.

The contributors do agree, however, that accountability is as important among NGOs as among any other set of institutions (no one here suggests that NGOs can 'rest on their laurels' because governments or businesses may be even less accountable than they are), and that effective accountability mechanisms always need to balance 'rights with responsibilities'. In other words, the space for independent citizen action must be protected in exchange for compliance with regulations that ensure that NGOs genuinely operate in the public interest. If the 'public interest' is too vague and amorphous a concept to be useful in any operational sense, then at least one can ensure that activities that are claimed to be charitable in nature are openly disclosed and accessible for public questioning. The opportunities to know what an organization does and to ask questions as a result are surely the bedrock of accountability.

Although this may sound like a perfectly reasonable equation, it turns out to be much more complex, controversial and politicized than was anticipated ten years ago in the first wave of writing about NGO accountability. This is partly because NGOs have their own equivalents to 'market sensitive information' among businesses and security concerns among governments – information, in other words, that may cause significant damage if released into the public arena at the wrong time, or at all (see Majot, Chapter 13). More importantly, NGOs today operate in a different, and often more hostile, political environment than was true for the 1990s, despite continuing high levels of public trust and government funding. This largely applies to NGOs in their roles as advocates and watchdogs – their role in the 'polity' as opposed to 'politics,' formally defined as the world of political parties and the struggle for control of the state. This is especially true in authoritarian regimes, but post-September 11th it can be an issue even in relatively open democracies like the United States. Concerns about the politics of NGO accountability turn out to be the most engaging theme of this book. Why is this?

In 1995, the first key text on NGO accountability concluded that:

> *the developmental impact of NGOs, their capacity to attract support, and their legitimacy as actors in development, will rest much more clearly on their ability to demonstrate that they can perform effectively and are accountable for their actions. It is none too soon for NGOs to put their house in order.* (Edwards and Hulme, 1995)

In the intervening years there have been some important innovations in this respect, many of which are documented in this book. In retrospect, however, NGOs did not heed this call with sufficient attention and are now suffering from it in a climate in which, unlike ten years ago, weaknesses in NGO accountability are being used as cover for political attacks against voices that certain interests wish to silence. NGO accountability has become a 'wedge issue' that appears uncontestable across different constituencies on the surface but disguises deep and often undeclared divisions of interest beneath. Examples of such attacks include the NGO Watch project at the American Enterprise Institute, the Rushford Report in Washington DC and the NGO Monitor in Jerusalem, all of which single out liberal or progressive groups for criticism while ignoring the same problems, if that is what they are, among NGOs allied with conservative views. It is no accident that hostility to NGO involvement in global governance forms a key element of neoconservative thinking in the US. Stronger NGO accountability mechanisms won't do away with politically motivated attacks like these, but they would surely help to expose them for what they are. Nevertheless, in such politicized climates, deeper innovations in NGO accountability may be more difficult to achieve because the results – gained through increasing openness to public scrutiny – may be used to destroy the organization or close off its access to influence and resources, rather than as an incentive to improve its performance.

The contributors to this book all struggle with the question of how to balance NGO rights and responsibilities in political climates like these, some of the climates being more openly authoritarian than others. The rights and responsibilities framework does seem to be useful across these different contexts, leaving lots of space for innovation according to the characteristics of different organizations, different types of NGO activity, and different times, cultures and places. Of particular importance is the recognition, made most strongly by Enrique Peruzzotti, that representation is only one of many routes to legitimacy, and for most NGOs not the most relevant one (unless, of course, they claim it for themselves). It is high time that this particular 'bugbear' was laid to rest. NGOs do not have to be representative to be legitimate, but they do have to be accountable for their actions, whatever they are, if their claims to legitimacy are to be sustained. This conclusion places the focus of the debate back where it belongs – on the costs and benefits of different, concrete approaches to accountability – and not on abstract criticisms about NGOs that supposedly compete with governments as representatives of the electorate, a goal that no NGO, to my knowledge, has subscribed to.

Accountability is the price to be paid (if price it is) for the freedom to exercise power and authority in a democratic society. NGO power may be 'soft' and NGOs' authority informal, but the principle remains the same. Most NGOs have accepted this conclusion, but the record of concrete innovation in NGO accountability remains patchy and shallow. It is difficult, and probably dangerous, to legislate for innovation at either national or international level, but it should be possible to encourage and reward good practice through additional funding, extra publicity and media coverage (good and bad), as well as through peer pressure – the 'market-driven improvements' recommended by Steve Charnowitz in this book. What one might call the 'first generation' of NGO accountability reforms reviewed here – such as the Philippines Council for NGO Certification and Uganda's NGO Law – are understandably showing some of the signs of their age and now require a further and deeper round of iteration. ActionAid's accountability system is a good example of a 'second generation' reform that builds on these earlier experiences, but goes much further. By analysing and disseminating such second generation reforms, this book should provide a much needed shot in the arm for the NGO community and for all those who see accountability as a platform to fulfil their mission to serve others more effectively.

Michael Edwards
New York
March 2006

Acknowledgements

The need for this book was first identified in a workshop on NGO accountability in January 2003, in Bandung, Indonesia. The workshop was hosted by Sawarung, a local NGO. Sawarung was one of the few Indonesian NGOs to have developed an explicit accountability mechanism tied to citizens in Bandung, as it had realized that in order for a citizens' group to hold local officials accountable, it had to be able to demonstrate the underpinnings of democratic practice.

Participants in the Bandung workshop discussed the purpose and origins of NGO accountability, effectiveness and performance, as one would expect, but also addressed the moral ground for accountability, trust, credibility and relations with other civic partners. The role of NGOs in empowering civil society, creating a public sphere and deepening democracy were important questions that were raised but not answered in this first workshop. While an analysis of the Bandung workshop was published (Jordan, 2005), one of the suggestions from the workshop was to develop a book on some of the deeper political questions surrounding NGO accountability. In the course of the next 18 months several papers from the Bandung workshop were elaborated, while others were newly commissioned.

In June 2004, an author workshop took place in The Hague, The Netherlands, convened by Hivos and hosted at the International Institute of Social Studies (ISS). A dozen draft chapters were jointly reviewed. Participants developed an improved framework for the book and insisted on the inclusion of two additional chapters relating to the role of donors as a dominant stakeholder in determining NGO accountability, as well as a chapter on the relationship between NGOs and local community-based organizations (CBOs) in transnational advocacy campaigns. After the Hivos/ISS workshop, several additional authors were identified and the book gradually obtained its final composition.

A Chinese version of Chapter 8 by Professor Kang has been published in *Ershiyi Shiji (Twenty-first Century)*, December 2004 (pp62–73), a journal published by the Chinese University of Hong Kong. Traces of an earlier paper by Rustam Ibrahim commissioned by the Asia Pacific Philanthropic Consortium (APPC) can be found in Chapter 9. We thank the APPC for its permission to publish. None of the other chapters have been published elsewhere. The co-editors are solely responsible for the contents of this book, which by no means represent any official viewpoint of either the Ford Foundation or the U.S. Government.

The elaborate process of the development of this book has involved many people along the way. We would like to thank, in particular: the staff of Sawarung; Hivos; ISS; Fundación Acceso; and the Ford Foundation, including Channapha Khamvongsa. The cooperation with all authors has been outstanding. We are grateful to Jan Aart Scholte, Hans Antlöv and Michael Edwards for reviewing draft articles and to Mia Serban for helping us out with the proofreading. Above all, we thank our respective families for their continued support and encouragement to undertake this endeavour.

Lisa Jordan and Peter van Tuijl
New York and Jakarta
March 2006

Section I

KEY QUESTIONS AND CONCEPTS IN THE CURRENT GLOBAL DEBATE

Rights and Responsibilities in the Political Landscape of NGO Accountability: Introduction and Overview

Lisa Jordan and Peter van Tuijl

INTRODUCTION

In the final decade of the 20th century, there seemed to be a broad-based consensus that non-governmental organizations (NGOs) were a good thing – as shepherds of development, as democratic agents and in making sense of globalization. NGOs were seen as the core of active civil societies, supporting the delivery of public services and contributing to an ever-stronger wave of democratization that appeared unstoppable after the fall of the Berlin Wall in 1989. However, since 2001, there has been a prolific attempt to build a case against NGOs suggesting that they are undermining national sovereignty and democracy, and have no relationship to any real public. As NGOs increasingly exercise their voice in public policy debates, and assert a pivotal role in defining both the problems (global warming) and the solutions (global treaty), the demand for NGO accountability is growing.

The bottom line in the discussion on NGO accountability is represented by the questions: what roles are valid for NGOs to play?; which responsibilities should be clearly articulated as part of these roles?; and to whom should NGOs be accountable? Related questions are where and how NGOs fit in structures of governance locally, nationally and internationally. The public, the media, academia and politicians have all begun to question who has entitled NGOs to assert such visible and apparently influential roles in different political arenas. One of the most succinct and powerful expressions levied against NGOs is 'who do you represent?'.

Unfortunately, these questions and the suspicion of NGOs are supported by people whose political views or interests are threatened by particular NGOs or the rise of NGOs as a political force. They are leading what has become an attack on the public policy advocacy roles played by NGOs. Borrowing from the handbook of NGO activists, NGOs themselves are now subject to watch-dogs and efforts to discredit the legitimacy of both their organization and their message.[1]

It would be a mistake, however, to disregard the current attack on NGOs as incited by political motives only. Accountability questions are on the rise for three reasons: rapid growth in numbers and size of NGOs, attraction of more funds, and a stronger voice in shaping public policy. NGOs may be the fastest growing form of civic association worldwide. All the growth in the sector has not been healthy. For example, many government officials establish NGOs alongside public office in order to receive public funds. There is the phenomenon of suitcase NGOs, which are made up of one person who travels from conference to conference. These unhealthy aspects of growth have attracted calls for accountability.

The growing NGO sector has attracted massive amounts of funding. Some Western NGOs have budgets that dwarf those of UN Agencies. Since the early 1980s, an important part of liberalization has been the privatization of services. NGOs have been the darling of social service delivery, preferred by donors over state entities. The attraction of more and more funds has also prompted calls for accountability mechanisms.

Working in greater numbers and benefiting from a larger resource base, NGOs have sought to shape public policy, especially within, but not limited to, the global political arena. NGOs are widely perceived to have set many of the global public policy agendas over the past ten years, including issues like unsustainable debt, environmental degradation, human rights law, landmine removal and corporate social responsibility. The more vocal NGOs become in articulating policy issues, the louder the call for their accountability from those concerned about the rising power of NGOs in setting the global public policy agenda and influencing the shape of markets (Manheim, 2003).

There are a number of real and important accountabilities to be addressed by NGOs, which stem from their responsibilities. NGO responsibilities can be categorized roughly in three ways. First, there are organizational responsibili-ties, which include transparency in decision-making and accounting, efficiency of operations and working within legal confines in a transparent manner. The latter responsibility, however, assumes universal rights are respected in the context within which an NGO operates. Second, there are responsibilities embedded in the mission of an NGO, such as promoting rights for the poor, the alleviation of hunger, children's rights, or saving the environment. Third, there is a category of responsibilities to different stakeholders that are impacted by or involved in the activities of NGOs.

The purpose of this book is to place the question of NGO accountability into the political framework from which it has arisen, a framework that is almost always missing in the technical discussions regarding certification, self-regulation and other operational accountability mechanisms. With this book, we argue that the response to these accountability questions depends on various considerations, foremost the political context in which NGOs operate, but also the particular mission of the organization and the demands of different stakeholders. Expanding on the first point, an NGO will be in a much better position to address accountability demands in an environment that is free, democratic and conducive to civic action, as opposed to a situation in which an authoritarian regime is repressing the basic freedoms of association, assembly and expression. Similarly, myriad issues arise around an NGO's responsibility when it operates in an environment where democratic institutions and practices are not fully formed. NGO accountability thus inevitably leads to discussing issues of human rights and democracy, not merely from a conceptual perspective, but as a basic human condition that either allows or prohibits individuals from associating with each other to promote their legitimate interests.

This book treats NGO accountability as an issue of plurality based on the need to apply common principles and universal rights in different contexts, as opposed to being an issue of common standards, tool-box techniques or mechanisms that can be applied universally. We do not believe that there are NGO accountability 'best practices' for sale.

Developing appropriate accountability mechanisms is a rather messy and lengthy process, as demonstrated by many chapters in this book. A discourse on accountability has been lacking among NGOs, perhaps out of a defensive reflex towards immediate political threats and addressing immediate needs, but also because seriously engaging accountability is expensive for almost any type of organization. Who has the time and the resources to start an in-depth participatory process to truly investigate the needs of key stakeholders, sort and rank them, and change the policies and the structures of the organization accordingly? Where is the incentive to do that? However, driven by both positive and negative imperatives and mixing organizational development with institutional survival and self-interests, NGOs are increasingly engaging accountability issues. Even though most NGO efforts to address accountability have emerged just in the last decade, they have begun to consolidate, within individual organizations and across national, global and regional networks. An additional aim of this book is to present these innovations in NGO accountability.

Our ultimate goal is to help NGO practitioners further develop the panorama of NGO accountability.

THE THREE Rs – RIGHTS, RISKS AND RESPONSIBILITIES

In response to the increasing calls for NGO accountability, standard accountability mechanisms have risen in abundance over the past ten years, such as certification-and-rating systems, developing infrastructure and management capacity and establishing codes of conduct. These accountability mechanisms often focus on the relationship between donors and NGOs, or governments and NGOs (Ebrahim, 2003). They can be helpful in upholding standards in particular fields, but they do not address the rights and responsibilities of NGOs. The discussion on accountability of NGOs rarely links responsibilities with the rights to associate freely, assemble and articulate a voice. The failure to review the question of NGO accountability within the framework of NGO rights and responsibilities has led to narrow technical solutions that often do not reflect the mission or values of an NGO or the multiple important relationships in which they are engaged.

NGOs have tested the boundaries of political systems by assuming a number of civic rights, especially in authoritarian regimes and emerging democracies. These include the right to a voice on policy decisions, the right to participate in political discourse, the right to mobilize and serve a public, the right to organize and the right to monitor and comment on the governance process. Such embodiment of rights has allowed NGOs to play a number of roles. Many have developed a voice to influence public policy, while others have missions to define, protect and defend the public good. Some monitor government performance with an eye to enhance it either through constructive critical engagement or by aiding social service delivery. NGOs also challenge majority populations by defining and defending minority rights or other groups that cannot speak for themselves. The universal freedoms of association, assembly and expression are essential rights for NGOs to provide public services, but, in particular, to allow them to inform public policy effectively.

Governments and multinational authorities welcome some of these roles, but find other activities of NGOs to be of concern, especially those which pertain to monitoring, commenting on or otherwise attempting to influence the market, political processes or the government and its authorities in day-to-day operations.

The more NGOs are contesting the status quo, the higher the risk that they will suffer from a violation of their fundamental rights. Violations are most commonly conducted by governments who are exercising their control over the political process and try to limit NGO rights beyond what is acceptable under international standards. NGO rights can be violated by other forces as well, such as inter-governmental organizations or corporate entities. Ironically, by now, there is a vast literature on how to promote an 'enabling environment' for NGOs and civic engagement.[2] However, in quite a lot of situations authorities are actively trying to disable such an environment.

The risks for NGOs involved in advocating public policies are varied and always depend on particular circumstances related to a specific context, a point most chapters in this book expand upon. A sharper realization of the potential dangers for NGOs who advocate public policies is a necessary contribution to the debate on NGO accountability, because the parameters for accountability are contextual and touch on the exercise of basic freedoms as well as on limitations of those freedoms. Governments or other power holders use different means and ways to compromise, disturb or stop NGO activities. We distinguish five categories of the most commonly used tactics, in order of egregiousness:

1 **Challenge credibility**: Authorities may try to challenge the credibility of an NGO by arguing that it promotes conflict (especially religious or ethnic conflict) or endangers stability by importing foreign values and foreign donor influences. NGO's voices in public policy discourse are often silenced by declaring them a threat to national security or against the national interest. Another common tactic is to suggest that an NGO is motivated by its own aspirations to garner state power or financial betterment, or that it represents no one. Challenging credibility may also include denying the value of information or denying the relevance of the policy advice as released by an NGO.

2 **Co-opt or corrupt**: Multinational authorities, governments and private sector actors try to co-opt or corrupt NGOs by bleeding their energies and resources away from key issues and towards governmental programmes, commissions or other bureaucratic obligations. They may also set up 'friendlier' competition by look-alike but bogus civic organizations, whose main mission is to support the official position, confuse the public and discredit the NGOs. Whether or not an NGO is co-opted is usually debatable and requires more of a judgement call than other risks or threats discussed here. Co-optation is in the eye of the beholder and where one stands often depends on where one sits. For one NGO, the opportunity to 'get a seat at the negotiation table' or otherwise engage in an official policy process might appear to be the best possible deal at a certain point in time. For another NGO, entering the same process might be a 'kiss of death' (Tandon, 1989).

3 **Challenge legality**: Governmental authorities can challenge the legality of an NGO by limiting the legal space for the operations of all NGOs. Governments can complicate access to, or limit sources of, financial support. They can purposely create ambiguity within the regulatory framework (Kang, in this volume) or require onerous bureaucratic paperwork. Many governments require annual governmental audits, which are intrusive. Sometimes governments will reserve the right to appoint NGO board members or officers, or reserve the right to appoint executive leadership. Some regimes have simply revoked registration and other legal rights.

4 **Disturb operations**: Governments can intervene at the operational level of NGO activities by refusing requests for information that are, by law, supposed to be in the public domain (Majot, Chapter 13). They can require information disclosure from NGOs even when there is no legal backing for the request, tamper with communications equipment, mail and monitor computer traffic, or plant an agent within the NGO. They can also impose travel bans for NGO staff and freeze bank accounts (Streetnet International, 2006).

5 **Intervene beyond the rule of law**: Lastly, rights or the rule of law have no meaning for some authoritarian regimes. These governments may decide to operate beyond the law to impede NGO activities through extortion, damaging property, framing staff as criminal, harassing volunteers or threatening the personal safety of persons affiliated with the NGO. NGOs are comprised of individuals and their rights can be severely compromised.

The issue of NGO rights, risks and responsibilities has taken on an even sharper edge in the post-September 11th world. It is beyond the scope of this book to discuss fully the implications of the so-called 'war on terror' for NGO rights and the space for NGOs to manifest themselves as civic organizations in different political arenas, but overall it has increased the stakes. More questions will be asked before NGOs are accepted as legitimate actors. NGO policy messages are scrutinized more severely. Specific sub-sectors, like Islamic NGOs, suffer in particular from a loss of the presumption of innocence. Donors have to prove that they are not a conduit for funding violence when supporting NGOs (Scott-Joynt, 2003). The war on terror has thus put additional pressures on the already increasing calls for NGO accountability. In our view, a firm line needs to be drawn between the spectrum of NGO accountability that we try to unfold in this book, which is based on the recognition of both NGO rights and responsibilities, and NGOs who for whatever reason deserve to be subject to a criminal investigation.

Resistance to granting NGOs the right to participate in public policy discussions is tantamount to resisting civic engagement in public policy or, in short, resisting democracy. In political arenas where democracy is not fully formed the tactics summarized above are often employed. However, questions like, 'Who do you represent?' and 'Why are you a legitimate stakeholder?' are asked as frequently by the UK and Indian governments as they are in Belarus or Zimbabwe. Resistance by NGOs to respond to these questions and address the issue of accountability not only poses a threat to the sector, but equally endangers furthering the role of civil society in expanding democracy and democratic practice in all political arenas, be they local, national, regional or global. In order to exercise what are basically democratic citizen rights, NGOs need to be able to articulate clearly to their supporters and to the public who they are, what their role is, where their support comes from and to whom they are accountable. The first responsibility of an NGO is to define its own accountability. That leads us into the substance of this book.

DEFINITIONS

The definitions of the key notions that we are using in this book are all subjects of academic and political debates with no clear winners. The main features of an NGO are: self-governing, private, not-for-profit and with an explicit social mission (Vakil, 1997). NGOs are embedded in civil society, as distinct from political society. While they can organize for a voice in political debates, they are not organized to participate in elections or control the levers of state power, like a political party. NGOs may provide services or advocacy to promote particular issues. NGOs are active in such fields as human rights, environment and conservation, development and peace, or they may have other social objectives. They are usually non-membership based and linked to each other in networks or alliances that sometimes take the form of more formal associations.[3]

NGOs can usefully be distinguished from community-based organizations (CBOs), on the one hand, and social movements, on the other hand. CBOs may have goals comparable to NGOs but are small, local and less absorbed into broader networks or alliances. Social movements are foremost qualified by their effective capacity to reach out to a mass-based constituency of support and do not share the characteristics of an organization. An NGO is generally an intermediary organization with a defined legal body and organizational shape, which qualifies it to receive assistance from donors. Both CBOs and social movements directly articulate the interest of their supporters and operate within less formal structures and receive less external financial assistance or none at all.

Civil society is the next big concept that figures prominently throughout this book.[4] We support the definition of civil society as the realm (that is, the public sphere) where citizens associate voluntarily, outside their families or businesses, to advance their interests, ideas or ideologies (Scholte, 2000). Any profit-making or governing activity is not included in civil society. NGOs, CBOs and social movements are all part of civil society, but the concept is broader and also includes religious organizations and professional or academic associations, none of which are the primary focus of this book.

Our definitions are in line with United Nations terminology (UN, 2004). The distinction between different types of organizations within civil society is not always easy to draw and the border lines are occasionally fluid, but the above categorization is sufficiently commonly accepted to communicate meaningfully about NGO accountability.

A SHORT HISTORY OF NGO ACCOUNTABILITY

Accountability at least points at a correspondence between actions and objectives that have been defined and agreed on. We refrain from defining accountability very tightly at the outset of this book, as its intent is to unfold a series of different angles, perceptions or conditions that may influence or determine whether or not an NGO is considered accountable. Although it may be grounded in legal obligations, accountability is a normative and socially constructed concept and it always requires interpretation of particular facts, circumstances, action or inaction. Much of the heat in debates on NGO accountability comes from those who believe that they are more entitled than others to establish such interpretations.[5]

Over the past 25 years, perceptions of NGO accountability began as a by-product of the prevailing paradigm regarding the role of NGOs in development. Changes in the development paradigm have produced a corresponding shift in emphasis in NGO accountability discussions. Today, debates regarding NGO accountability are embedded in multiple discourses around development, security, globalization and global governance. From a by-product of better performance management in the 1980s, accountability has become a hard issue at the centre of NGOs' political and organizational profile.

Below, we present a short history of NGO accountability by means of an evolving set of syllogisms that outline the prevailing perception of NGO roles, roughly in the last 25 years.[6]

The first syllogism: Complementing government (1980–1989)

1   Governments are not good at delivering public services.
2   NGOs are closer to the public.
3   NGOs are good at delivering public services.

Perceptions of NGO accountability focused on financial accountability, organizational capacity, efficiency and performance delivery.

In this era, privatization of major sectors of a national economy was a standard approach to development. Governments were seen to be part of the problem, market liberalization was understood to be the best way to achieve economic growth and structural adjustment was the dominant methodology for restructuring relations between the state and the market. The fashionable development paradigm was to rely on markets as much as possible, to actively downsize the state and to switch social service delivery to NGOs. NGOs were considered superior to the state delivery system because NGOs were private forces and had a reputation for reaching the very poor. The capacity, however, of NGOs to deliver large-scale services was in question (Gordon Drabek, 1987).

'One of the fundamental reasons that NGOs have received so much attention of late is that they are perceived to be able to do something that national governments cannot or will not do', wrote the editor of *World Development* in a special issue that provided a state-of-the-art overview of the debate on NGOs and development at the time (Gordon Drabek, 1987). After 20 years of development assistance provided by governments and multilateral agencies, the poor were not benefiting. The blame for entrenched poverty was placed squarely on the shoulders of developing country governments and justified through arguments that governments were too big and not efficient, or were corrupt. Aid and other financial resources were shifted away from government agencies to NGOs.

NGOs claimed a bigger portion of the assistance cake, and in so doing shifted from organizations focused on charity and emergency into carriers of people-centered sustainable development. It is striking how in the same issue of *World Development*, there is virtually no discussion of NGO accountability other than financial accountability. The focus is on how NGOs can improve their evaluation mechanisms and deliver more by 'scaling-up' the impact of their activities. Only Tim Broadhead raises the question whether NGO accountability can solely be to the sources of their funding, 'as presently is the case' or also to their partners (for Northern NGOs), or to their base (for Southern NGOs) (Broadhead, 1987).

The second syllogism: The rise of civil society (1989–1995)

1   Civil society is necessary for democracy.
2   NGOs are civil society.
3   NGOs are good for democratic development.

Perceptions of NGO accountability focused on quality of internal governance and the formalization of organizational intent and behaviour (codes of conduct and mission statements).

The second syllogism marks the first shift to a new paradigm, when NGO accountability began to be informed by questions of democracy and governance. For a short period, the fall of the Berlin Wall led many to believe that the age of democracy had begun, that civil society was critical to democracy and NGOs defined civil society. Even the crushing of the student revolt in Tiananmen Square was seen as an important signal of the 'thirst for democracy... ready to flare up again when the moment is right' (Clark, 1991). Improving the capacity of NGOs to undertake new responsibilities as harbingers of democracy became the dominant discourse on NGO management during this period (Aspen Institute, 1997). Dissenters were already hinting at the next paradigm shift through debates about scaling up impact or deepening the quality of the interventions and ensuing civic relations (Edwards and Hulme, 1995). Perceptions of NGO accountability focused on the quality of internal governance and the formalization of organizational intent and behaviour.

The third syllogism: The rise of good governance (1995–2002)

1   Good governance is necessary for development.
2   NGOs are not different from other organizations in civil society.
3   NGOs need to apply principles of good governance.

Perception of NGO accountability focused on legitimacy and establishing self-regulation or independent accreditation mechanisms.

The next period saw the gradual shift of the debate away from capacity building discussions and toward debates on the role of NGOs and civil society. In 1995, with the continued clear failures of the prevailing development model (the so-called 'Washington Consensus' built on structural adjustment), a new development imperative – good governance – began to appear (Kaufmann and Kraay, 2002). NGOs became embedded in the sweep for good governance as they were seen as agents of development, and needing to respond better to the public (World Bank, 2006). This half-decade also sparked a revolt against the rules of development, most famously in Seattle. The great globalization debates began to eclipse the development paradigms and changed the frame within which the NGO accountability discourse took place. NGOs as a phenomenon and the role of NGOs in globalization and development began to be debated among social scientists, advocates of economic liberalization and globalization and Southern governments. NGOs became fashionable foils for globalization. This period marked a more heated discourse on NGO accountability. NGOs responded with independent accreditation mechanisms and self-regulation through federations and associations.

The fourth syllogism: The return of state supremacy (2002 onwards)

1   Government is essential to ensure safety and development.
2   NGOs' influence is not in proportion to their credentials.
3   NGOs need to be kept in check by legitimate government frameworks.

Perception of NGO accountability focused on screening credibility and promoting external (state) control.

From 2001 through to today, the discourse on NGO accountability has two prominent strands. The first reflects greater themes in the development and globalization discourses. The return of state centricity or supremacy is one clear trend. Some states feel that they have ceded far too much authority to NGOs and other private agents. The US government, for example, has recently announced a new policy requiring all aid from the US to be clearly marked as American, regardless of how or where it is distributed (InterAction, 2003). Similar clear responsibilities to state interests are noted in myriad NGO laws, now on the increase at national levels worldwide (Kwesiga and Namisi, Chapter 5). The perception of NGO accountability in this view is focused on screening credibility and promoting external (state) control (Manheim, 2003). Even the World Bank has recently declared that states have a central role to play in development, which represents a complete shift from the 1980s development paradigm (Perry et al, 2006). The focus on terrorism among states is in part driving this new crackdown. Azerbaijan and Georgia, for example, have new laws governing NGOs that they have put into place as a response to the war on terror (Zullo, 2003).

The fifth syllogism: A rights-based approach (2002 onwards)

1   There is no democratic global governance supporting universal human rights.
2   NGOs assert and solidify human rights in different political arenas and regardless of the state of governance.
3   NGOs contribute to democratic governance by articulating public policy needs and practicing solutions resolving public needs.

Perception of NGO accountability focused on balancing multiple responsibilities to different constituencies or stakeholders, using a variety of mechanisms, servicing accreditation rather than regulation.

A competing fifth syllogism is also on the rise, based on principles of human rights and supported by the apparent differences of public trust in different institutions. The Edelman Public Relation Firm, for example, launched the 5th Barometer of Trust in 2004, stating: 'Why did we start this process five years ago? We had seen the Battle of Seattle and we started to see tremendous divergence between attitudes in Europe and the United States towards the NGO sector. That's the beginning of it'. (Edelman, 2005). Edelman's Barometer of Trust has consistently ranked NGOs as one of the most trusted forms of organizations, ranking above corporations, but also above governments, churches, the media and other authorities. This public trend of trust toward NGOs competes with the rise of state supremacy and the trend towards greater control over NGOs. Apparently, the global public (at least those bits that have been surveyed) believe that NGOs generally contribute to the public good.

Over the past five years, Edelman (2005) has found that the publics surveyed believe NGOs were the closest organizational form to their own personal social networks and offered more reliable information than leaders, experts, the media, governments and corporations. The public expectation of NGO accountability, we would posit, relates to the missions and services provided to beneficiaries. It may be far more sophisticated than the command and control mechanisms that governments and corporations are seeking from NGOs. A rights-based approach to NGO accountability could service this public expectation.

This book is oriented towards the fifth syllogism.

OVERVIEW OF THE BOOK

Section I: Key questions and concepts in the current global debate

This book consists of four sections. Different chapters in the first section elaborate the main concepts in the current global context. In the global political arena, an arena where the governance process has to be constructed with every issue (environment, terrorism, peace, internet, human rights), the call for NGO accountability from some sectors is an attack on NGOs. There are two main criticisms. The first are strong nationalistic critiques of NGOs that are seen to be working in cooperation with the United Nations and the Bretton Woods Institutions to undermine national sovereignty. The second line of critique suggests that NGOs are not representative and thus should step out of the way of the inter-governmental organizations that are getting on with the business of government. Steven Charnovitz provides the conceptual backdrop to defuse these critiques, first by pointing out that there is no simple analogy between domestic democratic politics and global policies, because in the global realm there is no such thing as democracy; and second, by turning the accountability question around by asking 'Who is entitled to influence the use of power and authority at the global level, or for that matter at any level of governance?'.

Charnovitz argues convincingly that considerations of public control of authority and power should begin with the individual and makes this point with some refreshing historical depth. He creates the necessary room to breathe for any civilized person, who today is governed by a seemingly choking multitude of decision-makers, from local to global levels. By focusing on the individual, Charnovitz also establishes a vital link with fundamental human rights. When individuals become engaged in policy debates, as they can choose to do via NGOs, the moral justification for their action may be unified. This approach helps to focus the accountability debate on the quality of the substance of the NGOs' message and allows for a compelling qualification of the demand for NGOs to have a certain representational value as 'a red herring'.

Enrique Peruzzotti further develops the argument on civil society, representation and accountability. He concurs with Charnovitz in identifying civic action not as a representative instance, but as a constituent one. Civil society enhances democratic governance by adding new voices and concerns to the political agenda and by demanding effective legal accountability. Being on the constituent side of the equation, civic actors cannot be subjected to the same yardstick employed to evaluate political parties or parliaments. Otherwise, they could lose their important function as a counterweight to the risk of a democratically sanctioned majority rule.

Active NGOs are exercising fundamental rights and they may very well enhance democracy, but operating in the public sphere also makes them vulnerable. Credibility in the public's eye is easily lost in an age in which 'reputation management' has become a self-standing business. Peruzzotti underlines the fact that many informal controls affecting NGOs are as strong as formal accountability mechanisms. Yet, there is a danger of NGOs losing sight of their mission or losing touch with the people they started out to work for. In order to prevent the risk of social authoritarianism, Peruzzotti concludes with a plea to make the democratization of associational life a key priority of civic engagement.

Section II: Traditional approaches: Legal accountability, certification and donor regimes

When the exercise of responsibilities is messy or seems to spin out of control, the intuitive response of those in power is to demand regulation. The second section of the book critically examines traditional attempts to address NGO accountability. Each chapter reviews a traditional approach to the question of accountability and concludes that these approaches can be flawed either through malfeasance on the part of more powerful authorities, a failure to take into consideration human rights or greater societal interests, or by inherent limitations to regulatory mechanisms.

The second section starts with an account by Patricia Armstrong of a controversy surrounding the attempt by the World Bank to support the production of a Handbook on Good Practices for Laws Relating to NGOs. The Handbook never made it beyond the status of a draft. When summarizing the discussion on the substance of the draft Handbook, Armstrong teaches us much about NGO accountability in relation to international law and universal human rights and standards, and the dire need to apply them carefully across different political realities. The chapter raises the question whether NGOs need special laws to be regulated. It queries whether it is the role of the World Bank to promote such laws. The chapter supports Steve Charnovitz's observation that government bureaucrats and politicians do not have any special competence to oversee NGOs and guide them towards attainment of the common good. When summarizing the discussion on the substance of the draft Handbook, Armstrong teaches us much about NGO accountability in relation to international law and universal human rights and standards, and the dire need to apply them carefully across different political realities.

In the next chapter, Professor Jassy Kwesiga and Harriet Namisi also support Charnovitz's observations. They depict the damage a new restrictive law and NGO Registration Board could inflict on NGOs in Uganda. In the Ugandan case, NGOs attempt to deflect the more onerous aspects of the proposed law through self-regulation by means of a voluntary code. This chapter illustrates a less luminous side of the Ugandan story, which is often depicted as a resounding success in development circles. NGO accountability is difficult to exercise and will not be enhanced if the Ugandan government's main aim in relating to NGOs is to assert political control, instead of correcting market or non-market failures. In the case of Uganda, NGOs so far have been able to avoid unwarranted political polarization and resist government pressures, mainly due to foreign support and by leveraging their sizeable contribution to the nation's GDP and employment. Still, what it produces is an unsatisfactory status quo, in which neither the government nor the NGOs are optimally strengthened. Democratic institutions are not developed and the burgeoning democratic culture is handicapped.

Stephen Golub reports on the case of the Philippine Council for NGO Certification (PCNC). It is one of the most outstanding and fully developed examples of NGO self-regulation in the world. Set up as a mechanism to provide a process of certification in order to secure the tax exempt status of Philippine NGOs, the existence of the PCNC has had a considerable spin-off effect in raising the stakes of NGO standards of operation. Golub appreciates the immediate contribution of the PCNC to improving NGO accountability as a moderate, yet valuable, by-product of its tax functions. He describes a number of roles taken on by the PCNC, which may not be directly oriented towards accountability, but do contribute to a climate of professionalism and shared organizational learning that enhances NGO accountability.

Reminding us of Peruzzotti's warning of social authoritarianism, Golub also describes how the PCNC negotiates internal Philippine NGO relationships and has to guard zealously its apolitical and unbiased reputation. The more successful the PCNC is in situating itself at the centre of assessing the performance of Philippine NGOs, the greater this need will be. The limits of NGO self-regulation will climax once PCNC certification becomes a condition for receiving donor funding, a possibility that at least some donors appear to entertain and that many NGOs and some other donors reject. Towards the end of his chapter, Golub highlights the particular concern that the PCNC might be drawn into assessing NGOs viability for the sake of preventing crime or terrorism. Clearly, NGO self-regulation is not suitable to become self-policing.

The lesson learned from the Philippines is that a structured and transparent process of self-regulation and certification can make important contributions to enhancing NGO accountability. But a spill-over into establishing a certified access to donor funding would be unwanted because it would create a hierarchy; wreak havoc among NGO relationships; reward conformity rather than diversified organizational behaviour; and limit the space for experimentation, start-ups or the promotion of newly identified interests. In other words, it would seriously endanger the potential added value of NGOs to contribute to development and it would violate the role of NGOs in civil society as constituents of democratic governance.

The last chapter in Section II is oriented towards donor accountability. This book includes a chapter on donor accountability because NGO actions and roles are subscribed more or less by their financial resources. Most NGOs lack a strong public base of funding and rely on a variety of resources that are channeled through donor agencies, corporations or philanthropists. These donors are now adopting new accountability mechanisms to apply to NGOs. Jem Bendell and Phyllida Cox explore the different types of donor agencies that fund NGOs and offer a concept of democratic accountability to be applied to donors themselves and to the relationship between donors and NGOs. Bendell and Cox argue that if democratic accountability is realized, the relationship between NGOs and donors could be far more supportive of democracy and democratic practice in society. As Bendell and Cox note, this area of accountability is underexplored, most likely due to the power that can be wielded by donors. This chapter is only the beginning of a richer conversation that is now underway within some donor circles.

Section III: The benefits of embracing accountability

Section III counters some of the cautions in Section II by highlighting the need for NGO accountability. The main message of Section III is that the interdependence between NGO accountability and the local context is critical to developing accountability mechanisms for NGOs successfully. Section III begins with a review of the current context for NGOs in China where, if rights are to be realized for NGOs, responsibilities have to be clearly defined and structured in a regulatory regime.

Professor Kang Xiaoguang and Feng Li explain how in a state-dominated society the concept of NGO has to be used with care. This chapter turns the story of NGO accountability upside-down. In many chapters of this book, we see a government or international organizations attempting to limit the space for NGOs, with regulations or by other means, as they see the growth of the NGO sector as a threat. NGOs rely on human rights and democratic norms to articulate their role in society and counter the authorities' attempts to limit their space. In China, the reality is quite the opposite. The lack of a regulatory enabling environment has resulted in stunting the potential role of NGOs. In most cases, the demand for NGO accountability from governments is reactive to growth and increasing political power. In China, the state has demanded regulations and accountability measures first, that is, for responsibilities to be defined. Accountability has been demanded pro-actively. Rights to exist might follow.

The story in China also shows that once accountability frameworks have been established, they have to be flexible enough to respond to new situations and create new space. NGOs in China may or may not obtain more independence from their parental institutions within government or the state-led corporate sector. The other important observation is that despite differences in context, people always wish to associate with one another, which demonstrates the vitality and universal appeal of fundamental human rights.

The overview of NGO governance and accountability in Indonesia by Hans Antlöv, Rustam Ibrahim and Peter van Tuijl shows the confusing impact of an abrupt and radical change in context. For more than 30 years, the Suharto regime worked on establishing a firm grip on a civil society trimmed down to a bare minimum number of umbrella organizations for different interest groups. NGOs were thus operating in a consciously disabled civil society and left with a tiny space, mainly for service provision. For Indonesian NGOs, working under such political pressures provided an excuse, in many ways justified, to avoid accountability questions. It also established NGOs as mainly urban and middle-class based, which proved to be a serious weakness once the political situation changed.

Since the fall of Suharto in 1998, Indonesian civil society has come out of the closet and many different types of organizations have been created. The number of NGOs has also exploded, but they have great difficulties in defining and asserting their role within the context of a country in transition to a more democratic political system and culture. From being a virtual political opposition, Indonesian NGOs now have to develop strategies of engagement, foremost with their government. At the same time, the classic NGO agenda, such as concern for human rights or the environment, has to be shared with more players, like political parties, religious organizations and universities, all able to speak out and publicize their views in a multitude of media outlets that have sprung up in recent years.

The greater public scrutiny of any organization in Indonesia has also raised the stakes of accountability for Indonesian NGOs. Donors have started to become impatient with some of their NGO counterparts, who have difficulties accepting that they now have to fulfill much greater demands for transparency and accountability. A number of organizational innovations and efforts indicate that Indonesian NGOs are beginning to respond to these challenges.

Section IV: Innovations: Expanding the accountability frontier

The final section of the book presents four innovative accountability cases that are already advanced in terms of substance, process, form and sometimes institutionalization. In each case NGOs live up to their task of prioritizing and developing innovations in associational life as first laid out by Peruzzotti. These cases are where the pioneers in social innovation are found. The accountability mechanisms are fluid, democratic and oriented towards learning. Many are framed in the global context.

We start with the struggle of an individual organization to ingrain accountability in its daily business. The chapter by Sarah Okwaare and Jennifer Chapman documents ActionAid Uganda's efforts to develop an Accountability, Learning and Planning System (ALPS). Information and how it is being used turn out to be vital elements in trying to establish accountability as a process of learning, reflection and evaluation carried out jointly with many different stakeholders.

The good news from this chapter is that accountability offers positive results for many stakeholders. The bad news is it takes an enormous amount of effort to go through a process like this and it requires the will to change fundamentally the way an organization works. ActionAid Uganda's experience provides encouragement for organizations to embrace accountability. It is also a reality check on the commitment and investments needed to do so. We believe the development of NGO accountability and its contribution to democratization will remain big concepts with little meaning without the footwork that is described in this chapter.

Agnes Callamard brings us back to the individual at the center of the accountability debate. She presents a concise overview of the Humanitarian Accountability Project International (HAP-I). The project emerged out of the ashes of the Rwanda Genocide, one of the worst cases of failure of international governance and lack of humanitarian assistance of the 20th century. The accountability approach developed by HAP-I resembles some of the principles and methodology of One World Trust's Global Accountability Project that is described in the next chapter, but is more like the ActionAid example in its attempts to encompass directly the populations that are affected by humanitarian assistance in the accountability assessment.

HAP-I developed a five-point framework to approach accountability: who is accountable; to whom; for what; how; and for what outcomes? It is a simple set of empirical questions that are hard to implement for many organizations. The first tests of the framework through research and surveys in Sierra Leone, Afghanistan and Cambodia provided some pretty shocking results. There were plenty of examples and even systemic patterns of a lack of accountability. More than most types of NGO activity, humanitarian assistance is provided in a context closer to life-and-death. Affected populations are completely dependent on NGOs who are often the first and sometimes the only responders to provide food, water and shelter. To avoid the risk of power abuse requires a conscientious effort that is grounded in institutional practice. Agencies participating in HAP-I have started to make adjustments to apply greater transparency in their operations. They have established mechanisms for affected populations to check compliance with common standards, file complaints and seek redress in case of shortcomings or violations of agreed commitments.

Where Steve Charnovitz makes the principle point that considerations of public control of authority and power should start with the individual, thereby grounding the debate on NGO accountability in fundamental human rights, Agnes Callamard articulates a complementary perspective. The exercise of such rights with the best of intentions under the most difficult circumstances still creates a responsibility that starts with the individual, who at that moment may be too tired, sick, hungry or afraid to even think or let alone believe in any form of association. It supports the establishment of a level playing field for NGO accountability in different political landscapes as characterized by the application of powerful universal principles to individual needs and aspirations.

Hetty Kovach describes how the UK-based One World Trust (OWT) has embarked on an attempt to create a new, self-standing accountability mechanism that serves the needs of organizations working globally. The accountability model has four dimensions: transparency, participation, evaluation and complaints and redress. Using extensive stakeholder surveys to verify the model, it is not only applicable for international NGOs such as Amnesty International, but also for international public organizations and global corporations. Stakeholders are broadly defined as 'any group or individuals who can affect or is affected by an organization'. Echoing Charnovitz's observation that there is no simple analogy between domestic democratic politics and global politics, an important innovation is that the OWT model at the global level equates NGOs with actors that they normally are not equated with in national democratic politics. Indeed, the deficit of effective democratic politics globally is equally felt among public, corporate and civil society organizations.

Establishing accountability is always political. The OWT Global Accountability Project (GAP) released its first report in 2003 and immediately raised controversy. Different organizations subjected to the GAP model tried to highlight those parts of the report wherein they figured well and obscured less welcome results. OWT has galvanized the debate among global institutions, providing both the carrot of assistance in developing meaningful accountability frameworks, and the stick of shame should efforts not measure up against other global actors that are similarly challenged in defining stakeholders. The OWT-GAP report has proven to be a rich learning experience and a step forward in view of Peruzzotti's call to strengthen the democratization of associational life.

The last chapter in the book looks more specifically at the practice of integrity within transnational NGO advocacy campaigning, covering a range of organizations, from internationally oriented advocacy NGOs to local CBOs. Juliette Majot allows us an insider's perspective on efforts to challenge the building of a dam in Uganda, as well as on experiences with the World Commission on Dams (WCD), a multi-stakeholder exercise to review the performance of big dams and their contributions to development. The chapter shows that even though questioning the representational value of NGO advocacy in the global political arena is a red herring, it does provide a powerful and frequently used tool to ridicule, belittle and ignore NGO messages.

Majot responds to NGO bashers by demonstrating that the quality of NGO accountability is often in the details of the relationships between people and organizations. How much effort is made to really understand each other; is there respect for differences; restraint where it is required; and equal sharing of successes and failures? The resources required to develop, implement and sustain the implementation of standards of accountability in the global context echo ActionAid's dedication at the national level.

Transnational NGO campaigns do raise one caveat. When it comes to transparency of information and disclosing internal debates within a campaign, the vulnerability and protection of the weakest partner, usually a few people in a local organization exposed to a hostile environment, is of overriding importance. Majot qualifies a limitation on outside scrutiny as a hallmark of responsible campaigning. It is a statement that leaves her open for the next undeserved attack by people who try hard to avoid understanding that in the absence of viable global democratic structures, NGO accountability in the global arena becomes the art of maximizing universal rights while taking responsibility for minimizing their violation. Her observations on transparency prove the point that NGO accountability must be developed in context, foremost related to the rights that are recognized in the political arena within which an NGO operates.

NOTES

1   For an example see www.ngo-monitor.org, which focuses on the legitimacy of human rights organizations.
2   'The enabling environment for civic engagement can be defined as a set of interrelated conditions (legal, fiscal, informational, political, and cultural) that fosters the growth of civil society and strengths its capacity to participate in public policy dialogue and program implementation' (World Bank Development Approaches and Initiatives, www.worldbank.org/civilsociety).
3   For useful discussions on the definition of an NGO see Cohen and Arato (1992); Keck and Sikkink (1998); and Edwards and Fowler (2002).
4   For discussions on civil society see Scholte (2000); Keane (2003); Edwards (2004).
5   To view contested definitions of NGO accountability see Edwards and Hulme (1995); Jordan and van Tuijl (2000); Chapman and Wameyo (2001).
6   A syllogism is a sequence of three propositions such that the first two imply the third, the conclusion. Defined by Aristotle, syllogisms are a mode of argument at the core of Western logical thought. They provide a simple format to support a discussion of the most important issues at hand and, at the same time, articulate the influence of Western approaches in identifying the role of NGOs in strengthening civil society and democratic development. They also help to explain how weaknesses in the prevailing propositions lead to new propositions and a new paradigm.

2

Accountability of Non-Governmental Organizations in Global Governance

Steve Charnovitz

INTRODUCTION

The issue of the accountability of NGOs in global governance has received increased attention in recent years. This chapter will analyse the issue, consider whether any public problems exist, and make recommendations on what could be done. The first part provides an overview of the current debate on NGO accountability, including the most significant commentary and scholarly work. The second part presents a new analysis of how to meet the challenge of enhancing NGO performance and accountability in the global arena. I will contend that accountability is needed and feasible where tasks are delegated to NGOs, but that accountability is an ill-conceived goal when the NGO acts autonomously to pursue its own interest. In general, NGO advocacy does not trigger a need for external accountability to the community and, in any event, no clear accountability holder exists. Certainly, one should not expect NGOs to be accountable to governments. Nevertheless, NGOs do need to be internally accountable (to directors, members and management), so it is wrong to say that NGOs are accountability-free actors.

I propose that the debate about NGO external accountability be reconfigured to seek better performance rather than accountability. Ideally, voluntary standards can be devised for discrete areas (for example, humanitarian work) and NGO performance can be independently rated. Such initiatives will help to place a check on NGO misbehaviour without relying on a form of control by government that would be inappropriate to a free society.

A SURVEY OF THE DEBATE ON
NGO ACCOUNTABILITY

In recent years, the participation of unofficial groups in international meetings has led to heightened concerns regarding the accountability of these groups. In this section I will examine these concerns. In doing so, I will take note of some historical moments relevant to addressing claims about accountability. NGO accountability is connected to the much larger topic of civil society and its relationship to the individual, the market and the state (Bucholtz, 1998; Ehrenberg, 1999). For reasons of space, I will not venture into the caverns of debate about the meaning and role of civil society. Instead, I will focus on one feature of civil society, the NGOs, particularly those that think and/or act globally.

Because NGOs have been internationally active for over two centuries (Charnovitz, 1997), there are many historical episodes one could use as a springboard into a discussion of NGO accountability. Yet, before NGO influence is strong enough on a global scale to spark demands for accountability, such activist NGOs must exist. Therefore, an appropriate place to start will be an authoritative statement articulating the legitimacy of NGOs.

The earliest I know of is *Rerum Novarum*, the 1891 Encyclical of Pope Leo XIII on Capital and Labour, which had an important influence on the development of liberal regimes to oversee labor unions (Pope Leo XIII, 1891). The Encyclical contrasts 'civil society' with the 'lesser societies', and indicates that the latter, the private associations, 'are now far more common than before' (paras 51, 54). The Encyclical offers 'cheering hope for the future provided always that the associations We have described continue to grow and spread, and are well and wisely administered' (para. 55). The societies described in the Encyclical are societies of working men, employers and benevolent foundations (para. 48).[1]

Entering into such societies is 'the natural right of man' (para. 51). Thus, the Encyclical explains that for a state to forbid its citizens to form associations contradicts the very principle of the state's existence, namely, to protect natural rights. The Pope concedes that the law should intervene to prevent certain bad associations, but counsels that 'every precaution should be taken not to violate the rights of individuals and not to impose unreasonable regulations under pretense of public benefit' (para. 52). Moreover, the state 'should not thrust itself into their [the associations'] peculiar concerns and their organization, for things move and live by the spirit inspiring them, and may be killed by the rough grasp of a hand from without' (para. 55). The Encyclical provides a philosophical underpinning for relaxed state regulation of NGOs.

The term 'non-governmental organization' came into use at least as early as 1920. In that year, Sophy Sanger employed the term in a discussion of how such organizations had not been able to participate in the first multilateral negotiations for labour treaties in 1906 (Sanger, 1920).[2] Sanger contrasted this pre-war practice to the advent of the International Labour Organization (ILO) in 1919. The constitutional provisions of the ILO set out in the Treaty of Versailles call for the participation of 'non-Government Delegates and advisers chosen in agreement with the industrial organisations, if such organisations exist, which are the most representative of employers or workpeople, as the case may be, in their respective countries' (ILO, 1919, Article 3.5). In the ILO, each member state sends four delegates – two from government, one employer and one worker. The employers and workers are not members of the ILO, however, because only nation-states are members.

A question regarding the representativeness of the ILO worker delegate from The Netherlands arose during the third session of the International Labour Conference (1921) when the Dutch Government's choice was contested by the Netherlands Confederation of Trade Unions. The ILO Conference extended the credential to the delegate chosen by the Dutch Government, but asked the ILO Governing Body to request the Council of the League of Nations to seek an advisory opinion from the Permanent Court of International Justice (PCIJ). This disagreement became the first matter to come before and be decided by the PCIJ. In 1922, the PCIJ held that The Netherlands had not violated the Treaty of Versailles in making its selection. In considering the matter before it, the PCIJ welcomed oral statements from the International Labour Office and two international labour union federations (1 World Court Reports, Advisory Opinion No. 1).

The openness of the PCIJ to statements by NGOs was an important episode in the history of NGO roles in international law. If an NGO-related question were to come to the International Court of Justice (ICJ) today, that Court would not allow NGOs to submit their own statements. No NGO participation in the ICJ has occurred since it was established in 1946, and the last requests by NGOs for an opportunity to submit amicus briefs in non-contentious cases were denied (Shelton, 1994).[3] The ICJ may be the only international arena in which NGOs have lost participatory opportunities since the 1920s.

The ILO Constitution is unusual in positing that the non-governmental delegates are to be 'representative' of specified constituencies within a country. Typically, the constitutions of international organizations that provide for NGO participation do not call for a representative body or suggest that the role of the NGO is to represent anyone in particular. For example, Article 71 of the United Nations (UN) Charter states that: 'The Economic and Social Council may make suitable arrangements for consultation with non-governmental organizations which are concerned with matters within its competence'. Thus, the stated rationale for NGO consultation is the concern of the NGO rather than the breadth of its membership or its representativeness.

Nevertheless, when it implemented Article 71 in 1950, the UN Economic and Social Council (ECOSOC) formulated a set of principles providing that the consulted organization 'shall be of recognized standing and shall represent a substantial portion of the organized persons within the particular field in which it operates'.[4] This requirement, to some extent, has been carried forward into the current ECOSOC Credentialing Arrangements, adopted in 1996.

These Arrangements state that the NGO 'shall be of recognized standing within the particular field of its competence *or* of a representative character'. The Arrangements also state that: 'The organization shall have a representative structure and possess appropriate mechanisms of accountability to its members, who shall exercise effective control over its policies and actions through the exercise of voting rights or other appropriate democratic and transparent decision-making processes'.[5]

Although most of the international legal agreements that provide for public participation in international organizations extend that participation to NGOs rather than to individuals, one prominent exception is the World Bank Inspection Panel that permits requests for inspection from 'any group of two or more people in the country where the Bank-financed project is located who believe that as a result of the Bank's violation their rights or interests have been, or are likely to be, adversely affected in a direct and material way'.[6] The Inspection Panel is a good example of a clear accountability mechanism for an international organization because the Panel reviews whether the Bank's actions are consistent with a prescribed set of standards – in this case, the Bank's own rules.

Overview of NGO accountability literature in international law and politics

A voluminous literature exists on the accountability (or lack thereof) of NGOs. Those writing on NGO accountability include lawyers, political scientists, economists, journalists and others. Some of the studies discussed below mix the issues of legitimacy, democratic accountability and plain accountability.

Starting with some opinion-shapers, in 2003 *The New York Times* (21 July) editorialized that: 'non-governmental organizations are now part of the power structure too'. They receive donations from the public and advocate policies that each group claims are in the public interest. As they become part of the established political landscape worldwide, 'these groups owe it to the public to be accountable and transparent themselves' (*The New York Times*, 21 July 2003). Pursuing a similar theme shortly afterwards, *The Economist* ran an influential essay 'Who Guards the Guardians?', which put forth the 'novel idea' of 'auditing NGOs' (*The Economist*, 20 September 2003). More so than any other general interest journal, *The Economist* has been attentive to the phenomenon of NGOs. In 2000, *The Economist* asserted that NGOs 'can get into bad ways because they are not accountable to anyone' (29 January 2000).[7]

Perhaps the most critical perspective on NGOs comes from John Bolton. Writing in 2000 before he joined the Bush Administration, Bolton expressed concern about the 'extra-national clout of NGOs' in global governance and worried that 'Civil society also sees itself as beyond national politics, which is one of the reasons its recent successes have such profoundly anti-democratic implications' (Bolton, 2000). The problem, as analysed by Bolton, is that NGO participation 'provides a second opportunity for intrastate advocates to reargue their positions, thus advantaging them over their opponents who are either unwilling or unable to reargue their cases in international fora'. Moreover, he contended that 'the civil society idea actually suggests a "corporative" approach to international decision-making that is dramatically troubling for democratic philosophy because it posits "interests" (whether NGOs or businesses) as legitimate actors along with popularly elected governments'.

Bolton, who is known for speaking his mind, went even further to claim that such corporativism is synonymous with fascism and that 'Mussolini would smile on the Forum of Civil Society' while 'Americanists would not'.[8] Yet this assertion by Bolton elides the fact that the Italian dictator and the fascist movement were seeking to control associations and to suppress any independence from the state (Tannenbaum, 1969). Bolton does not advocate suppressing NGOs, but he seems to want a government to shut its eyes to them. Bolton's article fails to explain why he thinks that 'Americanists' (a term he does not define) should not smile on a Forum of Civil Society. No other published criticism rivals Bolton's venom towards NGOs. All of the studies discussed hereafter offer criticisms of the NGO role within an analytical framework that accepts the legitimacy of voluntary, independent associations.

Several years ago, Kenneth Anderson wrote an article about the efforts by NGOs during negotiations for the treaty on landmines and he used that case study to offer more general observations on the NGO role (Anderson, 2000). Anderson's article made an important contribution to the international law scholarship on NGOs. Anderson calls attention to the development of a 'romance', 'partnership' or 'symbiotic' relationship between international NGOs, sympathetic states and international organizations. Anderson objects to this relationship because, in his view, 'international NGOs' are not conduits from the 'people' and do not operate from the bottom up.[9] Rather, he says, 'the glory of organizations of civil society is not democratic legitimacy, but the ability to be a pressure group' that will speak horizontally to other global elites. Such a horizontal conversation has a 'worthwhile, essential function in making the world – sometimes at least, a better place – but it does not reduce the democratic deficit' (Anderson, 2000).

These observations by Anderson about the NGO role show considerable insight and balance, but in more recent scholarship, Anderson seems to have lost that balance (Anderson, 2001). In offering advice to the Bush Administration, Anderson warns against a 'pragmatic conservative model' that would not oppose NGOs, but rather would merely seek 'to temper their extreme impulses and encourage them towards sensible actions and advocacy positions'. Instead, Anderson argues that stronger policies are needed because there are 'risks to democracy' from the activities of international NGOs. These risks ensue because there is a difference between NGOs operating domestically in a democratic society and NGOs operating in the international field. The alleged difference is that the NGOs do their domestic lobbying within a democratic structure, but that 'in the undemocratic international world' matters are different because the 'international system... has no democratic legitimacy'.

The degree of legitimacy declined after the international system began 'embarking on the path of downgrading democratic sovereigns and upgrading the supposed legitimacy of international NGOs'. Anderson (2001) points to two specific harms from NGOs. First, 'international NGOs muddy the waters of the critical question of how much power ought to be assigned to a system of international organizations that cannot ever be democratic'. Second, 'international NGOs actively seek to undermine the processes of democracy within democratic states whenever the results of those democratic processes produce, in the view of the international NGOs, uncongenial substantive outcomes'. As a result, he says, one should regard 'international NGOs, unlike their domestic counterparts – or unlike the international NGOs themselves when they work within sovereign democratic systems – as not merely undemocratic, but as profoundly antidemocratic'. Furthermore he asserts that international NGOs have felt themselves on the defensive with respect to the fundamental question asked by David Rieff (1999), namely, 'So who elected the NGOs?'.[10]

A number of unanswered questions leap out of Anderson's analysis. One is what is the difference between the criticized NGO activity of seeking to undermine or reverse the decisions taken by a democratic state and the uncriticized activity of NGOs working within the domestic political system to undermine official decisions? Why does Anderson think that the situs of NGO advocacy changes its democratic character? Another question is why could it be antidemocratic for international NGOs to focus their advocacy efforts on the decisions being made by and within international organizations?[11] I certainly do not share Anderson's view that the international organizations are undemocratic or cannot ever be democratic, but even if international organizations are undemocratic today, how can the NGO voice *reduce* the level of legitimacy since ultimately it is up to sovereigns to decide whether to follow any of the advice being offered by the NGOs? Another puzzle in Anderson's analysis is how NGOs could pose 'risks to democracy when international NGOs propose themselves as substitutes for democracy' if, as he believes, there is no democracy at risk anyway in the realm of international organizations? If Anderson's point is that NGOs pose risks to national democracy when they lobby in UN meetings, then he does not explain what that risk is.

Martha Schweitz offers a more positive view on the question of whether NGO participation in world governance is legitimate (Schweitz, 1995). She explains that the issue is not the legitimacy of a claim to obedience, but rather the legitimacy of participation by NGOs in distinct roles in the international governance process. A key myth to dispel, she proclaims, is 'the myth that NGOs must be representative organizations in order to be legitimate participants'. She explains that NGOs have at least three reasons for being that have nothing to do with representing anyone in particular: first, being sources of information and expertise; second, delivering services to people; and third, standing up for a core value. In her view, there is no minimum threshold for the number of people in the world that need to share a value for it to be heard in the international arena. Schweitz also addresses whether there should be some 'standards of conduct' pertaining to certain

NGO roles and suggests that 'We need to think about what makes an NGO a good world citizen'.

Gary Johns (2000) raises concerns about some of the assumptions underlying the NGO accountability movement. Johns argues that when NGOs posit that they are a new form of democratic legitimacy or the greatest expression of democracy, then NGOs may become subject to 'a policy of heavy-handed regulation of private associations'. Johns sees this path as undesirable from a 'liberal' perspective, and suggests that each NGO should 'claim no more than to represent a view' and should not seek to belittle the authority of representative democracy. In his view, the only scrutiny needed for NGOs is 'the ordinary scrutiny of any group or person who seeks to make claims on the public', that is, the 'integrity and truth of the proposal'.

Several analysts point to standards of conduct that NGOs violate or to general accountability problems with NGOs. For example, a decade ago, Julie Mertus warned of the 'dangers of NGOs that violate democratic norms' (Mertus, 1995). She notes that the operations of NGOs 'are at times decidedly opaque', and that the 'institutions of civil society may run against the most basic rule of democracy, namely, to govern with the consent of the governed'. One conclusion she reaches is that 'As long as international law fails to articulate a clear and consistent position as to the responsibility of non-State actors', these actors may continue to neglect human rights.

Jan Aart Scholte, a long-time scholar of 'civil society', observes that even though 'civil society groups have an obligation to answer to stakeholders for their actions and omissions', most of these groups 'have operated very limited and unimaginative accountability mechanisms in relation to their own activities' (Scholte, 2004). He sees such accountability shortfalls as being politically costly to 'civil society' work because authorities seize on missing accountability to reject the legitimacy of those groups in global governance. In contrast, Scholte reports on a number of innovative actions to promote accountability. For example, the Philippine Council for NGO Certification has developed a rigorous scheme of 'nonofficial oversight for civil society in that country' (Golub in this volume).

Peter Spiro (2002) seeks to unpack NGO accountability by asking to whom the accountability should be developed. His answer is that NGOs should be accountable both to their constituencies and to process, and he frames that distinction as internal versus external accountability. Regarding internal accountability to members, he suggests that the problem of accountability is exaggerated because there are practical constraints on NGOs (such as membership) that keep them in line. In evaluating NGO internal accountability, he cautions against the 'fetishization of other forms of association', such as the democratic state, which is 'implicitly idealized on the accountability metric, especially by virtue of periodic elections'. In Spiro's view, voting is a 'crude tool for keeping governmental authorities in line' and 'governments can get away with an awful lot before having to answer to their memberships'. Regarding external accountability of NGOs to 'the system', Spiro contends that this process now operates sub-optimally because, given the present infor-

mal arrangements for NGO participation, NGOs lack incentives to be accountable. Spiro's proposed solution is for states to accept 'formal inclusion of
non-state actors in international decision-making' in order to 'hold NGOs, as
repeat players, accountable to international bargains'.

Michael Edwards is one of the world's most thoughtful and experienced
analysts of NGO activities. Edwards (2000) explains that 'NGO accountability is weak and problematic, since there is no clear "bottom line" for results
and no single authority to which NGOs must report on their activities'.
Edwards advocates a 'New Deal' in which more participation in global governance is granted 'in return for transparency and accountability on a set of
minimum standards for NGO integrity and performance, monitored largely
through self-regulation' plus a 'much larger array of voluntary regulations and
other, non-coercive means of influencing destructive behavior'. Greater
accountability, in Edwards's view, is needed both upward, to donors, and
downward, to the poor. Edwards contributes the useful notion of vertical
accountability, namely, that on development issues, the claims made by the
large NGOs should be rooted in the experience at the local level. Another
constructive suggestion is to foster innovation in global governance through 'a
period of structured experimentation in NGO involvement'.

Hugo Slim offers a working definition of NGO accountability, which is
'the process by which an NGO holds itself openly responsible for what it
believes, what it does, and what it does not do in a way that shows it involving all concerned parties and actively responding to what it learns' (Slim,
2002). Slim proposes constructing a map of the NGOs' various stakeholders
in a given situation because NGO accountability cannot be expected to be
uniform across a wide range of NGO activity. The map may reveal conflicting
interests and will help in the design of the right accountability mechanisms,
such as social audits or a complaint procedure.

Benedict Kingsbury (2002) reflects on NGO accountability as a constitutional challenge. He explains that the struggle to articulate a useful approach
to establishing 'rigorous accountability of non-state actors suggests that international civil society has at present minimal conceptual resources other than
First Amendment liberalism for structuring thought about problems of
accountability'. Yet First Amendment liberalism, according to Kingsbury,
offers few means of NGO accountability except via markets, and it tends to
view demands for other forms of accountability with suspicion. Moreover, he
says, First Amendment liberalism is not very helpful in addressing the participatory claims of ascriptive groups, such as indigenous peoples exercising
governmental powers. Kingsbury calls for the development of 'a richer international constitutionalism' to help address accountability, mandate,
representation and participation.

An extremely impressive analysis of human rights NGO accountability has
recently been authored by Robert Charles Blitt (2004). Blitt takes a self-
described law and economics approach to the question of whether human rights
NGOs should be regulated in order to enhance their accountability. Blitt refers
to human rights NGOs as 'human rights organizations' or HROs. First, in order

to make a case for regulation of the HRO industry, there needs to be a problem. The overall problem Blitt sees is that the current market for HRO ideas and activism does not operate in a way so as to assure that the product is safe for those who consume or are affected by it. He suggests that HROs 'shoulder a virtual duty of care to the general public'. Blitt provides a number of reasons to be doubtful that the *internal* accountability controls on HROs are adequate – for example, he says that NGO reliance on government funding may operate to limit the independence of NGOs or, conversely, cause them to neglect their primary interests in reliability and objectivity. Then Blitt analyses the potential *external* controls, such as the media, donors, international organizations and the free market, and finds these controls to be inadequate. He devotes many pages to analysing the marketplace of ideas and argues that like any market, it may need regulation if there are dysfunctions. Among the harms he notes are the damage to an impugned body's reputation from misleading allegations, the futility of seeking judicial relief on small-size transactions and the difficulty of private law remedies because of extra-jurisdictional issues. Although I do not agree with every point he makes, his analysis is cogent on the whole and would be applicable to NGOs well beyond the human rights field.

Blitt's solution is industry self-regulation, in other words, the major HROs should establish detailed standards for operations, and invite all HROs to subscribe to them voluntarily. The standards would cover: professional staff and board membership criteria; financial and financial disclosure transparency; best practices for research, fact-finding and reporting; and protocols for issuing public retractions. Blitt makes clear that 'governments would have no role to play in setting HRO standards'. Once standards are adopted, they could be monitored and enforced in several ways, such as an independent monitoring agency, annual ratings of HROs, or best practices for financial agreements. He concludes that 'while individuals may remain free to establish fly-by-night HROs, recognized HROs will have an authoritative and objective tool that can be harnessed to credential themselves in the eyes of the media, governments, intergovernmental agencies, courts and the public at large' (Blitt, 2004).

NGO accountability is also being addressed in the reports of major international advisory commissions. In June 2004, the Panel of Eminent Persons on United Nations–Civil Society Relations appointed by Secretary-General Kofi Annan delivered its report and suggested that UN practices for engaging civil society should work to define 'standards of governance, such as those for transparency and accountability' (UN, 2004). In particular, according to the Panel, the UN Secretariat should discuss with the private groups advising the UN 'possible codes of conduct and self-policing mechanisms to heighten disciplines of quality, governance and balance'.

In January 2005, a Consultative Board appointed by the World Trade Organization (WTO) Director-General delivered an extensive report that included a brief section on NGO accountability (WTO, 2005). The Board noted the criticism that 'those lobbying for more access' are 'often neither especially accountable nor particularly transparent themselves'. Furthermore, the Board intoned: 'While there is now a broad recognition among member states of the UN of the substantial and proven benefits of non-governmental participation in intergovernmental debate on global issues, there are continuing concerns about the legitimacy, representativity, accountability and politics of non-governmental organizations.'

In reaching its conclusion, the Board of eight men neglected to hold any public hearings or to solicit public comments during its investigation, a period that lasted over 18 months.

RECONCEPTUALIZING NGO ACCOUNTABILITY

Centering accountability on the individual

Considerations of public control of authority and power should begin with the individual, and because I start with that assumption, I believe that the current debate about accountability in global governance should give more attention to the important contributions of Myres S. McDougal and Harold D. Lasswell. In their 1959 article in the *American Journal of International Law*, 'The Identification and Appraisal of Diverse Systems of Public Order', McDougal and Lasswell describe a 'world social process' in which the participants 'are acting individually in their own behalf and in concert with others' (McDougal and Lasswell, 1959). They emphasize that 'The ultimate actor is always the individual human being who may act alone or through any organization', and they talk of associations that 'do not concentrate upon power but primarily seek other values'.

By starting with the individual, McDougal and Lasswell avoid two analytical pitfalls. First, because individuals are seen as active participants, social and power process can be viewed as 'expanding circles of interaction' or as a 'series of arenas ranging in comprehensiveness from the globe as a whole... to nation states, provinces and cities, on down to the humblest village and township'. In this analytical approach, there is no need to explain why individuals should be able to participate at broader (or higher) levels of decision-making, just as they do in narrower (or lower) levels. Second, in positing the expanding circles, McDougal and Lasswell avoid the 'impossible separation of national and transnational law' (Lasswell and McDougal, 1997). The jurisprudence of human dignity they propose is applicable at all levels.

The notion of the individual being governed in a multitude of arenas is empirically convincing and normatively valuable. On any given day, the individual may be confronted with the dictates and decisions of his homeowner community, employer, local government, provincial government, national government and international organizations. The distance between the individual and his homeowner community may be closer than the distance to the UN, but the ability of the individual to influence any of the authoritative decisions may be very limited. Consider, for example, the innocent victims who suffer collateral damage as a result of sanctions ordered by the UN Security Council

(Reinisch, 2001), or the individuals dying of fatal illnesses who are being denied potentially effective drug treatments due to the precautionary approach used by the US Food and Drug Administration (Minor, 2005).

The normative value of seeing the individual as the object of simultaneous, multiple levels of lawmaking is that the truth becomes self-evident that an individual will have an interest in influencing all of the authoritative decisions that affect her, including not only those made by officials that she has elected, but also decisions made by others. From the perspective of the individual, the webs of authority enveloping her may be distinct in some ways, but the need to engage in politics is omnipresent. Although the strategies one uses in various political arenas will likely differ, the moral justification for purposive action will be the same – the pursuit of self-fulfillment and a just community order.

When is NGO accountability needed?

The literature on NGO accountability features a common thread, which is that internationally active NGOs should be subject to oversight and restraints by accountability holders. When a lens of democratic accountability is placed over NGOs, they can appear to be unaccountable because they are not publicly elected and because of the non-existence of a global public for ongoing valida-tion of NGO actions. Moreover, the restraints against abuse – fiscal, reputational and legal constraints – may not operate very well for some NGOs. The potential abuses include violating national laws, making false claims that tarnish the reputations of others, engaging in activities that abridge human rights, wasting financial contributions and misapprehending the public inter-est. I certainly agree that sometimes, some NGOs go agley. The question is what to do about it.

In answering, one should start with the individual. What accountability for an individual's actions is expected? We expect the individual to be account-able to her conscience, to her family, to whatever deity she recognizes, to the laws of the governments that have jurisdiction over her, to entities with which she has entered contractual relations (such as employers), and generally to those to whom she has made a commitment. This is an extensive range of accountability, but hardly seems all-encompassing in the sense that an individ-ual is to be accountable to all humans for all of her thoughts and deeds. In other words, my claim is that on a day-to-day basis, the individual engages in many acts of volition that are an exercise of her autonomy and for which no accountability is expected. If I am right about that, then when individuals act in concert, for example, through NGOs, we should not be surprised to see many decisions being taken for which there is no specific accountability to anyone outside the NGO.

Certainly, accountability needs to be in place for physically harmful NGO activities. Whenever an NGO engages in illegal or terrorist activity, then obviously it ought to be accountable to national criminal justice systems or to the UN Security Council. In recent years, the Security Council has often targeted non-state actors with economic sanctions (Hufbauer and Oegg, 2003).

Such retaliation against private persons through joint governmental action is not a new development, as multilateral legislation against dangerous organizations began with the Protocol of 1904 against the Anarchist Movement.[12]

Mundane illegal activity in NGOs can incur accountability under domestic law. An association committing criminal acts such as financial disruptions or eco-terrorism may be prosecuted (Crimm, 2004). Associations and their employees may also be liable under domestic law for potential torts such as negligence or defamation, and for violations of tax and corporate governance requirements.

A key question underlying the debate about NGO accountability is whether a new system is needed for oversight of NGOs, and if so, whether it should be formulated as a legal instrument. Ironically, the international organization on the cutting edge of applying international rules to NGOs is the WTO. The WTO has rules regarding public and private organizations that engage in standard-setting on products (that is, goods).[13] These rules appear in the WTO Agreement on Technical Barriers to Trade (TBT), which directs governments to 'take such reasonable measures as may be appropriate to them to ensure that local government and non-governmental standardizing bodies within their territories... accept and comply' with the TBT Code of Good Practice for the Preparation, Adoption and Application of Standards.[14] Among the requirements of the Code are that governmental and non-governmental standardizing bodies shall: first, play a full part in relevant international standardizing bodies with participation, whenever possible, taking place through one delegation representing all standardizing bodies in the territory; second, make every effort to achieve a national consensus on the standards to be developed; third, publish a work programme at least once every six months; fourth, before adopting a standard, allow a period of at least 60 days for the submission of comments by interested parties within the territory of that Member; fifth, take any submitted comments into account and, if so requested, reply to them as promptly as possible; and sixth, make an objective effort to resolve any complaints submitted by other standardizing bodies that have accepted the Code.[15]

Although the term 'accountability' is not used, the WTO TBT Code contains limited accountability norms of representation, consensus building, transparency, addressing complaints and giving a reply. The supervision of NGO operations through the TBT Agreement is a little-noticed phenomenon in WTO law. While there is nothing substantively wrong with the norms being demanded of standardizing organizations, some dissonance exists because the WTO itself does not practice what it preaches. The internal procedures of WTO committees do not provide for a public notice and comment period for WTO rule-making, and governments at the WTO can take positions without showing that their view is backed by a national consensus.

The WTO has increased the power of public and private international standard-setting bodies that devise international standards because such standards are now enforceable through the WTO. Under TBT rules, WTO member governments must use international standards where they exist as a basis for the government's own technical regulations.[16] Because a national government can be required to follow international standards even when it disagrees with them, governments may want to assure that national interests are well represented by the national organization that serves on the international body. Typically, the national organization is an NGO. A little-known US law, enacted in 1979, addresses this situation and provides authority to the Secretary of Commerce to oversee the adequacy of the 'representation' of US interests in standard-setting, and if necessary, to take steps to provide for adequate representation.[17] To my knowledge, no use has been made of this important administrative mechanism.

Beyond specialized WTO rules, no other multilateral discipline exists for NGO accountability. Should there be? Because NGO activity is multifarious, the answer to this question has to be highly textured. For operational activities by NGOs (for example, immunizations), one might demand more accountability than for advocacy by NGOs. For some operational activities, NGOs act as contractors. When NGOs are in a principal–agent relationship, certainly the NGO should be accountable to the principal. Yet much of NGO activity in world politics does not fit that typology because it lacks an external principal, and thus there is no ability to account to anybody. For NGOs, the key relationship is membership. The individual joins the NGO and puts time, money, voice and loyalty into it, and at some point exits the NGO.

Peter Spiro's (2002) distinction between internal and external accountability is a useful place to begin an analysis. When NGOs are in a corporate form, various internal governance obligations (in national law) ensue, such as accountability of the executives of the NGO to its trustees, accountability of employees to management and restraints against financial self-dealing. To enhance internal (and external accountability), governments often impose reporting and transparency requirements on NGOs. The UN has demanded that an NGO in consultative status 'possess appropriate mechanisms of accountability to its members' (note 7, Arrangements, para. 12). Stronger internal accountability can be responsive to the concern that NGOs are totally unchaperoned and are not accountable to anyone.

With respect to *external* accountability, funding agencies and foundations are likely to demand and obtain some degree of accountability (Ovsiovitch, 1998; Pettit, forthcoming). Sometimes in an NGO, there may be tension between accountability to the foundation giving it financial support and allegiance to the intended beneficiaries who may see the world differently than the foundation's grant officer. The most difficult issue regarding external accountability is the extent to which an NGO needs to be explicitly accountable to 'the public', or to the class of beneficiaries that the NGO purports to aid. When analysts criticize NGO activity, the criticism often takes the form that the NGO is not serving the cause it claims to serve. Assuming that such a problem exists, how can we address it through more intelligently designed accountability systems?

A key design consideration will be that if the concern is external global accountability of NGOs, then the optimal system may need to be transnational.

When legal measures are used, some harmonization of law or mutual recognition should be considered so that NGOs operating globally are not subjected to conflicting domestic laws.[18] When market or voluntary measures are used, there will be challenges of identifying the relevant stakeholders and sorting out inconsistent preferences among the stakeholders. For example, suppose an NGO in one country wants to preserve the wildlife in another, and yet the residents of the second country prefer development over preservation. In that situation, no unambiguous measure of NGO accountability seems to exist.

With so many different kinds of NGO activity in global governance, one promising approach is to distinguish various pieces. Consider a distinction between: first, delegated responsibilities; second, assumed responsibilities; and third, advocacy.

1 *Delegated* responsibilities occur when the international community delegates a task to an NGO. For example, the UN Security Council occasionally requests NGOs to provide assistance.[19] The Red Cross organizations are authorized and expected to perform various humanitarian functions (Forsythe, 1996–97; O'Connell, 2005). NGOs are used to certify vessel compliance with international rules regarding pollution from ships and safety of life at sea (Murphy, 2005). Although not exactly a delegated function, it is interesting to note that in June 2004, two NGOs were invited by the UN Security Council to give a briefing to the Council, meeting in regular session, regarding the role of civil society in post-conflict peace building.[20]

2 *Assumed* responsibilities occur when an NGO takes on a needed task that no one else is doing adequately. For example, Rotary International has launched a project to eradicate polio. Another example is election monitoring, which has been greatly facilitated by NGOs (Glidden, 2001). In the same way, the international regime to protect endangered species benefits immeasurably from constant monitoring by TRAFFIC, a joint program of the World Wildlife Fund and IUCN (The World Conservation Union) (www.traffic.org).

3 *Advocacy* is the NGO's use of its voice to influence world policy-making within international organizations and in national capitals. Just about every issue today experiences NGO advocacy.

The nature of an accountability system should vary depending on what is being carried out. As I see it, the external accountability requirements should be highest for the tasks delegated to NGOs, and lowest for activities that the NGO itself originates, with the assumed responsibilities lying somewhere in between.

The significance of making a person (a natural person or NGO) accountable is that the person owes a duty to a single or discrete set of accountability holders. For many NGO activities that duty exists, but for many others it does not. To suggest that an NGO should be accountable to the 'general public' or to the 'system' is doubly wrong – first, because drawing such dotted lines of accountability to the public itself is not feasible, and second and more importantly, because the general public is not the accountability holder of a free association of individuals. This is particularly so when the NGO activity at issue is the expression of ideas. The fact that NGOs may use their voice to call for intergovernmental organizations to be more accountable to the public does not provide a reason to turn the tables on the NGO and demand it to be equally accountable to the public. A similar problem would ensue in trying to make NGOs 'accountable' to beneficiaries. I would reformulate that goal to say that an NGO should better think through what it advocates so that its proposals will be more likely to help the intended beneficiaries and to do so without hurting others.

The real problem with NGOs is not that they are unaccountable, but rather that they suffer in various degrees from poor management and poor performance. Such behaviour often leads people to say that NGOs should be more 'accountable', but what they really seem to mean is that the NGO should act with more thoughtfulness, honesty, fidelity and probity. Recall the Encyclical of Pope Leo XIII in which he explained that associations need to be 'well and wisely administered'. The Pope also recognized that such ideal behaviour could not be forced by the 'grasp of a hand from without' (Pope Leo XIII, 1891, para. 55). That insight remains relevant in our own time as we consider how to achieve better NGO performance in global governance. The grasp of a hand from without should be avoided in favour of a steadier hand from within and the invisible hand of the market.

Let me suggest the following framework to enhance NGO performance, specifically with reference to international advocacy activities. Rather than try to control what NGOs say and do, we should be improving the quality of public discourse so that good ideas from NGOs are more likely to be accepted by elected officials and bad ideas are more likely to be ignored. The way to improve the marketplace of ideas is to make it as competitive as possible among bureaucrats, NGOs and business participants (Esty, 1998). When NGO outputs are poor, they are not wholly to blame because they receive so little advice on how to be constructive.

We live in an age of international standards and NGOs could certainly benefit from more refined standards as to what constitutes good practice in NGO advocacy. Some positive attributes are a high degree of transparency of NGO activities, an orientation toward data-driven analysis and strong internal governance mechanisms when an NGO operates in corporate form. In addition, governments owe it to the public and to the NGOs to enforce laws against NGOs that engage in illegal behaviour. Poor enforcement undermines the reputation of NGOs. In suggesting more attention be given to NGO performance, rather than to accountability, I am mindful that 'performance' is a quantity that should be measurable. Good analytical work is being done to construct such measures, but in the words of Michael Edwards and David Hulme, 'assessing NGO performance is a difficult and messy business' (Edwards and Hulme, 1995).

Debunking NGO 'representation'

Although the real issue in NGO accountability is whether the NGO is thoughtful, accurate and fair in its statements, most of the attention to NGO accountability has been on a different issue – that is, whether the NGO is representative of its members. To me, representation is simply a red herring. If the ideas being propounded are completely wrong, then the NGO for that reason may lack accountability to the community. In other words, I would give much more weight to how useful the ideas are that emanate from an NGO than I would give to whether the ideas faithfully represent the views of the NGO's membership.

If the adequacy of NGO representation of membership was ever a useful indicator of NGO accountability, surely the age of the internet and blogs changes that. For any powerful idea, a coordinator can put together many people in many countries who will support it. Such a virtual NGO might not have any organization in the traditional sense, but would be fully justified in saying that it faithfully represented its uniformly-thinking members. But surely the repetition or amplification of mistaken views is hardly sufficient for NGO accountability.

Although much NGO activity occurs in traditional affinity organizations, we often see a phenomenon whereby the potential impact of governmental decisions creates a new constituency concerned about it (King, 2003). Individuals who may have little in common with each other will join an organization to promote a particular cause that unites them. Such temporary, single-issue organizations may be highly representative of membership, but their accountability should be judged more substantively.

Another representational critique of NGOs seems to be that NGOs are pursuing merely a partial interest, special interest or single issue, and so perforce NGOs will not be accountable to the public as a whole, which is motivated by general interests. Yet as philosophers have noted for centuries, ascertaining the general interest is no easy task. The US Supreme Court has declared that 'The two houses of Congress are legislative bodies representing larger constituencies'.[21] Such representativeness is a source of the Congress's legitimacy, but the fact that there are two different houses suggests that neither was expected to be a perfect representative of the public. Acting in concert, however, they attempt to do so. Although NGOs may be a fixture of democracy, they are not themselves democratic institutions intended to represent the public in making decisions about the use of government power. NGOs do not compete with legislatures to represent public opinion.

At most, an NGO can represent a particular constituency or point of view. Yet the quality of its representation does not itself justify the NGO's role in influencing governmental outcomes. The representation of the public through elections is different from the nature of representing shared ideas and interests through an NGO. The root term 'represent' may get double duty, but representing ideas is different from representing voters.

Kenneth Anderson (2000; 2001) is right that some NGOs have made exaggerated claims that they represent civil society or the public and right again that NGOs sometimes assert that their participation in global governance makes it more accountable. Yet I do not worry about overreaching NGO rhetoric by NGOs as much as Anderson does. To the extent that NGOs do claim that their endorsement of a particular intergovernmental act gives it democratic legitimacy, I doubt that any government officials take that seriously. More importantly, I believe Anderson is wrong to call certain NGO advocacy anti-democratic merely because the NGO continues to try to change uncongenial policies of a government that the NGO has failed to convince regarding the merits of the NGO's position.[22]

The value derived from NGOs is not that they are better representatives of public opinion than are elected officials, or that NGOs supplement geographic representation via elections with interest group, pluralist representation. Those claims would not be justified and do not square with contemporary democratic theory. The true contribution of NGOs is that they seek to inform and influence the views of voters, elected officials and bureaucrats. That function of NGOs – to communicate information and values – fits comfortably in democratic theory because there is much more to democracy than the 'spasmodic majority vote' (Greaves, 1931).

As Alexis de Tocqueville postulated in *Democracy in America*, 'no countries need associations more... than those with a democratic social state' (De Tocqueville, 1988). His monumental book explains a number of advantages for democracy of political and civic associations, including that associations contribute to 'stimulating competition', and that they allow members 'to discover the arguments most likely to make an impression on the majority'. Thus, an NGO contributes to the democratic process by advocating its own view of the common good rather than by demonstrating that its view truly reflects the common will.

The basics do not change when policy discourse crosses national borders (Marks, 2001). NGOs are not created by governments to operate solely within a domestic political space. NGOs emerge through 'spontaneous creation' and will want to pursue their agendas at whatever level of government they need to. John Bolton claims that 'it is precisely the detachment from governments that makes international civil society so troubling, at least for democracies' (Bolton, 2000). Yet Bolton does not explain why he views voluntary associations as troubling when they detach themselves from government, other than to say that NGO participation in global governance 'provides a second opportunity for intrastate advocates to reargue their positions' and 'provides them at least the possibility of external lobbying leverage, to force domestic policy results they could not have otherwise achieved'. I do not share Bolton's fears about listening to competing views.

The approach that I offer here is to explain why there is no great need for special accountability for NGO advocacy functions in the public sphere. As voluntary organizations, NGOs depend on individuals who choose to belong to them, to work for them, to fund them and to listen to them. In 1999, the UN General Assembly endorsed strong freedom of association principles in the Declaration on the Right and Responsibility of Individuals, Groups and Organs of Society to Promote and Protect Universally Recognized Human Rights and Fundamental Freedoms. The Declaration states that 'Everyone has the right, individually and in association with others, to promote and to strive for the protection and realization of human rights and fundamental freedoms at the national *and international levels*' (UN, 1999, emphasis added). With respect to NGOs, the Declaration states, among other things, that 'Individuals, non-governmental organizations and relevant institutions have an important role to play in contributing to making the public more aware of questions relating to all human rights and fundamental freedoms'. This NGO role in making the public more aware is the key to understanding why NGO outputs injected into the marketplace of ideas are fully consistent with republican democracy.

Performance versus accountability in the marketplace of ideas

The best check on bad ideas from NGOs is criticism from others. Consider the recent episode of the spring 2005 report by Amnesty International that likened the US detention centers in Guantanamo to 'gulags'. President George Bush called that charge 'absurd' and Amnesty received considerable criticism for using a loaded term and making a claim for which they did not have evidence.[23] Personally, I do not know enough about the conditions at Guantanamo to judge whether Amnesty's claim was absurd or just exaggerated. This episode was valuable, however, in showing that a controversial statement by an NGO can be criticized by stakeholders and commentators, and that mistakes can hurt an NGO's reputation.

Such a market-like check is sufficient. The last thing the world needs is more governmental controls on Amnesty International to assure its accuracy and accountability. Common to the analyses by Edwards (2000) and Blitt (2004) is a conclusion that although NGOs could act voluntarily to develop standards to promote accountability, governments should not seek to impose such standards. NGOs tend to criticize governments, and so it will be difficult for governments to appear to be objective were they to police NGO statements as to whether they are honest and fair. Although I would agree with Edwards that 'structured experimentation' can be useful, I cannot endorse the recommendation of the UN Panel of Eminent Persons that urges the UN Secretariat to engage NGOs in discussion about codes of conduct and self-policing mechanisms. In my view, that would be an inappropriate role for international bureaucrats.

The right way to promote better NGO behaviour is by fostering the continuation of present trends of increased introspection by NGOs about their own performance and new efforts by NGOs to evaluate one another. Instead of seeking to coerce NGOs into being more 'accountable', we should instead seek ways to enhance incentives for NGOs to upgrade their performance. Today, NGO performance is being monitored more than ever before – but in the right way, by other NGOs. For example, the American Enterprise Institute and the Federalist Society for Law and Public Policy Studies have jointly set up 'NGO Watch' in 'an effort to bring clarity and accountability to the burgeoning world of NGOs' (www.ngowatch.org). So far, their web site is largely composed of news stories, related documentation and policy papers, but perhaps some serious watching will occur.

Getting real mileage out of monitoring, or 'auditing' NGOs, as suggested by *The Economist*, requires the availability of performance standards that have been accepted by many NGOs. Earlier I noted that Blitt (2004) had recommended 'self-regulation' by NGOs and some observers have suggested an NGO Code of Conduct. Defined standards are a prerequisite for any numerical ratings of NGOs.

Standards would be very difficult to devise for advocacy, but could be doable for the operational activities of NGOs. In 2003, the Humanitarian Accountability Partnership International (HAP-I) was launched to improve the accountability of organizations engaged in delivering humanitarian services (Callamard in this volume). HAP-I promotes and assists self-monitoring by member organizations, which include well-known organizations such as CARE International and the Danish Refugee Council. The motto of HAP-I is 'making humanitarian action accountable to beneficiaries'. Another recent development is that Social Accountability International (SAI) has been asked by InterAction, an umbrella group of international charities, to inspect and certify the tsunami-related child sponsorship programs of five major NGOs (for example, Save the Children US). The certification requires allowing SAI to inspect documents and field activities, and also examines some management issues such as director conflicts of interest, accuracy of advertisements and a 35 per cent cap on administrative and fundraising costs relative to total expenditures.

New techniques are now being tested by governments to gain the benefits of NGO participation. One is multi-stakeholder roundtables or dialogues, which are sessions held during an intergovernmental summit or conference in which persons from governments, business and NGOs participate together in a discussion. Such dialogues were held, for example, at the UN Monterrey and Johannesburg Summits. Another technique is joint statements by a broad range of NGOs that are submitted to international conferences. For example, in June 2004, at the United Nations Conference on Trade and Development XI, the Civil Society Forum submitted a Declaration that consisted of an analysis and several specific recommendations. The Declaration stated that the Forum 'represents social movements, pro-development groups, women's groups, trade unions, peasants and agricultural organizations, environmental organizations, faith-based organizations and fair trade organizations, among others' (Civil Society Forum, 2004). This technique is distinguishable from the traditional parallel summit of NGOs that meets alongside an intergovernmental conference (Pianta, 2001). The difference is that statements emanating from a parallel summit are not an official part of the intergovernmental meeting, as they were with the UNCTAD Forum. It may be too soon to tell whether these new forms of encouragement of NGOs to cooperate with each other will lead to more reasoned outputs. Yet such efforts are worth trying. After all, combining the value of autonomous groups with sustained cooperation among them is likely to contribute to economic and social progress.

CONCLUSION: THE FUTURE OF NGO
ACCOUNTABILITY

Democratic debate should not be subject to rigid zoning. Those who advocate ideas in one polity should be free to advocate them in another. When a transnational group gets together to promote a legitimate cause, it should be able to use its voice in any country or international organization.

The idea that NGOs active in global governance lack sufficient accountability has become conventional wisdom, and I would guess that the highest waves of accountability demands on civic society have yet to hit the shores. Because NGOs are extremely sensitive to threats to their influence, they can be expected to take steps to obviate those threats. Recognizing that NGO influence is now being undermined to some extent by the mantra for greater NGO accountability, NGOs will be eager to cooperate in the expansion of 'accountability' mechanisms.

An attempt to formulate a plan for greater government regulation of NGO political activities would run into many problems, starting with the trammels of statism. Government regulation tends to be territorial and yet this does not match up well with the domain of NGO action that can be global, or with the membership and participants in an NGO that can be transnational. The difficulty of this spatial challenge tends to be underestimated by those who would like to see greater NGO accountability to someone or something. It is one thing to say that Global Witness, for example, needs to be more accountable, but quite another to specify to what sovereign authority or global public accountability is to be owed.

Governments should not try to regulate directly the quality of advocacy of NGOs, but rather should improve it indirectly by establishing mechanisms that give NGOs an incentive to upgrade their own performance. NGOs are very likely to be criticizing governments and it will be difficult for governments to appear to be objective were they to supervise NGO statements.

The idea of providing better mechanisms for NGO debate works well whether the issues are technical/scientific or hinge on values. The WTO benefited enormously from the intellectual contributions of health NGOs who pointed out that the trade rule for compulsory licensing of patents could prevent a supply of essential medicines from being available to countries without a manufacturing capacity.[24] That point was an economic and technical one. The NGO critics of WTO Agreement on Trade-Related Aspects of Intellectual Property Rights (TRIPS) also raised more general concerns about whether the WTO rules for patenting took sufficient account of health values. Over many decades, NGOs have shown themselves to be adept in advocacy on both the narrower technical points and the broader claims on values.

In the critiques of NGOs, one subtext seems to be that NGOs are pursuing only a 'partial' interest (or a single-issue campaign), and perforce NGOs will not be accountable to the public as a whole, which is motivated by general interests. Assuming that this is true and a problem, the solution might be to pay less attention to the NGOs or to mandate group altruism. In my view, that is the wrong diagnosis and the wrong solution. It is the wrong diagnosis because partiality or private interest can operate as a virtue not only in markets but also in polities. Constitutional rules may be valuable to tie a government's hands in order to make it less susceptible to the entreaties of special interests, but in my view, such constitutional rules should not include muzzling the private voice. It is the wrong solution because authoritative decision-makers need a constant infusion of competitive ideas and values in order to make the right public policy decisions. To quote De Tocqueville (1988), 'A government, by itself, is equally incapable of refreshing the circulation of feelings and ideas among a great people, as it is of controlling every industrial undertaking'. Government bureaucrats and politicians do not have any special competence to oversee NGO operations and guide them towards attainment of the common good. Ideally, any ensuing regulatory or accountability mechanisms should be devised by NGOs themselves as voluntary measures.

NOTES

1 Thus, the Encyclical considers both mutual benefit and public benefit groups. The Encyclical does not specifically address lobbying activities of NGOs.

2 Sanger was one of the drafters of the provisions on labour in the Treaty of Versailles and she became the first head of the ILO's Legislative Section (Oldfield, 2004).

3 I am not aware of any formal requests by NGOs since Shelton's article was written.

4 Review of Consultative Arrangements with Non-Governmental Organizations, E.S.C. Res. 288(X), Feb. 27, 1950, para. 5.

5 Arrangements for Consultation with Non-Governmental Organizations ('Arrangements'), E.S.C. Res. 1996/31, para. 9 (emphasis added). The disjunctive 'or' seems to imply that not all NGOs given status have to be of a representative nature.

6 World Bank Inspection Panel Operating Procedures, para. II.A.4.a, available at: http://wbln0018.worldbank.org/IPN/ipnweb.nsf/WOperatingProcedures. The request may also come from an organization, association, society, duly appointed representative, or foreign agent in some circumstances (Boisson de Chazournes, 2005).

7 'Sins of the Secular Missionaries' (2000) *The Economist*, 29 January. See also 'The Non-governmental Order' (1999) *The Economist*, 11 December.

8 According to Bolton, the Forum of Civil Society would be an annual conference of worldwide NGOs that would meet at the United Nations in New York.

9 The concept of 'international NGOs', which is at the center of Anderson's analysis, is not explicitly defined, as far as I can tell. As I read Anderson, he is discussing two phenomena: first, NGOs based in one country that act on global issues; and second, transnational NGOs that contain members (or subunits) from different countries.

10 Rieff (1999) has criticized NGOs by saying that the 'leaders of such groups, unlike politicians, do not have to campaign, hold office, allow the public to see their tax returns or stand for re-election'. In a recent study, two social scientists note the irony of complaints by journalists and academics that civic society associations are

not democratically elected because, as they explain, no one elected the journalists and academics either (Verweij and Josling, 2003).

11 Perhaps a more basic question about Anderson's thesis is why lobbying by an NGO to a group of governments poses more risks to democracy than the same lobbying by that NGO to its 'home' government.

12 Protocol respecting Measures to be Taken Against the Anarchist Movement, Mar. 14, 1904, 195 Consol. T.S. 118. Earlier multilateral treaties acted against the slave trade, a profit-making enterprise.

13 The rules to be discussed below apply only to goods, not to services. See WTO Agreement on Technical Barriers to Trade ('TBT Agreement'), art. 1.3. Thus, a standard programme regarding services – such as the 'Equator Principles' on project finance – is not covered by these WTO rules.

14 TBT Agreement, art. 4.1. In the WTO lexicon, a standard is something approved by a recognized body with which compliance is not mandatory. TBT Annex I, para. 2.

15 This rule seems to include the possibility of complaints by bodies in any WTO member country.

16 TBT Agreement, art. 2.4. An exception exists in situations 'when such international standards or relevant parts would be an ineffective or inappropriate means for the fulfilment of the legitimate [national] objectives pursued, for instance because of fundamental climatic or geographical factors or fundamental technological problems'. In the one dispute so far (dispute WT/DS231, EC – *Trade Description of Sardines*), this exception was applied strictly.

17 19 USCS § 2543 (2005). The procedure provides for private persons to initiate complaints.

18 One successful mutual recognition initiative occurred in the European Convention on the Recognition of the Legal Personality of International Non-Governmental Organizations, Apr. 24, 1986, ETS 124. International NGOs are defined broadly as those carrying on activities with effect in at least two states (art. 1). Once it has gained recognition in one party, the NGO has the right to invoke the Convention in another party to acquire recognition there (with some exceptions) (arts. 2, 4).

19 The earliest episode was Complaint of Aggression Upon the Republic of Korea, S. C. Res. 85 (July 31, 1950) requesting appropriate NGOs to provide such assistance as the United Command may request.

20 The two NGOs were CARE International and the International Center for Transitional Justice. See Arria and Other Special Meetings between NGOs and Security Council Members, available at www.globalpolicy.org/security/mtgsetc/brieindx.

21 United States *v.* Ballin, 144 US 1, 7 (1892).

22 Daniele Archibugi calls for 'institutions which enable the voice of individuals to be heard in global affairs, irrespective of their resonance at home' (Archibugi, 2000).

23) See 'Amnesty Insufferable', *New York Post*, 29 May 2005, p26; Applebaum, A. (2005) 'Amnesty's Amnesia', *Washington Post*, 8 June, p.A21; Riley, J. (2005). 'Human-rights Group Says US Runs "Gulag of our Times"', *Chicago Tribune*, 26 May, p.15.

24 See the Agreement on Trade-Related Aspects of Intellectual Property Rights (TRIPS), art. 31(f).

3

Civil Society, Representation and Accountability: Restating Current Debates on the Representativeness and Accountability of Civic Associations

Enrique Peruzzotti

INTRODUCTION

In recent years, a very lively debate on the public status of civil society organizations has emerged as a result of the increasing questioning by governments and multilateral agencies of the role and activities of NGOs and civic associations. The impressive proliferation of a multitude of advocacy organizations and of different sorts of NGOs in the domestic and global arenas has generated concerns about the nature and consequences of their activities on domestic representative institutions. Doubts have been raised about the representative claims and the accountability of those civic associations. For many years, particularly when those organizations largely operated in authoritarian environments, the issue of the representativeness and accountability of civic actors could easily be brushed aside given the illegitimate nature of many domestic governments and the continuous threat they presented to any form of autonomous social activity that dared to challenge and expose their abuses of power and human rights. However, the increased presence of democratically elected governments in developing countries makes it difficult to keep avoiding an analysis of the relationship between civil society actors and representative institutions.

In many of the new democracies, elected officials are skeptical of the claim of NGOs and advocacy organizations to 'represent' the citizenry, civil society, 'the poor' or any other specific constituency. After all, they claim, they are elected in honest elections in which the whole citizenry participates (under the equalitarian principle of one citizen, one vote). The behaviour of elected officials is under the constant supervision of accountability agencies to assure that their policies and decisions are responsive to the public. In contrast, they argue, most of the organizations that operate in civil society are directed by a cadre of self-appointed leaders, many of them are not even membership organizations, and are not subject – as politicians are – to the scrutiny of formal mechanisms of legal and political accountability. Similar arguments are made for civic organizations and networks that operate in the transnational arena and that conceive of themselves as part of a global civil society. While at this level there are doubts about the representativeness of *all* organizations given the absence of global-level sovereign institutions, the increasing visibility of global civic networks has contributed to putting in the spotlight questions about their accountability and alleged bonds with a supposedly global citizenry (Anderson and Rieff, 2004).

Debates on the accountability of civic associations and NGOs are often framed in language that resembles the relationship between citizens and elected politicians. It makes it important to have a closer look at the nature of the ties that link civic associations to the citizenry at large, because it helps to understand how NGO accountability is often approached from a flawed angle. Can civil society organizations or NGOs be equated to political parties? Should they become part of representative institutions? Or should they remain in the constituent side of the representative equation? These are some of the questions that will guide the analysis.

The first section of this chapter will focus on the conceptual links between accountability and representation, and will show that the concept of accountability is intrinsically linked to the delegation of power by citizens to politicians. The second section analyses the relationship of civil society to representative institutions, arguing that civic organizations are located not on the representative, but on the constituent side of the democratic bond. The chapter then critically reviews existing debates about the representative claims of civil society organizations, arguing that analyses that simply stretch the concept of political representation to civic associations overlook the crucial differences between these two types of organizations. Finally the chapter focuses on the issue of the accountability of civic organizations and explores alternative ways to improve the institutional environment and organizational quality of the plurality of associational forms that characterize contemporary civil societies.

REPRESENTATION AND ACCOUNTABILITY

The concept of accountability is intrinsically linked to that of representation. It refers to a particular type of bond that politicians establish with the citizenry in so-called 'representative democracies' as a result of the periodical act of delegation of power that the electorate makes to elected representatives. In contrast with authoritarian regimes and non-representative forms of democracy,[1] representative democracies combine an institutional framework of authorization of political power with one oriented to ensure the responsiveness and accountability of those authorized agents. The citizenry as the sovereign instance of democracy temporarily delegates its power to a group of representatives appointed through free elections. The representative is someone who has been authorized to act with relative independence of the electorate. Insofar as representative democracy implies the existence of a fundamental gap between political representatives and citizens, it requires the existence of institutional mechanisms to ensure that such separation does not result in unresponsive or illegal governments. The central question addressed by the concept of accountability is precisely how to regulate and reduce the gap between representatives and represented while simultaneously preserving the distance between political authorities and citizenry that characterizes the relations of representation (Pitkin, 1978).

The concept of accountability refers to the ability to ensure that public officials are answerable for their behaviour, in the sense of being forced to inform and justify their decisions and of being eventually sanctioned for those decisions. It involves a certain type of exchange or relationship between two autonomous actors, one of which holds a claim of 'superior authority'. As Richard Mulgan (2000) argues, accountability is *external*, that is, it entails an act of control by someone that is not part of the body being held accountable. Accountability refers to a certain type of *interaction*: it is a two-way social exchange (the seeking of answers, response, rectification, and so on). Finally, accountability presupposes *rights of superior authority*, in the sense that those asking for accountability have the authority to demand answers and impose sanctions. The latter must not be interpreted as necessarily having the ability of formal enforcement or sanctioning power, it can also refer to a moral claim to assert rights or to denounce wrongdoing based on the normative claims that legitimize the representative contract.

The accountability of political power can be established on legal or on political grounds. The notion of legal accountability refers to a set of institutional mechanisms aimed at ensuring that the actions of public officials are legally and constitutionally framed. Through the separation of powers, the recognition of fundamental rights and the system of checks and balances, modern constitutionalism establishes the institutions that enable curbing the arbitrariness of state power. The constitutional grounding of state institutions in public law parcels state power into judicial, legislative and executive branches, and delimits state activity into rigorously circumscribed competencies. In addition, fundamental rights provide institutional safeguards to protect citizens from unlawful encroachment by state officials. While these constitutional and legal regulations might generate compliance, they require mechanisms of accountability for those cases in which public officials engage in improper or illegal actions. As Mulgan (2000) argues, in its core sense, mechanisms of legal accountability 'are confined to that part of the law which lays down enforcement procedures'. For mechanisms of legal accountability to function effectively, there must exist institutions with the capability to call to account and to impose sanctions for those cases where officials step outside due process or constitutional prescriptions. The latter can refer to agencies specialized in demanding accountability (like audit offices, administrative tribunals or ombudsmen) or institutions that while not primarily agents of accountability – since they perform a variety of functions – play an important role in upholding constitutional and procedural rules (legislatures and the legal system).

The concept of political accountability refers instead to the responsiveness of governmental policies to the preferences of the electorate. Political accountability is intimately intertwined with the concept of democratic representation. It refers to a particular type of relationship that results in the act of delegating authority to a representative body, where the represented holds a claim to superior authority over those to whom it has temporarily delegated its power. A government is politically accountable if citizens have the means for punishing unresponsive or irresponsible administrations. It is usually assumed that political parties represent the essential institution of political representation and that elections are the main mechanism of political accountability that the citizenry has at its disposal to reward or punish politicians. Elections provide a regular mechanism for citizens to hold governments responsible for their actions, forcing out of office those incumbents who did not act in the best interest of voters and reelecting those who did.[2] It is from this position of representatives of the citizenry at large that political society questions the alleged political representativeness of civil society organizations.

CIVIL SOCIETY AND REPRESENTATIVE GOVERNMENT

The concept of civil society refers to the associational dimension of citizenry. It points to the self-constituted activities of associated citizens, be it in the form of social movements, voluntary associations, advocacy organizations, NGOs, informal publics, and so on. The concept of civil society entails not only a plurality of associational forms that emerge as a result of the self-constituting forms of action of autonomous citizens, but also a specific set of institutions that makes those activities possible. Two different aspects of the term 'civil society' must then be distinguished: first, an 'active' dimension that refers to the multiple associational forms that act within the terrain of civil society; and second, a 'passive' dimension that refers to the establishment of a system of fundamental rights that guarantee the free unfolding of the actors and associations that operate within the realm of civil society, as well as an autonomous public sphere. 'The rights to communication, assembly, and association, among others, constitute the public and associational spheres of civil society as spheres of positive freedom within which agents can collectively debate issues of common concern, act in concert, assert new rights, and exercise influence on political (and potentially economic) society' (Cohen and Arato, 1992).

The associational dimension of the concepts of citizenship and civil society clearly stands on the constituent side of the representative equation. While analyses of representation have tended to focus on the role of the individual citizen as voter (Manin, 1997; Przeworski et al, 1999), it is important not to overlook civil society as a crucial social arena that contributes in manifold ways to ensure accountable government. Representative government presupposes a dynamic interaction between the political system and the represented; to understand adequately the forms assumed by such dynamic, we should focus on the complex set of in-put/out-put relationships between citizens and politicians that contribute to feed, shape and reproduce relations of representation. It is necessary to go beyond individualist and election-anchored models of representation to include the self-constituting associative practices and politics of civic associations, social movements, NGOs and informal publics, that is, the activities that the constituents unfold to assure that representatives remain responsive and accountable to them. In brief, proper functioning of representative arrangements requires both active representatives and constituents.

There are two ways in which civil society complements and enhances the workings of existing mechanisms of accountability. First, civil society enhances representative government by adding new voices and concerns to the political agenda, thematizing novel issues, and criticizing existing public policies and legislation. Second, civil society can also contribute to improve the quality of representative arrangements by demanding effective legal accountability. By denouncing violations of rights or breaches of law and due process by public officials, as well as through efforts to develop strategies oriented to improve the workings of the mechanisms and agencies that regulate and frame the behaviour of political representatives, civil society complements and often activates mechanisms of legal accountability.

The first group of activities and initiatives revolve around issues of political accountability and has been widely analysed by the literature on social movements and on civil society (Offe, 1987; Tarrow, 1994; McAdam et al, 1996). Many of the social movements that have emerged in different democratic societies in the past three decades (ecological, feminist, peace, youth, anti-globalization, and so on) express identities and claims that were not represented or adequately processed by the existing mediating structures of political and economic society.[3] The role of parties and interest group organizations as instances of political aggregation and mediation has been challenged increasingly by new social movements, NGOs, transnational organizations and civic associations, that is, by a variety of forms of self-constituted associational forms that developed innovative forms of civil society-based politics. Major goals of the new forms of civic engagement were the reconstitution and strengthening of an autonomous civil society and the struggle to open up existing structures of representation to new voices and demands. Those actors develop new venues of social expression against what they perceive to be an ossified set of political mediations that became incapable of providing a focus of symbolic identification and an effective mechanism for the collective articulation and aggregation of social identities and interests (Dalton and Kuechler, 1990). Environmental organizations, the peace movement, feminist organizations and anti-globalization protesters illustrate efforts to include into the political agenda concerns that had been largely overlooked by the screening structures of interest pluralism and competitive party politics. Such a broad spectrum of civic actors provide a 'sounding board' that, by developing campaigns to draw the attention of decision-making authorities to previously ignored issues, plays a crucial sensor role that helps the political system to remain responsive to the current concerns of the citizenry.

There is a second group of societal initiatives that focus instead on the legal dimension of the concept of accountability. This sort of demand has been recently analysed by the literature on social accountability (Peruzzotti and Smulovitz, 2002). The concept of social accountability draws attention to initiatives of control exercised by actors such as civic associations, NGOs (both local and transnational), social movements and the media that were commonly neglected by the literature on accountability. Traditionally, analyses of mechanisms of legal accountability focus exclusively on the interactions that take place within a group of intra-state actors and on mechanisms (such as parliamentary investigative commissions, the courts, electoral authorities) that belong to a broader system of division of power and of checks and balances within the state. However, the emergence of strong human rights movements in different national and regional contexts and of a variety of civic initiatives organized around a common concern for *constitutionalizing* the workings of the state called attention to innovative forms of civil society-based politicization organized primarily around demands for accountable government (Pérez-Díaz, 1999; Peruzzotti, 2002; Goetz and Jenkins, 2001).[4]

The politics of social accountability involve civic efforts whose goals are: first, to monitor the behaviour of public officials and agencies to make sure they abide by the law; second, to expose cases of governmental wrongdoing; and third, to activate the operation of horizontal agencies, such as the judiciary or legislative investigative commissions that otherwise would not be initiated or would be initiated in a biased way. By exposing cases of governmental wrongdoing, human rights violations, activating reluctant state agencies of control and monitoring the operation of those agencies, civic actors are making a crucial contribution to the enforcement of the rule of law.

In brief, and returning to the question of accountability, the concept of civil society stands on the constituent side of the representative bond; it is not a representative instance but rather it indicates a terrain where multiple constituencies organize to demand accountability from political society. Constituent politics are different from representative politics in the sense that the former are not bound by the formal rules and accountability mechanisms that constrain and regulate the interaction of the latter (Montúfar, 2005). Social movements and NGOs are not forced to compete and win elections or court different constituencies, nor are they subject to the formal procedures that regulate the interactions among the different instances of representative government. In contrast to representative politics, the constituent politics of civil society leave great room for creative and innovative action, allowing social movements or NGOs to challenge present identities or existing constituencies without being concerned about electoral accountability or due process. As Anderson and Rieff have recently argued:

> *because they are not electoral institutions (not representative in the electoral sense) they are free to be pure, unabashed advocates of a point of view; free to ignore all the contradictory impulses that democratic politics requires and the compromises and adjustments and departures from principled purity that politicians must make; and free to ignore entirely what everyone else, the great democratic masses and their leaders, might think in favor of what they themselves believe is the right, the true, and the good.*
> (Anderson and Rieff, 2004)

There are several schemes, however, that aim at placing domestic civil society organizations in a role that goes beyond the place it is usually assigned to it under representative democracy. This is the case of certain strands of neo-liberalism, of advocates of 'co-governance' or of proponents of 'associative democracy'.[5] Such models presuppose a devolution to civil society of some of the functions delegated to political society, that is, they aim at integrating certain civic actors into the existing structures of interest intermediation. The latter implies a profound redefinition of the role attributed to civil society in a representative democracy: civil society organizations cease to be constituent organizations to become mechanisms of intermediation.

If civic associations assume public functions and act as partners in governance, a different yardstick should apply and formal mechanisms to regulate and monitor their activities must be established to be able to hold these actors accountable. Yet, if that is the case, we can no longer speak of a model of representation based on accountability, because the basic distinction at the base of the representative relationship between represented and representative has been eroded or replaced by direct forms of social participation in decision-making procedures. Civic organizations that 'co-govern' or that have assumed decision-making responsibilities are no longer on the side of the citizenry, that is, they are no longer external to political power; they have migrated from the constituent to the representative side of the equation and are consequently in no position to monitor political power externally. They should be subjected to formal mechanisms of accountability, as any other representative body would.[6]

WHO DO YOU REPRESENT? QUESTIONS ABOUT THE REPRESENTATIVE CLAIMS OF CIVIC ACTORS

On many occasions, economic and political elites react to the different forms of civil society-based politics by turning the civic claims for greater accountability and responsiveness against the claimers and questioning their legitimacy, as well as their representative character. Who do they represent? Who appointed them? To whom are they accountable? Those are common questions raised by elected authorities, corporations or bureaucrats when confronting challenges by specific social actors. The following excerpt from an editorial in *The Economist* helps to illustrate the type of counterclaims that are raised against civil society movements and associations:

> *The increasing clout of NGOs, respectable and not so respectable, raises an important question: who elected Oxfam, or, for that matter, the League for a Revolutionary Communist International? Bodies such as these are, to varying degrees, extorting admissions of fault from law-abiding companies and changes in policy from democratically elected governments. They may claim to be acting in the interests of the people – but then so do the objects of their criticism, governments and the despised international institutions. In the West, governments and their agencies are, in the end, accountable to voters. Who holds the activists accountable.* (*The Economist*, 23 September 2000)

What are the representative claims of civil society organizations? The question raises an important problem that is at the heart of current debates about the legitimacy and accountability of civil society actors. Elected officials, it is generally argued, are periodically appointed through regular and contested elections and are therefore representative of society at large and accountable to the citizenry. Civic organizations, instead, can never make such a claim to universality; the groups of civil society inevitably always refer to a far narrower world of citizens than representative authorities. They are self-appointed and self-constituted associational forms and, unlike political representatives, they are not formally obliged to give periodic accounts to the citizenry.

It would be erroneous to extrapolate mindlessly from the conceptual framework employed to analyse representative relations to civil society. As argued in the previous section, civil society is not a representative instance, but a constituent one. Being on the constituent side of the equation, civic actors cannot be subjected to the same yardstick employed to evaluate political parties or parliament. To subject civic organizations to the criteria of political representation that are applied to electoral organizations negates the very specific features that make civic organizations valuable for representative democracy: the freedom that citizens enjoy to associate voluntarily with others who share similar interests and values irrespective of how extended or appreciated those values or activities are in the citizenry at large (Gutman, 1998). A major tenant of civil society studies since Alexis de Tocqueville sees in civil society a crucial sociological counterweight to the potential threat of democratic majoritarianism. To subordinate its associations to such logic would suppress one of the most valued democratic functions of civil society in representative regimes. It would be as erroneous for civil society to claim or abrogate a representative role, as it is to demand 'representativeness' from civic actors.[7]

It is also misleading to analyse civic actors through the theoretical lenses of pressure- or interest-group politics. Pressure groups representing the socio-economic interests of their members are a parallel tier of organizations whose goal is to lobby government to advance and protect these special interests. The role of interest-group organizations in democracy, as well as the tensions and challenges they pose to representative institutions have been extensively analysed by the literature on pressure groups' politics, pluralism and neo-corporatism.[8] To equate civil society to the logic of interest group-politics is an unfair and inadequate simplification of the immense forms of collective action and association that develop within the social arena. In fact, a main theoretical goal of the new social movements and civil society literature is to differentiate the former interventions in the political process from the established literature on parties and interest groups. The proliferation of new forms of politicization by civic groups is seen as the principal innovation that new social movements and civic networks have made to representative politics. These value-driven organizations thus differ in their structure and claims from private interest representation; their agenda is not necessarily driven by the defense of specific economic interests, nor are their actions likely to benefit their members directly.[9]

The associational terrain of contemporary civil societies is diverse, containing in its womb an ample variety of organizational forms and different understandings of what they claim to *represent* as civic organizations. Usually, the literature distinguishes between membership and non-membership organizations. Grassroots or membership organizations differ from other forms of civic associations by the fact that they are internally organized around a classic representative structure: there is a clear constituency, a process of delegation of power to a set of representatives, as well as instances and mechanisms by which the former can make the latter accountable. As with political parties and interest-group organizations, membership or grassroots associations are organized around a clearly defined constituency, which they claim to represent. In this type of organization, numbers matter: the size of their membership is usually taken as a measure of their 'representative' weight by government and political parties. A large massive organization will certainly command more attention from them than one that only represents a politically insignificant proportion of the electorate. The fact of being membership organizations does not place them, however, on the representative side of the equation; even if they democratize their internal structure, these organizations are still constituent organizations and can only claim to represent themselves and their membership-based constituencies.[10]

Other forms of civic organizations like social movements or NGOs, instead, are built on a different type of claim. They are generally non-membership organizations and in many instances are driven by a small cadre of activists and self-appointed leaders. Their voice is neither the voice of numbers or votes, nor the voice of already constituted private interests; they do not claim to represent a certain percentage of the citizenry or electorate, nor specific interests (as private-interest organizations). They entail a different sort of organization – a public-interest organization – whose role and interventions can be subjected neither to the representative logic of parties, nor to forms of private-interest representation. They do not claim (and do not want to be) representative of existing constituencies. Rather, they want to transform the latter's identities and behaviour; they want to mould a new type of constituency. New social movements, for instance, do not necessarily compete for the allegiance of an existing electorate; their public interventions are aimed at challenging majoritarian beliefs and forms of self-understanding (Melucci, 1996).

Similarly, many self-appointed NGOs act as advocates of constituencies that do not yet exist, they claim to speak for the unorganized and the voiceless. They engage in what Warren Nyamugasira (1998) has termed an 'interim representation' – they are not actually representing a constituency, but rather speaking for a constituency that has yet to be organized and empowered. As mentioned above, representation requires both active constituents and representatives. In the case of 'interim representation' a crucial side of the equation is missing: this sort of advocacy is not an exercise of representation, nor can we frame it within an accountability model. These sorts of NGOs are actually attempting to enhance representation by acting as temporary spokespersons of constituencies that have yet to be created; the very success of their job of empowerment will make these organizations superfluous. 'The ultimate objective against which success must be measured', Nyamugasira rightly argues, 'is that the people's voice increases while that of NGOs themselves declines' (Nyamugasira, 1998).[11]

It is this transformative and future-oriented logic that sets many civil society organizations apart from the representative activities of parties and interest-group organizations. While the latter struggle to represent existing constituencies properly, be it a percentage of the electorate or a certain economic sector, many civil society organizations do not attempt to aggregate already constituted interests and groups, but rather to challenge them. It is a future-oriented politics that is initially carried out in loneliness by very 'unrepresentative' groups and organizations.[12] The work of human rights organizations in authoritarian contexts, for instance, often is carried out by minor groups that must confront the hostility of both the regimes they are denouncing and of society at large. The significance of such politics rests precisely on its unrepresentative character, that is, in the refusal to abide by the predominant standards of an existing political culture that welcomed or tolerated human rights abuses and on their efforts to trigger processes of political learning that would eventually reshape social identities and behaviours.

In conclusion, civil society should not be forced to be in a representative relationship to the citizenry the way political parties are. A great deal of civil society politics entails broadening the scope of existing representative structures and generating new constituencies, not simply mirroring existing political constituencies. To attempt to make civic organizations politically accountable to the citizenry at large would destroy one of the most valuable assets of the notion of civil society: its role in generating cultural and political innovation by challenging predominant forms of self-understanding. The question that is frequently asked of civic organizations, '*Who do you represent?*', is inadequate to weigh the claims of civic actors. The question we should rather ask is '*What do you represent?'*. It is not numbers, but the force of their arguments that gives legitimacy to their claims.[13]

TO WHOM ARE YOU ACCOUNTABLE?
THE ACCOUNTABILITY OF CIVIC ORGANIZATIONS

The notion of accountability cannot be separated from the concept of the representative contract that binds elected authorities to the citizenry. It presupposes, as argued in the first section, a form of interaction in which one of the actors holds claims to superior authority and the capability to demand answers and impose sanctions because it has temporarily delegated its authority to a certain group of representatives. No equivalent to such delegation exists in civil society organizations; most of them are self-organized and self-appointed, and consequently are not tied to give formal accounts to the citizenry the way elected officials are.

The fact that civic organizations are not formally politically accountable to the citizenry as elected representatives are does not mean that they can be completely oblivious to public beliefs and sentiments, and that they cannot be subject to informal sanctions. Given that these organizations fundamentally operate in the public sphere, where they develop counter-arguments that challenge official or predominant interpretations, their credibility and public reputation is crucial to the success of their mission and activities. It is in their best interest to uphold high standards of behaviour and to develop a solid reputation. In this respect, civil society organizations and movements are subject to the same informal controls and threats as political parties (and for that matter, as any organization that needs to build and sustain symbolic capital to operate successfully in the public sphere). The fact that these mechanisms are informal does not mean that they are weak; a scandal can have devastating effects on any civic organization since it could irreparably damage its public image and prestige (Gibelman and Gelman, 2001). Once the credibility of an organization is undermined, it is very difficult to reconstruct it. The informal sanction can have more devastating effects than losing a grant or having to pay a fine to a governmental agency, for it destroys a resource that takes many years to build and that is very unlikely to return once it is gone (Thompson, 2002).

There has been much discussion on specific forms of accountability that NGOs can develop with their multiple stakeholders (Edwards and Hulme, 1995). Such debates usually distinguish among three main types of stakeholders: donors, members and those who are the subject of an organization's intervention. Sometimes the problem is posed in terms of external and internal stakeholders. Many view the development and/or improvement of the internal structure of governance as a way to increase the accountability or the representativeness of an organization. Better standards of internal governance, however, do not make an organization more 'representative' in the strong sense of the concept. Rather, they make the leadership of the organization more accountable and responsive to the goals and needs of the organization's members or board. While it is usually assumed that there already exist a variety of mechanisms by which members, boards and donors can hold the leaders or a certain organization accountable, there is a consensus about the underdevelopment of mechanisms of 'downward accountability'. Consequently, a large part of the debate has evolved around the need to develop and strengthen mechanisms of downward accountability. It is important to distinguish among these three different types of relationships, since it is only the first two – the relationship to members and to donors – which really fit an accountability model. What are described as forms of downward accountability are often far from constituting a real accountability relationship.

Why can we speak of a real accountability relationship only in certain specific cases, like those that refer to the relationship of members, boards or donors to the leadership of an organization? Because only in those instances is there a delegation of power, be it from the board or from the membership to the leadership through internal elections, or of economic power from a donor to an organization. The examples that are frequently used to illustrate cases of downward accountability, instead, refer to situations in which the basic elements of an accountability relationship are missing. This is the case, for example, of many humanitarian NGOs or of social organizations that provide specific services to the poor. In such situations, there has been no delegation of power from the constituencies that are the subject of the intervention to the organization that is implementing the services or programmes. Not only are the basic conditions of an accountability relationship not present (exchange among two actors one of whom holds rights of superior authority, autonomy of the account holder, and so on), but we are frequently confronted with a situation that is the very opposite of an ideal accountability relationship: it is the NGO or multilateral agency which is clearly in a power position while the targets of their intervention not only lack equal standing, but too often stand in a relationship of extreme dependency with regard to the material goods or services that the organization provides.

What is referred to as 'downward accountability' usually describes either strategies of self-control or self-evaluation on the part of an organization, or strategies of empowerment 'from above'. For example, the World Bank uses the concept of social accountability – a concept that was initially developed to analyse independent forms of civic engagement aimed at making public authorities accountable – to describe techniques of self-evaluation or of empowerment from above that bear no resemblance to an accountability relationship. The development of scorecards, communications campaigns, consultations or other forms of obtaining feedback from the beneficiaries of a development assistance programme stop short of being an exchange between equals, and even less an exchange where the beneficiaries are exerting rights of superior authority because they delegated their power to the representatives of certain NGOs or to some multilateral agency, like the World Bank. In this respect, one should wonder whether, in the strict sense of the word, there could be something like 'downward accountability'. Accountability, to use the same metaphor, is always 'upwards'.

When, then, can we properly speak of an accountability relationship in the realm of civic organizations? First, in the relationship that many organizations establish with donors. In this case there is a clear act of delegation of power (not political, but economic power) that conditions the NGO–donor exchange. The economic dependency of NGOs on external sources forces them to compete in an international market for funds. Consequently, this type of organization is subject to a form of market-driven accountability; in general, donors impose certain conditions that grantees have to meet in order to be eligible for funding, such as the existence of an independent board, transparent mechanisms of accounting, internal appointment procedures, or certain standards regarding their performance and the quality of their service delivery. Donors have the opportunity to exercise ex ante and ex post accountability. In the first case, the establishment of filtering mechanisms to the pool of prospective applicants plays an important screening function. In the second case, the existence of evaluation procedures, as well as the possibility of exercising sanctioning power also act as important mechanisms of accountability. Donors usually evaluate the performance of certain organizations to determine whether or not they will continue to support them and their activities. This provides a clear incentive to guide the organizations' actions and take into consideration the eventual reaction of the funding source. As with elections, the 'rule of anticipated reaction' applies: anticipating the likely response of the donor agency at the moment of evaluating the final report, the organization decides to behave in a responsible manner (Friedrich, 1963). The second case is some sort of internal delegation of power to the leadership either from the organization's membership or from a board of directors.[14]

IMPROVING THE INSTITUTIONAL QUALITY OF THE ASSOCIATIONAL TERRAIN OF CIVIL SOCIETY

This chapter centered on some misleading applications of the concepts of accountability and representation to NGOs and civic associations that do not contribute to a better understanding of the nature of those organizations and of the types of bonds that they establish with the public, their constituencies or clients, and with political parties. Three lessons can be drawn from our review of the problem of the representativeness and accountability of civic organizations. First, the reproach that is usually made against civic organizations about their lack of representativeness is misleading, for civil society organizations are not representative but constitutive institutions. Second, that being on the constitutive side of the equation means that these organizations are free of the formal accountability constraints that regulate the interactions of representative institutions and that such a condition is essential to give them ample room for free and creative action. Attempting to subject them to a variety of formal accountability mechanisms would inevitably undermine one of the most valuable features of civil society. Lastly, there should be a cautious use of the term accountability, especially when civic organizations are engaged with disempowered and needy populations.

The above stated caveats do not mean that the question of the institutional qualities of civic associations should be discarded altogether, or that the search for ways to make them more open and transparent should be abandoned. Civil society politics should not relinquish the arena of associations but should make it a central concern of its politics. So far, civil society demands for institutional betterment have fundamentally focused on limiting arbitrary government; it is necessary to broaden such politics to address the problem of social authoritarianism within civil society as well. If civil society represents a specific form of society that aims at moulding social relationships around the normative principles entailed in modern constitutionalism, the question of how to democratize social beliefs, practices and associational life should become a key priority of democratizing forms of civic engagement.

Efforts to improve the quality of the associational terrain of existing civil societies should not simply transplant solutions or mechanisms that are adequate for other spheres, as that would compromise civil society as a field of creative self-constitution of new actors and voices. It would be erroneous to establish government- or privately run certification boards or to institutionalize formal structures of civic representation that grant the status of 'representative of civil society' to a group of organizations. Instead, efforts should go, first, in the direction of establishing more open and transparent organizations and developing civic actors whose behaviour is subject to more demanding ethical and legal standards. Second, efforts should be made to improve the quality and openness of the public sphere to prevent its capture by a small group of corporations, the government, political parties, private interest associations and 'the usual suspects' that as civic organizations tend to abrogate for themselves the voice of civil society.

Such two-tier politics would mirror the politics that some civic actors are promoting to increase the accountability, openness and transparency of representative institutions. Could we turn some of those initiatives inwards to raise issues about the lack of transparency of certain organizations, to question unethical behaviour by civic leaders or organizations, to expose cases of civic corruption and wrongdoing, or to implement measures that would translate into a much more open and accessible public sphere? A politics of social accountability turned inwards is not only feasible, it is also the most adequate way of dealing with the quality and integrity of the associational structures of civil society. By adopting a societal road to institutional transformation, civil society can avoid the dangers of a statist approach to the problem, with the associated risks to its autonomy that this type of solution always entails. It could also serve to moderate some of the undesirable 'side-effects' of market-driven mechanisms, like the dangers of organizational self-encapsulation and the development of a class of detached civic officials that live off funding from the public, donors, governments or multilateral agencies. Such politics will require a sustained effort aimed at self-transformation and organizational betterment, and a determined will to promote changes to improve the quality of the space for civic associations that provides the central arena to its manifold forms of public intervention.

NOTES

1   This is the case in plesbicitarian and direct forms of democracy. For some of the features of the representative bond in those regimes see O'Donnell (1994); De la Torre (2000).

2   For a recent and rather skeptical discussion on the role of elections as mechanisms of political accountability see Przeworski et al (1999) (particularly Chapter 1).

3   As an arena of social interaction, civil society differs from forms of associational mediation that stand between the individual citizen, the market and the state, mainly political parties and interest groups. Political parties and interest groups represent two types of strategically-oriented mediating organizations that dominate the arena of representation of contemporary democracies. Many usages of the term 'civil society' fail to make this distinction and consequently include within the former concept political parties, trade unions or business organizations. I will maintain the distinction made by Cohen and Arato (1992) since it contributes to a better understanding of the complex terrain of economic and political mediations that are present in today's representative democracies and of civil society's links to those mediating structures.

4   For analyses of similar developments at the transnational level see Fox and Brown (1998); Khagram et al (2002).

5   On 'associational democracy' see Cohen and Rogers (1995); Hirst and Bader (2001). On the neoliberal notion of civil society see Meyer (1992). On 'co-governance' see Ackerman (2004).

6   One might wonder whether these societal actors actually represent a new organizational tier aimed at expanding the system of private-interest representation with a new category of public-interest organizations. If this is the case, can they still be legitimately considered a part of civil society? We may be witnessing the migration of some actors that originally emerged from civil society to the intermediary structures of political and economic society. Those organizations would eventually become the latest tier of intermediary organizations, adding new voices to a space that had been previously dominated by interest groups and political parties. The answer to the question about the accountability of such actors must consequently differ from the solutions that are being proposed for civil society organizations.

7   A similar argument has been recently developed by Kenneth Anderson and David Rieff (Anderson and Rieff, 2004). In a very interesting article, Anderson and Rieff argue against the pretension of assigning civil society organizations any representative role: civic organizations represent no one other than themselves. In their view, the term 'global civil society' has a built-in pretense to representativeness and should be consequently challenged. Their argument establishes a divide between domestic and global NGOs and advocacy organizations; in their view, the issue of representativeness emerges fundamentally at the global level because certain international NGOs seem to place themselves in a representative role they can never fulfill. However, the claim to representativeness crosses civic society organizations

at both the domestic and global level. At the bottom of this debate, there is a clash between conflicting visions about the role that civil society organizations play in a representative democracy and at the international level. The models of associative democracy or co-governance, for example, attribute a representative and intermediary role to domestic civic organizations that must also be challenged.

8   On interest-group politics see Latham (1952); Eckstein (1960); Schattschneider (1960). For a more recent contribution, Gerber (1999). On pluralism, see Dahl (1961). On neo-corporatism, see Schmitter and Lehmbruch (1979); Offe (1985).

9   In fact, when speaking of NGOs, particularly developmental NGOs, it is usually argued that they are organizations geared to serving the needs of third parties (Atack, 1999).

10 This is the position, for example, of Frank Vibert (2003). He views the developments of standards to improve the internal accountability of organizations as a way to solve the 'representative' status of NGOs. While certainly the establishment of internal ballots or consultation might help to improve the representativeness of the organization's leadership vis-à-vis its members, such measures do not make such an NGO a representative one (Vibert, 2003).

11 In these exercises at creating a constituency from above, as opposed to a process of self-constitution of societal actors, there is always the risk of organizational paternalism towards the population that is the subject of the NGOs' intervention. In many instances, there will be resistance to developing forms of intervention that would eventually lead these organizations to work themselves out of their job.

12 Ideological parties once played this transformative role before being electorally displaced to the margins of political competition by the advent of catch-all-parties. Such transformation is partly responsible for the weakening of current parties' capacity for symbolic integration. Increasingly, political parties encounter the competition of new contestants that seem to be more successful in attracting public attention and mobilizing considerable sectors of the citizenry. For an analysis of the actual decline of parties see Schmitter (2001).

13 Michael Edwards refers to the principle of 'a voice not a vote' to differentiate the logic of NGOs from that of political parties (Edwards, 2000).

14 Many see these accountability mechanisms as problematic for they tend to gear NGOs or civic organizations to the agenda of foundations, governments or multilateral agencies, undermining the contentious and creative side of civil society. Mary Kaldor, for example, speaks of a troublesome trend toward the *NGOization* of civil society to emphasize how 'accountability' to donors is distorting the logic and priorities of civil society organizations and taming its contentious character (Kaldor, 2003). Such arguments serve to highlight the problems of attempting to make civil society accountable. As I have been trying to argue, a more accountable civil society is not necessarily a better one.

Section II

TRADITIONAL APPROACHES:
LEGAL ACCOUNTABILITY,
CERTIFICATION AND DONOR REGIMES

4

The Limits and Risks of Regulation: The Case of the World Bank-supported *Draft Handbook on Good Practices for Laws Relating to NGOs*[1]

Patricia Armstrong

INTRODUCTION

Calls for greater accountability by NGOs have come from many quarters in recent times, some motivated by legitimate and important concerns, and some not. This paper examines one of the tools often cited for promoting accountability – the use of law – as recommended by one particular document, the World Bank's *Draft Handbook on Good Practices for Laws Relating to NGOs*. While the Bank did not ultimately finalize the document, its story intertwines debates on a number of key issues regarding NGO accountability in relation to international law and human rights, and universal rights and standards versus the specificity of the political context. It illustrates and clarifies not only the limits of legal regulation under international human rights law, but also challenges more generally the use of law to address accountability concerns in diverse, complex and sometimes difficult circumstances. Finally, it raises questions on the role of international institutions in promoting these kinds of standards and demonstrates how contested they are.

   With the growth in the number and role of NGOs in client countries in the early 1990s, the World Bank recognized the potential importance to the success of its efforts of constructive contributions by NGOs to development activities and sought ways to encourage more effective participation of NGOs. One of the issues identified as undermining NGO contributions in many countries was an operational environment, including laws, that was overly restrictive (World

Bank, 1994). Thus, in 1995, the Bank undertook a project entitled 'Developing Global Standards for NGO Laws' that focused on the legal aspects of enabling environments, the centerpiece of which was the production of a handbook that would provide suggestions of global standards for the development and improvement of laws and regulatory systems for NGOs. The stated purpose of this effort was to promote a more supportive legal environment for NGOs that would also make them more transparent and accountable:

> *In order for the Bank to be able to work effectively with NGOs, and to benefit fully from the contributions they can potentially make to successful development, it is essential in any particular country in which the Bank works that the NGOs that are or might be involved in projects financed by the Bank be freely established and operate without undue constraints; that such NGOs be independent of the government; and be transparent and accountable.* (World Bank, 1997)

The envisioned handbook was produced, ultimately entitled the *Draft Handbook on Good Practices for Laws Relating to Non-Governmental Organizations* (hereinafter Draft Handbook), the primary draft of which was issued in May 1997 as a discussion document.[2] The Draft Handbook proved to be controversial and in the end, some five years later, the Bank decided that it was not an appropriate tool for it to use.

The account of the World Bank's road to this conclusion illustrates the nature and complexity of NGO accountability issues that are still relevant, particularly regarding the role that law should and should not play in this effort. Many of the means currently proposed to increase accountability are much the same as those put forward by the Draft Handbook, and there is often a conflation of concerns related to NGO credibility, legitimacy and representativeness with accountability issues.

This chapter recounts, at least from an outsider's (and critic's) point of view, the history of the Draft Handbook. It discusses why the Bank, a large international development finance organization, decided to give attention to these issues; the nature of the Handbook project, both as originally conceived and as it developed; key aspects of the Draft Handbook's approach to regulation, particularly as it related to NGO accountability; selected criticism of the Draft Handbook's text and the Bank's response; and finally, some lessons that might be drawn from this experience.

WHY THE WORLD BANK?

An initial question is why the World Bank thought it was appropriate and useful for it to become involved in issues related to NGO legal frameworks. First, some background is helpful. In the 1990s, NGOs gained increasing prominence on both international and national stages, and in both operational and advocacy arenas. The enormous growth in the number of NGOs was one of the hallmarks of the post-cold war era. NGOs came to be viewed by many in the donor community as more reliable recipients of financial support than governments, about which there were often serious doubts about capacity, intention and honesty. Simultaneously, new technology permitted NGOs to coordinate and organize with each other on a myriad of often controversial issues.

With these developments, NGOs became the target of criticism, sometimes as a result of their success ('Who elected them?') and occasionally as a result of problems created by the misconduct of some NGOs, whether illegal, unethical or simply inappropriate. While such misconduct was limited, it was a natural concern of the donor community. The Bank was increasing its interaction with NGOs, in part as a result of its conclusion that involving NGOs in its work would increase its effectiveness. During the 1990s, the Bank sought to expand operational collaboration with civil society organizations in Bank-funded projects. For example, in the 1990 financial year projects in which civil society groups had some operational role were only about 10 per cent of the total, while by the 2001 financial year, more than 70 per cent of the projects considered by the Bank's Board included some intended civil society involvement (World Bank, 2000/2001). At the same time that the Bank was seeking to encourage greater NGO participation in development activities, many governments, particularly in Eastern Europe and the former Soviet Union, were not relating well to the NGO sector, reacting either not at all to calls for greater openness and reform regarding civil society, or, in other cases, with a heavy, often authoritarian, hand.

The World Bank, assessing this situation, concluded that one problem was the absence of good national laws that foster, support and regulate NGOs and, in some cases, there was also an absence of the implementation of those laws that existed. The Bank also indicated that it had received specific requests for this work from local NGOs. The head of the Bank's NGO Unit that initiated the project later stated his thinking:

> It would not be effective for the World Bank to try and press governments to introduce progressive laws in this area. Governments who introduce laws unwillingly are likely to have little intention of implementing them. So what is more effective for the Bank is to focus on the knowledge aspect and to use the trust it enjoys amongst governments to encourage a more enabling legal framework. The very factors that lead some to question whether the World Bank is an appropriate organization to be in this field lead others to suggest the converse, since it is generally trusted by governments around the world, as is its advice and analysis on a whole range of government activities.[3]

The Bank viewed the legal aspects of an enabling environment as fundamentally technical in nature, a matter of legal drafting for consideration by experts.

In 1995, the Bank engaged the International Center for Not-for-Profit Law (ICNL), an NGO based in Washington DC to work with it on these issues, and the Developing Global Standards for NGO Laws Project was born.

THE PROJECT: AN OVERVIEW

The Developing Global Standards for NGO Laws Project had several elements: it called for the World Bank and ICNL to collect and analyse laws governing NGOs in countries around the world; create a publicly available archive and database of NGO laws and related reports; and produce a handbook with suggestions for 'standards and best practices guidelines for the development or improvement of laws and regulatory systems for NGOs', as well as for NGO self-regulation. Legal experts would be consulted and 'at least one major seminar would be held in connection with the release of the Handbook'.

The project was formally launched at a meeting at the Bank in January 1996. As the meeting coincided with a CIVICUS (World Alliance for Citizen Participation) meeting in Washington, representatives of a number of non-US-based NGOs were able to attend. The Bank described the project and presented a 40-page preliminary working draft of guidelines. Reaction to the project was generally positive, although limited given its newness. Subsequent drafts of the Handbook followed, in February and November 1996 and February 1997, leading to a 'discussion draft' in May 1997 that was 126 pages in length.

The 1995 Project Description did not include a timeline for the preparation of the Handbook, but initially it appeared to be quite short. At the January 1996 meeting, the Bank stated its hope that the document would be completed by the following summer, that is, within about six months. However, by the November 1996 draft, the need for further consultation was acknowledged, with completion anticipated after receipt of comments and additional research 'over the next year or so'. This time period was repeated in the May 1997 draft of the Handbook. In May 1998, the plan again changed when the Bank agreed to prepare an additional draft for further review before finalizing the document. That revision did not appear until September 2000 and a decision was thereafter made not to release it at all. The Bank decided to end its association with the Handbook all together in 2002.

As to consultation on the Handbook, while the preliminary working draft of guidelines distributed in January 1996 'enthusiastically encouraged' any 'additional experience, information, or analysis that would throw additional and helpful light on this attempt to arrive at global standards and best practice guidelines', the time for this to occur – approximately six months – did not appear to permit anything extensive. Instead, the draft noted its reliance upon earlier work: 'the guidelines are the result of years of research and experience by many people' and had been 'developed through formal and informal processes involving literally thousands of hours spent by hundreds of lawyers, NGO leaders and government officials'. The Project Description did not set out plans for a consultative approach to the development of the Handbook. While the Description discussed the preparation of country studies by local experts, there was no mention of the circulation of the draft Handbook to them or any broader consultation or translation of drafts into other languages.

Until the May 1997 draft, it appears that distribution of drafts of the Handbook was limited, primarily to groups and individuals viewed as experts. With the May 1997 draft, the Bank undertook a concerted distribution of the document, made plans for its translation and organized consultations. Later in 1997, a six-week 'virtual' (online) consultation on the Handbook, now in Spanish, took place with NGOs and others from Latin America. In November 1997, a meeting for NGOs from East and Southeast Asia occurred in Bangkok to discuss the Handbook. There were also plans for additional meetings in East and West Africa, but they never occurred, apparently due to a lack of funding. By 1999, several thousand copies of the 1997 draft had been distributed and it had been translated into a number of languages.[4]

THE DRAFT HANDBOOK: AN OVERVIEW

The Draft Handbook was a lengthy and complex document. Its recommendations were set out in the form of statements of principle followed by a discussion that explained the policy rationale, and often provided examples of how issues were dealt with in different legal systems. The Draft Handbook was not intended to be a model law or code 'because the legal systems of the world differ in large and small ways, and local traditions of law draft are also varied'. Its provisions were also not intended for use in all countries, but rather only in those governed by the rule of law. While acknowledging the possibility of government abuse, it stated that the Draft Handbook was intended as an 'aspirational set of guidelines rather than practical advice about how to survive in a repressive legal atmosphere'.

As one of the Draft Handbook's stated aims was to encourage and support the creation and growth of a vibrant NGO sector, it contained language, often eloquent, in support of that objective. For example: 'The Bank believes that restrictive NGO laws are inappropriate and would, in the long term, erode public support and confidence in national development objectives'.

The Draft Handbook acknowledged the relevance of the international law of freedom of association and endorsed many principles that were consistent with its exercise, for example, that 'the presumption behind all NGO laws should be that individuals, groups, and legal persons are *entitled* to form associations for any legal, nonprofit purpose' (emphasis in original); that there should always be a presumption in favour of establishment; that the establishment process should be simple, no more difficult than that for a commercial entity; and that establishment should involve a minimum of bureaucratic discretion, that 'it is... not necessary for a government official to decide whether there is a need for the organization to exist or not'.

THE DRAFT HANDBOOK'S APPROACH TO REGULATION

Two features of the Draft Handbook were particularly important to the regulatory scheme it proposed: first, its categorization of NGOs; and second, the relevance to regulation of NGO activities that sought to benefit a public interest.

As to the first, the Draft Handbook distinguished between two general types of NGOs: 'public benefit organizations' (PBOs) and 'mutual benefit organizations' (MBOs). The PBO–MBO terminology was critical to the suggested regulatory scheme since it was used to determine the recommended level of regulation.[5] Those NGOs that sought to serve some public benefit were usually to be subject to greater scrutiny by, and accountability to, government. The Draft Handbook's justification for this approach was that there is a legitimate public interest in the regulation of activities of NGOs that sought to benefit 'the public interest', for that reason alone: 'The activities of PBOs – and the public interest activities of MBOs – affect the public interest, and the public is entitled to know about them'.

Once NGOs to be regulated had been identified, the Draft Handbook called for them to be transparent and accountable, 'the basic trade-off for relatively easy establishment... in exchange for protection of the laws allowing easy establishment as a legal person'. Greater transparency and accountability were seen as fulfilling several objectives, including: to guard against unscrupulous NGOs and the fraud and illegal actions they may commit; to promote NGO integrity; to promote informal regulation by an informed general public; to make NGOs more accountable to the groups they purport to represent; and to promote self-regulation.[6]

Reporting, both internal and external, was the main vehicle to ensure NGO transparency and accountability. The Draft Handbook called for NGOs to report regularly on their finances and activities to the government; for the government to have the right to enter an NGO's premises, inspect and audit books and records, sometimes at random; and for more detailed reporting from NGOs that were engaged in activities that 'significantly affect the public interest'.

While the Draft Handbook presented a detailed statement of principles for legal regulation by governments, it was also intended to enhance the climate for self-regulation. This was accomplished primarily in the Draft Handbook's final chapter and an appendix containing examples of self-regulatory schemes, with a small number of references appearing in other parts of the text.

CRITICISM OF THE DRAFT HANDBOOK

Criticism of the Draft Handbook fell into three general areas: first, that the World Bank was not the appropriate institution to be addressing NGO legal framework issues, particularly in the development of prescriptive regulatory mechanisms for use by governments; second, that the process for developing the Draft Handbook was severely flawed and inadequate; and third, that the content of the Draft Handbook was similarly flawed and not consistent with international human rights law, particularly freedom of association.

There were three detailed critical NGO reviews of the Draft Handbook. The first, in August 1996, came from the Civil Rights Movement of Sri Lanka (CRM, 1996, hereinafter CRM Critique). This initial comment was important, not only because it was early in the Draft Handbook's development and came from a country where NGOs could be affected by its terms, but also because the concerns expressed by CRM were at the heart of later critiques from others. Second, in September 1997 and in October 1998, the Three Freedoms Project, an initiative comprised of seven Asian NGOs, issued detailed statements, including Ten Minimum Requirements for the Independence of NGOs (Three Freedoms Project, 1997).[7] The Three Freedoms Project also organized a Handbook-related event at the 1997 World Bank/International Monetary Fund (IMF) Annual Meetings in Hong Kong. Finally, in November 1997, the Lawyers Committee for Human Rights, an NGO based in New York (now named Human Rights First) produced a detailed critique (Lawyers Committee for Human Rights, 1997a, hereinafter LCHR Critique).

The role of the World Bank

While most NGOs welcomed the World Bank's interest and desire to promote an enabling environment for NGOs, many felt strongly that the Bank was the wrong institution to take the lead in setting out a desirable legal regulatory framework for NGOs.[8] The Three Freedoms Project NGOs articulated this view clearly:

> *We do not believe that advising governments on the sensitive and politically-contested matter of how to organize civil society is an appropriate role for the World Bank; it is a subject which is not within the Bank's particular competence or experience and the Bank's staff are generally unfamiliar with the ramifications of such issues. For these reasons, if governments are in need of advice on NGO laws from an international body, we would encourage the Bank to urge governments to make use of the Office of the UN High Commissioner for Human Rights' program of technical assistance.* (Three Freedoms Project, 1998)

Central to this concern was the fact that many of the Draft Handbook's recommendations were prescriptive in nature and, more importantly, that international law relevant to NGO legal frameworks, that is, the parameters within which such national laws should be framed, was not well developed.[9] The Bank, in presenting to governments a host of regulatory recommendations, risked being the means by which such legal development would occur.

While the Draft Handbook tried to limit problems related to its prescriptive nature by stating that its recommendations should only be used where the rule of law was established, this condition did not exist in many of the countries where legal frameworks were most deficient and where the Draft Handbook could have been expected to be most used, namely, new or transitional countries with a history of neglect or authoritarianism in relation to civil society. Indeed, a number of countries not meeting the Handbook's rule-of-law prerequisite were then in the midst of reforms related to NGO laws. For example, in China (Human Rights in China, 1998), Egypt (Human Rights Watch, 2000) and Pakistan (Zia, 1996; Mufti, 2000), governments would no doubt be pleased to be able to cite the World Bank as the authority for imposing new restrictions on NGOs. Critics thus called the Bank's rule-of-law limitation of the applicability of the Draft Handbook as not only unrealistic, but also naive.

The Handbook's development process

It seems clear that, at least at the beginning of the project, the World Bank had no plan for any broad-based consultation on the Draft Handbook. This is also consistent with its view that the Handbook project was primarily a technical exercise. If such a plan for consultation did exist, it was not set out in the 1995 Project Description.

One group that was consulted throughout the process was the World Bank-NGO Committee, a group comprised of NGOs, many from developing countries, and World Bank staff members, and its NGO Working Group (comprised of the NGO members of the Committee). This group met annually in Washington and periodically held regional meetings. In October 1996, Bank staff made a presentation to the NGO Working Group about the project. Concerns about the Draft Handbook were reportedly raised. The Bank also included the Draft Handbook on the agendas of the Asia, Africa and Latin America regional meetings of members of the Working Group. While interaction with the Working Group was important, it did not provide the focused attention that was needed, as its members were primarily development-oriented NGOs without a specific focus on law or legal issues. More generally, in many NGO circles the Working Group lacked credibility as a legitimate NGO voice in relation to the World Bank (Bello, 2000), which undercut whatever value there might have been in the wider NGO community with the limited consultation that occurred.

The difficulty in obtaining a useful consultation on the Draft Handbook was evident from those efforts that did occur. The online consultation organized for Latin American groups took place over a multi-week period and had the benefit of a Spanish translation of the Draft Handbook. While it reportedly involved several hundred groups and individuals from 17 countries, it was later acknowledged that the number of substantive comments received was very low.[10]

The Asia consultation fell far short of what was needed, amounting to an informational rather than consultative exercise. NGOs invited to the meeting in Bangkok did not receive copies of the Draft Handbook before the meeting, meaning the time available for review was woefully insufficient. And when distributed, the Handbook was only in English. Moreover, some NGO critics of the Draft Handbook, such as Human Rights in China, an NGO based in Hong Kong and New York, and the Hong Kong Human Rights Monitor, based in Hong Kong, were not invited to the meeting despite the suggestion of an organizer. Both NGOs had reviewed the Handbook as participants in the Three Freedoms Project mentioned earlier.

The problem of late distribution of the Draft Handbook that occurred in Bangkok was not unusual. The September 2000 revision of the Draft Handbook, long in preparation (since at least May 1998), was to be the subject of a 2–3 October 2000 meeting in The Hague, which had also been long in preparation. However, the new draft was provided to meeting participants only in late September, with some not receiving it before their arrival at the meeting. Concerns were raised by meeting participants as to how an informed discussion could occur under these circumstances and some participants refused to attend the meeting for this reason.

There is no question that consultation on the Draft Handbook was diffi-cult and presented significant (and to some degree, expensive) challenges, particularly if it was to involve local groups that could be affected by its provi-sions. But meaningful consultation was critical to the preparation of the clearest and most appropriate text and to finding approaches that would not oversimplify issues that may have universal applicability in diverse national, legal, cultural, political and social circumstances. Such consultation would have also been an important way to build NGOs' own capacities on these issues.

It seems clear that the World Bank failed to anticipate, plan and budget to meet those challenges from the outset of the project. And the Draft Handbook's length, detail and complexity made consultation with those who could be affected even more difficult. For whatever reason, financial resources for these needs were inadequate through the life of the project. Meetings in Africa to discuss the Draft Handbook never took place, apparently due to a lack of funding. And as seen, when meetings did occur, they often lacked the advance planning necessary to facilitate and promote a useful discussion.

The Draft Handbook's content

It is useful to note at the outset what was not disputed about the Draft Handbook. Critics acknowledged that some regulation of NGOs was not only proper, but also important when there was a legitimate government or public interest in an NGO's affairs that requires protection, for example, where NGOs receive tax concessions, raise money from public donations or operate in a regulated area, such as schools or health care. In addition, critics noted that minimal reporting was appropriate where the legal system provided limited liability to an NGO with a grant of legal personality, for example, the name and address of an authorized representative that would be available to protect the rights and interests of those who interacted with legally established entities.

Critics' primary complaint about the Draft Handbook's text was that its provisions were inconsistent with fundamental principles of international human rights law. Freedom of association, as a right, necessarily means there will be limits on the degree of regulation that can be applied. Indeed, under settled standards, there is a presumption *against* regulation and the burden is on those who would impose it to establish its justification (Lawyers Committee for Human Rights, 1997b). Restrictions must also meet a number of tests, that is, in general, they must be prescribed by law, necessary in a democratic society and imposed to preserve the interests of national security or public safety, public order, the protection of public health or morals, or the protection of the rights and freedoms of others.[11] In addition, limitations must be related and proportionate to a specific public policy interest and must be necessary, not merely useful or desirable, to achieving that purpose. Finally, any restrictions must be precise and framed as narrowly as possible in order to avoid ambiguities that would lead to misinterpretation or manipulation.

In the view of its critics, the Draft Handbook, particularly its transparency and accountability provisions, failed to meet international standards in several respects. Among the concerns were a lack of clarity in the terms and concepts that were central to the proposed regulatory scheme, and the overarching role of 'activities intended to benefit the public interest' in justifying greater regulation and scrutiny. Those provisions were part of an overall approach to regulation that was problematic, putting some NGOs, particularly those that were often critical of governments, at risk. The Draft Handbook acknowledged that regulatory powers could be misused by governments:

> *There is, of course, the ever-present danger of over-regulation by government, or, indeed, the use of reporting and audit requirements to harass NGOs that are critical of the government or otherwise unpopular. There is no certain protection against governmental abuse, and it exists to some extent in every society. One of the most important reasons why every country should have sound administrative laws that permit actions by organs of the government to be challenged in court, and independent judges to hear those appeals, is to provide a correction for governmental abuse and a deterrent to future abuses.*

While acknowledging the problem, the Draft Handbook provided opportunities for unwarranted government intrusions. A means by which this was accomplished was the fact that key terms in the Draft Handbook were loosely defined if at all, particularly PBOs/MBOs and the 'public interest'. The Draft Handbook relied heavily on the PBO/MBO distinction, the definition of which was not precise and was in fact confusing. PBOs were groups with purposes and activities that affected or were intended to affect the interests of the public or a significant portion of it. Generally, MBOs were membership organizations, but such groups could also be PBOs, and a PBO could be formed as either a membership or a non-membership organization. Just as a PBO could serve membership interests, a membership organization could engage in significant public interest activities. As the Lawyers Committee's Critique of the Draft Handbook pointed out:

> *To say that a PBO is one which is 'involved in activities... that... affect or are intended to affect... the public or a significant portion of it' is really only to re-state the definition. Neither is it particularly illuminating to suggest that everything that is not a PBO is therefore an MBO, particularly if MBOs are not necessarily membership organizations. For example, if an organization is not a membership organization, but is intended to benefit 'a defined group of individuals,' how does one distinguish that defined group of individuals from a 'significant portion' of the public, which is the essential characteristic of a PBO? Is the difference only a function of the size of the group of intended beneficiaries, or is it that with an MBO the intended beneficiaries are (presumably) 'identified'?* (Lawyers Committee for Human Rights, 1997a)

The Draft Handbook's use of 'activities intended to benefit the public interest' as a key regulatory criterion presented similar problems. The level of government or public scrutiny recommended was to vary according to whether an NGO was engaged in such activities or those that 'significantly affect the public interest'. However, the Draft Handbook did not define 'public interest' and did not explain why an NGO's orientation toward the public interest justified increased obligations, or what was meant by 'significantly affect'. The lack of clarity ran squarely into freedom of association principles that require that limitations on freedom of association should be narrow and specific, not general and sweeping.

Moreover, the proposition that the public had an interest in the activities of a private organization that sought to benefit the public, and that therefore that organization must be transparent and accountable by reporting to the government and to the public at large is inconsistent with international law. An intention to benefit the public does not, *by itself*, constitute a threat within the permissible limitations on freedom of association, namely, to democratic society, the public order, the rights of other citizens to exercise their rights and freedoms, or public health or morals. Neither national security nor public safety needs to be preserved by regulating the activities of public-spirited citizens and the groups they form to carry out their work. Only with particular activities that implicate those concerns would a possible justification arise. But this nexus between activities or operations and a legitimate government or public interest was missing from the scheme proposed by the Draft Handbook.

Reporting mechanisms were the Draft Handbook's 'main vehicle' to achieve transparency and accountability: 'In exchange for protection of the laws allowing easy establishment as a legal person, an established NGO should accept reporting requirements and enforcement mechanisms that are appropriate and proportional to the legitimate interests that the public may have in its operations and activities'. Thus:

> ... *any established NGO that has activities that significantly affect the public interest should be required to file reasonably detailed reports annually on its finances and operations with the agency responsible for general supervision of NGOs. In certain specialized situations more frequent reporting may be appropriate.*

The Draft Handbook went further, recommending that the government have power to examine the books, records and activities of an NGO, and the power to audit NGOs randomly and annually for 'very large NGOs', which suggested that size alone could be a sufficient trigger for greater government attention.

Critics also pointed out that the Draft Handbook's suggestion that the 'basic trade-off' between the establishment of an NGO and the imposition of mechanisms designed to achieve transparency and accountability was not consistent with international law. First, the exercise of freedom of association is a right and the government is obliged to facilitate the enjoyment of that right by making it possible for people to form organizations – there is no *quid pro quo* to obtaining legal personality. Second, transparency and accountability to the government necessarily amount to regulatory intrusions on freedom of association, which must be specifically linked to a legitimate government or public interest.

The 1996 CRM Critique spoke directly to this point and the place of regulation to achieve accountability and transparency:

> *There is nothing intrinsically good, or bad, in accountability and transparency; one must be careful to always look at the context in which they are sought to be applied. There are situations in which accountability and transparency are essential (never more so, by the way, than when they concern the workings of governmental bodies); where they are desirable (in varying degrees); and where they may be nothing more than a pernicious cover for interference with a person's right to self expression, individuality or privacy... In general, it may be said that NGOs are accountable: to their members in every respect; to donors in respect of funds given by them; to the public only where there is a legitimate public interest (e.g. you collect money in the streets); to the government only where there is a legitimate government interest (e.g. say you are a charity and get tax exemption).* (CRM, 1996)

The Draft Handbook suggested that transparency and accountability would provide an added benefit by making NGOs more accountable to the groups they purport to represent:

> *Adequate disclosure can also go far towards providing the public a base of knowledge against which it can determine whether and the extent to which an advocacy NGO really listens to and speaks for the group it purports to represent and benefit and whether it has a solid basis in research and experience for the claims and statements that it makes.*

The Draft Handbook did not state why this was necessary in the context of international legal standards – indeed, many advocacy NGOs do not purport to be representative of any group other than their own. Critics pointed out that in a society that respects and promotes freedom of association, people will form all kinds of NGOs, some of which will succeed, and others fail, depending on the 'market place' of needs for what NGOs can provide. Whether or not NGOs accurately reflect the needs and views of their selected constituency, and whether their claims are accurate and verifiable will be critical factors in whether they attract support from donors, government and their chosen constituencies, or gain the credibility to achieve their objectives. Compulsory public reporting requirements are not needed to bring that about. On the contrary, a much better way to achieve this end would be to ensure respect for the basic freedoms of expression, association and assembly. Moreover, there is no reason why the government should play the role of ensuring that NGOs accurately represent their constituencies' views and make claims that have a 'solid basis in research and experience'. In the absence of some particular government interest, these are matters for NGOs, their members, their funders and the NGO 'marketplace' to resolve (see also Charnovitz and Peruzzotti, in this volume).

In conclusion, criticism of the Draft Handbook's text was centered on its inconsistency with basic principles of the international law of freedom of association and the risks thus presented to NGOs, particularly those trying to exist and operate in repressive environments. The central concepts on which the Handbook was based were open to easy manipulation by governments that had little or no interest in promoting and protecting a vibrant civil society. And the fact that the Handbook came from an international institution with considerable influence on governments, as well as other institutions and donors, only heightened concerns.

THE WORLD BANK'S RESPONSE TO THE CRITICS

In reaction to critics, the World Bank modified the Handbook project at several points, with key developments in May 1998, April 1999, July 1999, October

2000 and at the end of the Bank's involvement with the Draft Handbook in 2002.

With regard to the earliest substantive criticism of the Draft Handbook from CRM in August 1996, the Bank provided assurances to CRM that its concerns had been heard and that CRM would 'be pleased to see in the next draft how significantly we have responded to your comments'. However, the Bank characterized the changes suggested as 'being ones of tone and emphasis, more than content' and reiterated its continued commitment to one issue at the heart of the CRM's complaint that governmental regulation of NGOs is a justifiable *quid pro quo* for granting legal personality. While some changes were indeed made in the succeeding text of the Draft Handbook, they were superficial in nature and did not address the core of CRM's concerns.

The Bank's response to CRM was typical of subsequent reactions to other critics, namely, there was a willingness to consider, and often make, line-edit changes in the document, but there was no willingness to revisit the overall approach of the scheme suggested or to discuss the appropriateness of the Bank's role in undertaking the project.

Over the life of the Draft Handbook, the Bank responded to critics in various ways, including:

- *That only human rights groups had raised concerns about the Draft Handbook.* Implicit in this assertion was a view that the interests and concerns of human rights NGOs were different from and not relevant to those of other groups, a proposition that is difficult to sustain. Attention by human rights groups to the Draft Handbook should have been expected: human rights are their business, of course, and freedom of association, the relevance of which was noted by the Draft Handbook, is the core principle protecting all NGOs. Moreover, such groups, by their nature, are often critical of and therefore unpopular with governments, often the first targets of repressive governmental action and victims of violations of the right to associate. As they were potentially the NGOs most immediately affected, human rights groups naturally took the lead in reviewing the Draft Handbook.
- *That the PBO and MBO terminology was appropriate and useful in articulating legitimate objectives.* The Draft Handbook acknowledged the newness of its approach: 'Most legal systems do not use the terms PBO and MBO as such. These reflect an attempt to generalize and to put on a sounder theoretical footing the actual, more fragmented practices that exist in various legal systems'. However, as originally designed, the PBO/MBO terminology was primarily intended as a tool to assess the potential appropriateness of tax benefits (Salamon and Toepler, 1997), a more limited and different use than was proposed by the Draft Handbook. The Draft Handbook thus converted an analytical tool into a regulatory mechanism. Finally, even if the PBO and MBO nomenclature had been appropriate for use in the Draft Handbook, as noted earlier, it was not clearly defined despite being primary criteria for the regulatory scheme proposed.

- *That freedom of association was enjoyed by individuals, not NGOs.* This was an overly narrow interpretation of international law. It is of course correct that the law protects individuals, but NGOs are a vehicle through which individuals avail themselves of that right. The Bank stopped making this claim in 1998 following two decisions of the European Court of Human Rights,[12] apparently on the basis that these decisions changed international law. While those decisions were welcome and important, the European Court's articulation of the rights of European NGOs in those cases was not described as a change in or a new interpretation of basic legal principles.
- *That criticisms were a misunderstanding of the purpose and intent of the Handbook.* Most critics did not dispute the Bank's intention or motives in undertaking the Handbook project, but this response did not address the flaws in the detail of the proposals by which the Draft Handbook sought to achieve a commendable end.
- *That criticisms often used the Draft Handbook's text out of context.* The Draft Handbook's use of ill-defined terms meant that they were subject to manipulation and differing interpretations. Imprecision opened the door to arbitrary application of laws, the risk of the imposition of unwarranted burdens on NGOs and unnecessary intrusions into their affairs. It took no stretch of the imagination to envisage a government making a determination that an NGO it did not like was engaged in 'activities that significantly affect the public interest' and therefore should be subject to greater scrutiny. Such governments could pick and choose provisions as desired without regard to their context, but could, nonetheless, declare the World Bank as the authority for its action.
- *That the overwhelming number of NGOs that expressed views about the Draft Handbook welcomed it and had no significant criticism of its content.* This was no doubt correct and not surprising. The Draft Handbook was a long, complicated and often legalistic document, intimidating to non-experts and non-English speakers. Moreover, its terms drew on legal traditions that were unfamiliar in many parts of the world. And perhaps most importantly, the Draft Handbook, in non-technical language, extolled the value and importance of NGOs in ways that were very welcome to the ears of all NGOs, particularly when they came from an institution with the ability to influence governments. The problem was that the Draft Handbook's detail undermined the support expressed.
- *That the Draft Handbook was being successfully used in many countries.* This assertion was difficult to dispute, as the claim stood on its own without supporting evidence, at least available to outsiders. Among the countries cited where the Draft Handbook supposedly had a positive influence were Bangladesh, Nepal and the Philippines. However, at least some NGOs in other countries, for example, Egypt, Yemen and Namibia expressed serious objections to the Draft Handbook. Critics' fears were not that the Draft Handbook, with well-intentioned rights-respecting inclinations, could not be a useful resource. Rather, they had concerns related

to governments of a quite different sort, those that neither respected freedom of association, nor sought to encourage the growth of an independent NGO sector.

- *That the Draft Handbook's primary emphasis was on self-regulation, not regulation by governments.* Both the title (*Handbook on Good Practices for Laws Relating to NGOs*) and details of the Draft Handbook belied this assertion. While the Draft Handbook stated that it 'favors self-regulation', self-regulatory mechanisms were addressed primarily in only one chapter at the end of a long document, with limited and sometimes ambiguous references in other text. More importantly, the Draft Handbook set out a detailed system that recommended government regulation of a wide range of NGO activities and operations.

- *That NGOs can avoid government regulation by simply not seeking legal status, something expressly permitted by the Draft Handbook, or some other type of legal form.* This may be true, but ignores two things. In many jurisdictions, NGOs effectively have no choice but to seek legal status if they are to be able to undertake the most basic of activities, for example, opening a bank account, renting an office, taking a case to court or attracting financial support. And to suggest that they establish themselves as some other type of entity, for example, a commercial organization, does little to advance openness for NGOs. Finally and most importantly, as noted earlier, freedom of association requires governments to take positive steps to enable groups to organize.

- *That repressive governments do not need the World Bank to assist them in taking wrongful actions against NGOs.* That may be the case, but the World Bank should not be in the position of strengthening arguments of authoritarians or putting an (unintended) imprimatur on their actions.

- *That, in any event, there is no evidence that the Draft Handbook had had any negative effects.* This is difficult to disprove, as the Draft Handbook was only a draft and the Bank's connection with it ended in 2002, with its proactive distribution ending earlier (by mid-1999). However, it would seem self-evident that the World Bank should not be making recommendations that are inconsistent with or inappropriately develop international law. To take one example, while the Draft Handbook generally recommended that governments permit funding of NGOs from sources that were not domestic, it suggested that an exception might be necessary in 'certain rare and highly sensitive circumstances', language that was imprecise and open to easy manipulation. First, this provision (which was not changed in the 2000 version of the Draft Handbook) is not consistent with the 1998 UN Declaration on Human Rights Defenders, adopted by consensus by the UN General Assembly.[13] Second, restrictions on funding of domestic NGOs by foreign organizations continue to be used by many governments as a tool to limit the legitimate activities of NGOs and, in some cases, put them out of business.[14] While it may be unlikely that these laws were an unintended result of the Draft Handbook, had the Draft Handbook gone forward, its provisions could have been used to justify the inappropriate laws, even though they would be inconsistent with the UN declaration. In a report to the UN General Assembly, the Special Representative of the Secretary General on Human Rights Defenders noted:

> *A common feature of many newly adopted NGO laws of concern to human rights defenders is restrictive provisions regarding funding. An increasing number of domestic laws place restrictions on the origin of the funds that NGOs receive and require prior authorization for NGOs to access international funds from nationals abroad or from foreign donors... Given the limited resources available for human rights organizations at the local level, legal requirements of prior authorization for international funding have seriously affected the ability of human rights defenders to carry out their activities. In some cases, they have seriously endangered the very existence of human rights organizations.*[15]

THE END OF THE DRAFT HANDBOOK

The Handbook project was affected by the criticism from NGOs. In July 1999, the Bank stated that no decision had been made whether another draft of the Handbook would be issued; that comments on any further draft would be sought prior to release; and that the May 1997 draft would be taken out of circulation and no additional copies made, except for specific requests for foreign language translations.

The Draft Handbook remained in doubt into 2000, when the Bank decided to present a revised draft to a group of NGOs and intergovernmental organizations for consideration. After several delays, a meeting finally occurred in The Hague in October 2000, organized by the Bank, with CIVICUS and the Institute of Social Studies. As a result of discussions in The Hague, the Bank agreed not to release the revised draft and to consider other approaches to supporting the growth and development of an enabling environment for civil society beyond the Draft Handbook. Among the principles the Bank stated would guide its development of a new strategy were that 'it should not harm existing civil society organizations in developing countries' and freedom of association should be respected and fostered by the strategy and all resulting initiatives. In 2002, the Bank formally ended its association with the Draft Handbook and transferred ownership of the document to ICNL. The Handbook was not subsequently revised or reissued by ICNL.

CONCLUSION

The account of the *Draft Handbook on Good Practices for Laws Relating to NGOs* described here provides insight into some of the challenges in developing approaches to the legal regulation of NGOs, particularly those that seek to respond to demands for NGO accountability. While the Draft Handbook was in many ways on the mark in stating the relevant principles, those principles were not consistently reflected in its details. The fact that the source of the document was the World Bank, an institution with considerable influence with governments, as well as other multilateral and bilateral groups, increased the risks it presented.

Lessons from the Handbook experience that have broader applicability include the following:

- Human rights, particularly the freedoms of association and expression, must be at the center of the thinking about the regulation of NGOs. Recommendations of prescriptive rules, particularly those intended to have universal applicability, will seldom be appropriate.
- Legal regulatory schemes for NGOs should generally focus on NGO activities or operations that warrant attention, whether to protect a legitimate and defined public or government concern or the rights of others, rather than on the nature or characterization of the entity concerned, whether not-for-profit or for-profit.
- Initial questions when devising a regulatory scheme to promote accountability should be: accountable to whom and for what purpose and why should the government have a role?
- The fact that other approaches to promoting accountability in the NGO sector, for example, self-regulation, greater oversight by donors or members, may be difficult, flawed or present other challenges should not be sufficient to justify a regulatory role for government.
- The development of regulatory systems for NGOs is a complicated process made more so when approaches are intended to be appropriate in diverse national, legal, cultural, political and social situations. There are no quick or easy solutions. The meaningful involvement of local NGOs is essential not only to the development of appropriate approaches, but also for the growth and development of the capacities of those groups.
- Consultation on the development of accountability systems must be adequately planned and budgeted at the time a project is conceived.
- The value of new or better laws should not be overestimated. Hindrances to the growth and development of civil society may have little to do with the presence or absence of good law.
- The World Bank lacks the mandate and competency for the development of prescriptive rules for the regulation of NGOs by governments. As the NGO Working Group on the World Bank suggested in April 1999, the Bank's role would best be limited to the facilitation of others, particularly organizations with the appropriate mandate and expertise, such as UN agencies.

In many ways, the Draft Handbook was eloquent in its support for NGOs and the importance of a vibrant civil society to national development. It sought to support the growth of civil society and address genuine and growing concerns about the need for greater accountability by NGOs. These factors, together with the worthy intentions of its drafters, led many to overlook the details of its largely generic approach to complicated issues that were fraught with risks to some NGOs.

Accountability of NGOs is important, indeed, sometimes essential, in a wide range of situations so that members, donors, the general public and governments can play an appropriate role. In addition, NGOs may also find accountability mechanisms to be useful strategic tools to gain credibility or leverage in promoting their own programme and activities. But accountability is a relative value. As the CRM Critique stated: 'There is nothing intrinsically good, or bad, in accountability and transparency; one must be careful to always look at the context in which they are sought to be applied' (CRM, 1996).

NOTES

1   This chapter draws on documents and notes growing out of the author's work from 1995 to 2002, first as a staff member and then a consultant with the Lawyers Committee for Human Rights (now Human Rights First), an NGO based in New York. The author is grateful to Colin Fenwick, Stefanie Grant and Peter van Tuijl for their insights and suggestions. She would also like to thank John Clark, Lead Social Scientist, World Bank East Asia and Pacific Region, and Jeff Thindwa, Acting Coordinator, Participation and Civic Engagement Group, World Bank Social Development Department for their comments and criticism of an earlier draft of this paper. Finally, the comments of Leon Irish and Karla Simon, both of whom were actively involved in the Draft Handbook when they were with the International Center for Not-for-Profit Law and, for part of the period, Lee as a consultant to the World Bank, are very much appreciated. While sharp differences in views remain, their perspectives improved and clarified the paper overall. This chapter has been abridged for publication in this book. An extended and fully refer- enced version is available at: www.civilsocietybuilding.net/csb. All documents referred to in the full version of the paper are in the author's possession. The views expressed here are solely her own.

2   References to the Handbook in this chapter refer to the widely distributed 1997 draft, unless otherwise noted.

3   John Clark, World Bank, 'Legal Dimensions of the Enabling Environment Seminar', The Hague, October 2, 2000, CIVICUS Transcript, pp320–321.

4   The May 1997 draft was translated into Spanish, Russian, Chinese, French, Arabic, Albanian, Ukrainian, Bulgarian, Vietnamese and perhaps other languages.

5   The PBO/MBO distinction is familiar in some legal systems, although the Draft Handbook noted that 'most legal systems do not use the terms PBO and MBO as such'. The problems presented by their use in the Draft Handbook were ones of definition and recommended use, as described later.

6   The Draft Handbook noted: 'A constant challenge for the Bank and others is to determine whether and the extent to which an NGO really listens to and speaks for those whom it purports to represent and benefit'.

7   The NGOs involved in the Three Freedoms Project were: Alternative Law and Development Center, Inc. (AlterLaw, the Philippines); Cambodian Association for Human Rights and Development (ADHOC, Cambodia); Hong Kong Human Rights Monitor (Hong Kong); Human Rights in China (China and US); Institute for Policy Research and Advocacy (ELSAM, Indonesia); Law and Society Trust (Sri Lanka); and the Union for Civil Liberties (Thailand).

8   Until April 1999, the view of the Lawyers Committee for Human Rights was that if the Handbook was properly prepared, it could be a useful tool in promoting greater openness and respect for freedom of association for NGOs. The Lawyers Committee's view changed in April 1999 after proposals were made to the NGO Working Group on the World Bank that were seen as evidence that necessary changes in the Draft Handbook were not likely and that there was a desire to expand inappropriate activities, most notably the promotion of a sample NGO law (which ultimately appeared as an appendix to the 2000 Draft Handbook).

9   While not well developed, freedom of association was and is widely protected. In addition, during the period that the Draft Handbook was under consideration, the UN General Assembly adopted the UN Declaration on the Right and Responsibility of Individuals, Groups and Organs of Society to Promote and Protect Universally Recognized Human Rights and Fundamental Freedoms (Human Rights Defenders Declaration, 1998), which clarified a number of issues addressed by the Draft Handbook.

10   It was noted that the Bank had received comments or contributions from only 12 groups or individuals as a result of the 6-week virtual consultation.

11   See particularly the International Covenant on Civil and Political Rights, Article 22 and the European Convention on Human Rights, Article 11. In addition to these two treaties, there are more than 13 other international treaties that protect freedom of association, including those related to economic, social and cultural rights, race, women and children. For a detailed discussion of the international law of freedom of association, see McBride (2003).

12   United Communist Party of Turkey and Others *v.* Turkey, Application No. 19392/92 (30 January 1998); and Sidiropoulos and Others *v.* Greece, Application No. 26695/95 (10 July 1998). Both references are available at http://hudoc.echr.coe.int/hudoc.

13   Declaration on the Right and Responsibility of Individuals, Groups and Organs of Society to Promote and Protect Universally Recognized Human Rights and Fundamental Freedoms, adopted 9 December 1998, the negotiation of which started in 1985. It was a notable development in the understanding of the law of freedom of association and expression for NGOs. Article 13 states: 'Everyone has the right, individually and in association with others, to solicit, receive and utilize resources for the express purpose of promoting and protecting human rights and fundamental freedoms, through peaceful means'.

14   See, for example, existing or recently proposed laws in Angola, Belarus, Egypt, Jordan, Kyrgyzstan, Russia, Turkmenistan, Uzbekistan and Zimbabwe. These laws are in addition to general laws that exist in all countries that address illegal activities, whether committed by an individual or for-profit or not-for-profit organization.

15   UN Doc. A/59/401, §§ 75, 77 (1 October 2004). This concern has been raised by the Special Rapporteur since her first report following the creation of her position in 2000. See UN Doc. E/CN.4/2001/94, p.32 (26 January 2001).

5

Issues in Legislation for NGOs in Uganda

Jassy B. Kwesiga and Harriet Namisi

INTRODUCTION

This chapter seeks to highlight the character of current debates on issues of NGO accountability and other related questions, such as legitimacy and credibility, through a case study of the NGO Registration Amendment Bill 2000, already tabled in the Ugandan Parliament. For four years now, NGOs have marshalled and mobilized every possible argument and strategy to get the bill amended because it threatens NGOs' rights and freedoms of speech and association. Eventually, NGOs decided that the best course of action was not to seek the amendment of the bill, but rather to produce and advocate an alternative bill. This alternative bill is already in place and being marketed to stakeholders, alongside initiatives to promote NGO self-governance through voluntary certification. The purpose of this chapter is to argue that the status of NGOs in Uganda would be better regulated under an alternative legal apparatus that recognizes rights along with responsibilities.

We have deliberately written on NGOs and not on civil society. Civil society is composed of many organizations that operate under different laws. Except for the media, civil society organizations other than NGOs do not seem to be active in influencing the government to change the laws that govern them. Either they are comfortable with these laws or they probably use different methods to satisfy their needs. Civil society organizations that normally do articulate a political role have been oppressed. Trade unions, for example, have been disempowered to the extent that even big private enterprises like hotel establishments in cities do not allow their formation. We therefore concentrate on NGOs.

THE NGO LANDSCAPE

The colonial period in a country like Uganda did not encourage the growth of autonomous people's organizations or voluntary associations. There was no room to challenge the power structure of the colonial system. When Uganda attained its independence from the British in 1962, it did not improve the fortunes of civic associations in the sense of increasing peoples' participation in governance. There was a tendency for the post-colonial masters to argue that the severity of the post-colonial problems required a united front. What should have grown into autonomous voluntary associations were 'swallowed up' by the state and firmly subordinated to ruling party ideology and machinations. These included workers', women's and youth organizations, cooperatives and even the media.

The advent of dictator Amin into power in 1971 sealed the NGO coffin. It was inconceivable that any civic organization could have the courage to raise a political finger to Amin and his government. The consequences were known. Faith-based organizations, for example, experienced them in a most bitter manner when the Anglican Archbishop was murdered in cold blood. After the overthrow of Amin in 1979, post-Amin governments failed to organize the establishment of an orderly transition that could lead to the birth of democracy. The country was again involved in wars between Museveni 'bush' fighters and the Obote government, leading to the capture of state power by the Museveni forces, which formed the National Resistance Movement (NRM) government in 1986.

The formation of the NRM government was based on a Ten Point Programme, a kind of manifesto, which clearly advocated peoples' participation in the development of the country, the promotion of human rights and redefining the state in a way that would increase the freedoms of individuals to go about their business, guided by the rule of law. The 1995 Constitution is by and large embraced by civil society organizations as one of the best in Africa because of its emphasis on human rights, which include issues of affirmative action and decentralization; for giving prominence to the role and independence of civic organizations; and for the fact that it was democratically conceived. No wonder that such increased democratic space led to the proliferation of many NGOs in the country. In 1986 there were 160 NGOs; in the year 2000, this had increased to 3500; and currently there are 5200 registered NGOs (Sebtongo, 2004).

A recent study underlines the contribution that the NGO sector makes to the economy and employment. The expenditures of the civil society sector in Uganda are equivalent to 1.4 per cent of gross domestic product (GDP). The work force in the civil sector numbers over 230,000 workers, which represents 2.3 per cent of the country's economically active population and 10.9 per cent of its non-agricultural employment (John Hopkins, 1999). To put this in perspective, the civil society workforce is over one-and-a-half times the size of the public work force and over half as large as all sectors of manufacturing combined. It is estimated that 23 per cent of the adult population is involved in volunteer work.

The Constitution of Uganda recognizes the role of civic organizations and accords them autonomy. It states that 'Civic organizations shall retain their autonomy in pursuit of their declared objectives' (Articles II (i); (iv) and 32 (I)). It furthermore refers to affirmative action in 'favor of groups marginalized on the basis of gender, age, disability or any other reasons created by history, tradition or custom, for the purpose of redressing imbalances which exist amongst them' (Article 32 (I)). These provisions, accompanied by the provision that all citizens shall be empowered and encouraged to be active participants 'at all levels in their own governance', lay the legal support for civic organizations' work in the country.

In addition to these provisions in the Constitution, most of the government's development work plans also boldly recognize the role of civic organizations. The recent Poverty Eradication Action Plan, for example, recognizes the role of civil society and specifically states that:

> government enjoys productive partnerships with civil society
> (NGOs) in a number of areas and there are five general roles that
> they play: (1) advocacy, particularly for the interests of groups
> who might otherwise be neglected; (2) voluntarily financed
> service delivery in sectors not covered by government
> programmes; (3) publicly financed service delivery, subcontracted
> by government; (4) support to conflict resolution; and (5)
> independent research on key policy issues. (Ministry of Finance,
> Planning and Economic Development, 2004)

Professional voluntary associations, in particular, seem to have succeeded in attracting the attention of the policy-makers, for example, the associations of lawyers, doctors, engineers, business groups, sometimes the teachers and others working in specialized fields like those for children, people with disabilities, health or the environment. Several donors, principally the World Bank, the United Nations Development Programme (UNDP), the Danish International Development Agency (DANIDA) and the United Nations Children's Fund (UNICEF) also extend invitations to relevant NGOs. As far as invitations and consultations are concerned, the situation has improved with most stakeholders.

At the decentralized level, NGOs have initiated serious dialogue with local authorities to establish modalities for working together, especially in setting priorities for work plans, monitoring and sharing information and facilities. An initial resistance, not unexpected, is beginning to wane and positive results are beginning to show. It should be noted that there are many NGOs with leadership positions in the various local government councils. This is a sign that participation in NGO activities can act as a training ground for democratic leadership. NGO leaders in different councils are working on modalities for more interaction with NGOs (outside the councils). Emerging district NGO networks will enhance this process.

Within this broadening scope of institutional relationships, NGOs have raised issues as they see them on the ground, especially those relating to poverty, governance and social development. They have argued that every one is entitled to a minimum standard of living and requested the government to address such issues as food security, education, health, shelter, HIV/AIDS, agriculture, environment, water, sanitation and employment. They have talked about human rights, conflicts and conflict resolution, and the need for disaster preparedness. People with disabilities have continued to argue their cases along with other issues of marginalization. All this has been based on the premises of social, economic, political and cultural rights and justice.

More than anyone else, NGOs have firmly drummed up the case of the debt crisis and how the money saved should go into the promotion of social services as part of the poverty action fund. This debate has been expanded and intensified to revisit the issue of national resource management and corruption. In summarizing the range of NGO activities, the role of women's groups has to be mentioned as well. They have addressed hard issues of land tenureship, domestic relations, representation and teenage pregnancies. There is evidence that the creation of the original Ministry for Women's Affairs was partly due to advocacy and lobbying by women's groups in the country. Generally speaking, Uganda is well ahead of many countries in recognizing the role of women in development.

NGOs have also continued to raise issues of a global nature. The Ugandan government has committed itself to fulfilling several international obligations. NGOs consider it their responsibility to enhance the domestication of such obligations. These covenants and conventions are about different types of rights, discrimination, degrading treatment and many facets of social development. There are many other emerging issues that NGOs are beginning to get interested in, such as influencing the process of negotiating international and regional trade agreements to promote poverty policies and other issues related to international trade and financing. It was most revealing that during the summit in Geneva to review the Copenhagen recommendations on social development, only the Ugandan NGOs had a country report (Robert, 1999).

NGOs AND THE LAW

The Constitution accords positive legal support for the role of NGOs. Unfortunately, there are many other laws in place, which are at variance with the provisions of the Constitution. One such problematic law, which has not been harmonized with the Constitution, is the law on accessing official information, passed by the Parliament of Uganda in 2004 without incorporating comments from civil society organizations. This bill does not encourage a culture of openness within government and public bodies. Therefore, principles of open government with mechanisms for monitoring and reporting, creating awareness and the management of records are not in place to facilitate the implementation of the law (Coalition for Freedom of Information, 2004). In this case, transparency and accountability, good governance and the strengthening of democracy are strongly affected. Another prominent problematic law is the Local Government Act, which empowers district local government officials to 'coordinate, supervise and monitor' the work of NGOs. However, the interpretation and actual behaviour of local government officials is more towards the need to control NGOs, and even to close them, if they do not listen to what these officials tell them to do. To them, NGOs cannot be autonomous in a district that has clearly elected leadership. They ask, 'Autonomous from whom and what?'. All such laws remain thorny to NGOs. However, the emphasis of the rest of this chapter will be on the NGO Statute of 1988/89 and the subsequent NGO Registration Amendment Bill of 2000.

The NGO Statute of 1988/89 and NGO Registration Amendment Bill 2000

The proliferation of NGOs led the government to put in place an NGO Statute (1988/89), which clearly reflected its anxiety about them. First, it set up an NGO Registration Board, located in the Ministry of Internal Affairs – alongside police, prisons, security agencies and immigration. Second, the Statute required NGOs to go through cumbersome bureaucratic procedures for their annual registration with the Board. Third, Registration Board members were appointed by the Minister of Internal Affairs, which implied that representatives of the security agencies sat on the Board, with the responsibility to vet NGO registration applications. Obviously, these members of the Board looked at NGOs as a security risk, to be carefully watched, monitored and controlled.

NGOs are not against legislation as such. It is the way it is done, its content and implications that have to be agreed on. The introduction of the NGO Registration Amendment Bill in 2000 came as a surprise and raised many worrying questions. The draft bill is opposed by NGOs. The NGOs were surprised that despite their current status and in many ways acknowledged contribution to development, the government appeared unwilling to put in place legislation that promotes NGO–government partnerships and recognizes the NGOs' watchdog role and other tested attributes.

The NGOs oppose a number of specific sections of the draft bill. The objectives of the bill see the investment of a large degree of power in the NGO Registration Board, which will have a mandate to monitor NGO operations and turn into a National Board for Non-Governmental Organizations. The new Board will develop and issue policy guidelines for NGOs and CBOs, and provide permits for any duly registered organization. The bill supports an expansion of the minister's power to make regulations prescribing the manner in which organizations shall be wound up when they cease to operate and also prescribes the duration and form of a permit issued to an NGO when it is registered. The draft bill specifically states that: 'no organization shall operate in Uganda unless it has been duly registered with the Board and has a valid permit'. This is a requirement in addition to the registration certificate, however, the precise nature, function and duration of these requirements are not defined. This could introduce unnecessary costs to the NGOs. It is also very unfortunate that an NGO that has already been registered must obtain a permit in order to operate. This clearly contradicts the purpose of registration. Centralized NGO registration may lead to processes of bureaucracy and unnecessary delays in obtaining a certificate.

The draft bill also states that 'an organization shall not be registered if the objectives as specified in their constitution is in contravention of government policy, plan or public interest'. This could create unintended consequences for NGOs. These grounds have not been clearly defined and could give unnecessarily wide, discretionary powers to the NGO Board. Who exactly defines the 'public interest'? Assuming that an organization is to lobby and campaign against the death penalty or human rights abuses like domestic violence or human torture of any nature, which may be public policy, plan or public interest, is it a strong ground to deny registration to an organization? The concern is that the draft bill does not conform to the requirements of a free and democratic society.

The draft bill further states that 'an organization which contravenes any provision of this section commits an offence and is liable on conviction to a fine not exceeding 20 currency points'. Besides, where an organization commits an offence as earlier stated, 'any director or officer of the Organization whose act or omission gave rise to the offence also commits the offence and is liable on conviction'. The bill threatens NGOs and their officers who breach its provisions with fines and imprisonment. This will be infringing on the legitimate exercise of the recognized right to freedom of association. Also, the legal personality of a registered non-governmental organization should be distinct from that of its officers, founders or members. The liability of an NGO should be separated from the fact that an organization actually operates through its officers. This dual liability contradicts the Penal Code Act, which states that 'a person shall not be punished twice either under the provisions of any law for the same offence'.

The proposed NGO Board is almost exclusively composed of government members and includes members of the internal and external security organizations. This is highly suspect and tends towards maintaining the view that NGOs are a 'security threat' that must be handled with an iron hand. Instead, the selection of board members should be based on knowledge of and familiarity with the NGO sector. Whereas the NGO sector agrees with the inclusion of two members from the public sector on the Board, the mode of their identification is not visibly spelled out for the purpose of transparency. NGO representatives should be identified in a transparent fashion.

No independent appeal procedure has been stated. The draft bill states that, 'A person aggrieved by the decision of the Board may within one month of the date he is notified of the decision, appeal to the Minister'. Incidentally, it is very interesting to note that the minister is the person who appoints the Board. Therefore his/her neutrality is highly suspect. NGOs therefore suggest that if room for appeal must be enforced, then there ought to be a right of appeal from the decision of the Board to the courts. Courts provide justice and in any case NGOs must have an arbitration mechanism where they can be sure of fair play.

What are the reasons for the draft bill?

How is it that a government that on the one hand recognizes the contributions of NGOs, invites them to meetings and seeks their policy input, on the other hand wants to put in place such an unfriendly law? If one goes by the various pronouncements by government officials in media reports, a number of considerations may indicate possible underlying forces behind the character of the draft bill. NGOs admit that there may be some truth in some of them, but not to the level of dwarfing the good achievements highlighted above.

According to the 1988/89 Statute, NGOs are expected to state their mission, geographical area of operation and objectives clearly. It is, however, reported that some organizations have attempted to divert from their original intentions. The government is very passionate about this because there is a fear that these organizations may cause a security threat in the long run. The argument that NGOs are a 'security threat' has been echoed many times by different government officials, but no concrete examples are given to support the statement. Next, the issue of transparency has always been a point of contention. NGOs have been accused of being very reluctant to disclose how much funding they receive for their organizations and even their expenditure levels. Some organizations have also been accused of mismanagement of funds, supposedly based on donors complaining to government. Therefore, the new regulation would assist the government in weeding out some of these organizations by denying them permits.

Government officials also sometimes refer to the need to prevent the emergence of 'briefcase NGOs'. This refers to individuals moving from one meeting to another while claiming to represent an organization. However, the organization in question exists only on the paper they carry in their bags. They have no office, staff or physical address. Some of them have been accused of 'conning' vulnerable groups out of their money, promising them a number of incentives, including paying fees for their children. Then they disappear without a trace. It has also been tough going for NGOs since the year 2000, when a religious 'cult' in a remote area of the country, apparently registered as an NGO, persuaded its followers to gather in their usual meeting place and accept immolation as a faster means to go to heaven. Over 1000 people perished in the inferno.

It is also believed that some individuals and even institutions have been aggrieved by the advocacy role of some NGOs, for example, in the areas of exposing corruption among individuals in government or by openly accusing the government of human rights abuses, lack of commitment to ending the war in Northern Uganda and by revealing irregularities during presidential elections. Misunderstandings between NGOs and local politicians have been recorded in almost all districts and even at the national level. The NGOs' performance is, in many cases, ranked highly and appreciated by local communities. This has not gone unnoticed by local politicians, who sometimes have responded by questioning the mandate, transparency, legitimacy and accountability of the NGOs compared to their own credentials as elected officials.

The decision by parliamentarians not too long ago to reward themselves with huge sums of money in the form of salaries, allowances and, at one point an attempted pension scheme was challenged by NGOs. This may not have been well received by the legislators. The process of privatization of government institutions and the arrival of foreign investors was also challenged by NGOs. Not that NGOs were against it per se, it was more a question of how it was done and the implications on the lives of the poor. As a result of the above alleged 'sins', the government may have decided to propose the restrictive law as a means to control the NGO sector that appeared more accountable to the donors than to government.

NGO opposition to the draft bill

Whatever the underlying causes, NGOs have continued to oppose the Non-Governmental Organizations Amendment Bill. The NGOs have argued that the impact of the proposed bill on NGOs must be fully analysed to avoid unintended consequences. The bill must provide flexibility for the future because this is a growing, dynamic, heterogeneous and diverse sector. Sufficient time for consultations and notification of key stakeholders must be allowed before the bill is presented to the parliament. The government must ensure that key resources for achieving compliance have been spelled out at the lowest cost and risk possible.

The bill has continued to linger in parliament, partly because of the sustained advocacy efforts towards the passing of a favourable law for NGO operations, partly because of pressure on the government by donors, and also because the NGOs have the support of several sympathetic members of parliament, especially those with a civil society background. The majority of these are members on an affirmative ticket, such as those representing people with disabilities, women and the youth.

In order to make the bargain clearer, NGOs drafted an alternative bill with new proposals. But while the views from the political wing of government were that the bill should be sent back to the cabinet and adjustments made to incorporate the new proposals, the concerned technical officials could not entertain this because it would mean restarting the process of law-making.

It is also important to note that, for the moment, parliament is preoccupied with debates on the transition process, debating the stipulations contained in the current Constitutional review, including whether the Constitution should be amended to allow the current president to have a third term of office. Hence, parliament is too busy to deal with the NGO bill. However, NGOs will not be very surprised if the bill sails through one afternoon, amidst all this.

NGOs AND THE QUEST FOR SELF-REGULATION

As mentioned before, Ugandan NGOs are not against legislation, as is sometimes suggested by government officials. In fact, as of now they are discussing 'voluntary certification' as a mechanism for self-governance. This means that the NGO sector would be:

> *able to control its own activities and is not under the effective control of any other entity. To be sure no organization is wholly independent. To be considered self-governing, however, the organization must control its management and operations to a significant extent, have its own internal governance procedures and enjoy a meaningful degree of autonomy.* (UN, 2002)

In promoting this argument for self-control, NGOs are pleading the support of the provisions in the 1995 Constitution that guarantee the autonomy of civic organizations.

During the last four years, NGOs have seriously revisited issues of self-regulation, held several meetings and hired a researcher who has reviewed voluntary certification in many countries. In response to the NGO Amendment Bill 2000, which stresses government control, NGOs have sought an option also indicated in the NGO alternative bill to establish a national NGO council to take care of all opportunities, challenges and questions arising from or directed at NGOs. The current national NGO networks, which include the Development Network of Indigenous Organizations (DENIVA) and the NGO Forum, agree that a national council has a role to play above that of the umbrella organizations and networks. Reference has been drawn from a number of countries including Kenya, where a national NGO council is entitled to establish its own structures, rules and procedures for networking purposes and establish a regulatory committee in the council to enforce the NGO code of conduct, also referred to as the process of voluntary certification.

There is broad agreement that there is a need for voluntary certification as a mechanism to clean up the NGOs' own house, increase their credibility and accountability and demonstrate seriousness of purpose. In addition, voluntary certification would give NGOs security. It is argued that if this is not done, the government is likely to come in with its own control measures in the name of 'shaping up' NGOs. References were made to cases where district chairpersons have closed district NGO networks on the spurious grounds that NGOs are not harmonizing their work with that of the district administration and have credentials that are suspect.

If imaginatively crafted, voluntary certification could put in place 'minimum standards' to guide all NGOs on standards that they should aspire to achieve. There is even an inconclusive debate on whether certificates of standard achievements should be issued to raise motivation and to guide other stakeholders (including donors) who want to work with credible NGOs. It is being likened to the international certification given to goods.

The issue of voluntary certification enforcement is crucial, but who should enforce it? This has been a contentious issue with NGO codes of conduct in many countries. It revolves around questions of neutrality and fairness, but also whether enforcement is in the spirit of 'voluntarism'. Rather than enforce, why not create benefits, which will automatically attract NGOs to respect the demands and standards agreed on? Is there something to learn from the African Peer Review, where the African Union worked out governance indicators that African countries were free to subject themselves to and agree to address whatever shortcomings were identified?

Besides voluntary certification, NGOs in 2003 and 2004 developed an agenda with minimum standard values. These are values that can be observed and respected without incurring any costs or forfeiting anything. The values mentioned in the standards for voluntary certification include: integrity and accountability, transparent decision-making, active citizen participation, peaceful coexistence, tolerance and reconciliation, effective sharing and separation of powers, openness to change, willingness to negotiate and equitable distribution of resources. The public is expected to hold their leaders accountable based on these principles.

The idea to develop a minimum agenda is not only to target leaders. NGOs must also uphold these principles in their own organizations and translate them into a code of conduct to hold themselves to account because they cannot preach what they do not practice. For each of these principles, benchmarks have been developed as practical undertakings that NGOs expect any leader or political entity to undertake, whether in power or vying for power. These benchmarks will be used to measure, evaluate and appreciate leaders' or political entities' behaviour, actions and programmes. In other words, they will be used to hold them accountable, NGO leadership included.

As much as the government is concerned about regulation, NGOs are trying hard to find means of upholding accountability and self-regulation using common values. Lastly, looking at what is happening in other countries and within Ugandan professional associations, and bearing in mind discussions on the current NGO bill in Uganda, it was agreed that NGOs should ensure that there is legal support for NGO self-governing measures and for the discipline of errant ones in a manner supported by the law. Any stakeholder with a complaint about an NGO should report it to the recognized organ put in place by the NGOs for 'interrogation', or go to a court of law.

CONCLUDING REMARKS

Accountability and transparency are issues for building up democratic institutions and democratic culture. What NGOs are asking for is room within the responsibility of the state. The Constitution clearly articulates 'the State shall be based on democratic principles which empower and encourage the active participation of all citizens at all levels in their own governance' (Article II (i)). The challenge for NGOs is to build a united front to defend their rights and autonomy. This is only possible if they are firmly rooted in a social base that is politically alert.

Both colonialists and early post-independence African leaders never encouraged or supported the growth of autonomous voluntary associations, especially those with a tendency to challenge power relations. As observed, 'we have inherited in Uganda a strong tendency towards control in many areas of life, private or public. Very many aspects of our lives as citizens are regulated, and most often regulated by the state rather than by the citizens themselves' (De Coninck, 2005). It is regulation by citizens that Ugandan NGOs are fighting to achieve. Accountability cannot be for communities, donors and the state alone. It should also be for the NGOs themselves.

6

NGO Accountability and the Philippine Council for NGO Certification: Evolving Roles and Issues[1]

Stephen Golub

INTRODUCTION

This chapter examines the work of the Philippine Council for NGO Certification (PCNC), whether and how PCNC promotes NGO accountability, and the Council's other evolving roles and related issues. These other matters include:

- PCNC's original and continuing function, as authorized by Bureau of Internal Revenue (BIR) Regulation 13-98 (BIR 13-98), which is to certify a tax-deductible 'donee institution' status for applicant NGOs and other non-stock, non-profit organizations (such as universities and religious institutions) receiving donations from Philippine corporations (typically through Philippine foundations);[2]
- by virtue of this tax deduction provision (which also applies to individual donations), PCNC's help to NGOs generate financial support in an environment of diminishing foreign funding;
- the organization's role in certifying for foreign as well as domestic donors that NGOs are in 'good standing', including the potential that donors may require PCNC certification for NGOs receiving their funds;
- PCNC's effect of either closing or opening the door to excessive government regulation of NGOs;
- its role in inhibiting the flow of funds to terrorist organizations and other criminal activities;

- PCNC's advice to NGOs to strengthen their structures, operations and professionalism;
- its provision of opportunities and incentives for NGO self-assessment and improvement; and
- PCNC's facilitation of inter-NGO contact across sectoral and philosophical lines, in ways that broaden perspectives and strengthen civil society.

PCNC is important not just because of these roles, but because it serves as at least a partial model for current and potential efforts in other countries. Given that the Council has only existed since 1998 and that the nature and scope of its work are in flux, it would be premature to reach firm conclusions on the issues this chapter considers. Nevertheless, it is fair to offer some initial impressions of PCNC, the issue of NGO accountability and the overlap between the two.

THE GENESIS OF PCNC[3]

The genesis of PCNC dates to 1995. In the context of a general overhaul of Philippine tax law, the Philippine Department of Finance (DOF) and BIR set up a joint task force that, among many other recommendations, proposed eliminating the tax code provision that permitted full deduction of donations to certain non-stock, non-profit organizations, including NGOs. The Philippine tax system is the only avenue through which the government could be said to regulate NGOs, other than the requirement that NGOs register with the Securities and Exchange Commission in order to acquire legal status.

The task force proposal stemmed from its broader mandate to recommend systemic changes that would increase revenue collection. Another factor underlying the proposed change was the widespread abuse of the tax system by politicians and other wealthy individuals who have exploited the tax-deductible and tax-exempt status of NGOs to set up fraudulent organizations that serve private and often corrupt ends. Changing the tax code therefore aimed to both increase revenues and close a commonly abused loophole. It is to the credit of DOF and BIR, and a positive reflection of the civil society–state relations in the Philippines, that the proposal surfaced through an official consultation process in which its elements were shared with corporate and NGO leaders.

Although this proposal was a relatively minor part of a potentially sweeping overhaul in tax policy, it was of considerable concern to Philippine corporations that make legitimate donations to NGOs. Numerous corporations make such contributions, typically through foundations. For example, a leading NGO, Philippine Business for Social Progress, acts in part as a grant-making foundation that channels private sector support to non-profit activities.

The proposed tax code revision also stood to affect individuals who make such donations to NGOs, although they constitute a smaller and far less organized pool of support.[4] Still, there is considerable potential for such persons to increase their contributions. Particularly since international funding for Philippine NGOs will likely decrease in coming years (as foreign foundations, bilateral donors and multilateral sources focus more on impoverished, conflict-ridden or strategically sensitive societies), the need to maintain tax incentives for individual and corporate donations will increase.

The potential revision spurred leaders of corporate foundations to pick up the pace of discussions among themselves and with the government concerning the status of NGOs under Philippine tax law. Together with leaders of the NGO community and in consultation with government personnel, they began to fashion a mechanism through which legitimate NGOs would retain their donee (that is, tax-deductible) status.

For both substantive and political reasons, the DOF and BIR were responsive to the concerns of their corporate and civil society counterparts. Non-governmental groups play a major role in delivering development-oriented and welfare services to Filipinos, services that the government is less adept at providing. Even at the expense of sacrificing potential tax revenue through perpetuating deductions for donations to NGOs, the government did not want to undercut organizations contributing to societal well-being. In addition, Philippine commercial and civil society interests are powerful political voices on many issues, not least those that directly affect their financial status.

Recognizing the government's legitimate concerns, as well as the BIR's severely limited capacity to separate the legitimate wheat from the bogus chaff in the non-profit community, foundation and NGO leaders sought a non-governmental mechanism that would address the interests of both parties. Toward this end, PCNC was launched and registered as a non-stock, non-profit organization in January 1997. But its role regarding deductibility was unclear. The Tax Reform Act of 1997, which took effect on 1 January 1998, allowed donations to accredited organizations. However, the Act did not specify the process and even the agency for deciding on accreditation. These decisions were left to the Act's implementing rules and regulations.

Both before and after the adoption of the Act, a series of negotiations among corporate foundations, NGO federations, the DOF and BIR addressed whether and to what extent PCNC would play a role in accrediting NGOs for tax-deductible status. The many issues with which the negotiators grappled included whether:

- BIR could or should delegate any authority and responsibility to an NGO;
- BIR should delegate that power to a new NGO with no track record, such as PCNC;
- PCNC should be the sole agency with accreditation responsibilities; and
- there should be limits on the kinds of NGOs that could qualify for donee status (with DOF initially aiming to restrict that status to disaster relief groups).

A January 1998 Memorandum of Agreement between the DOF and PCNC established the initial parameters of the latter's role. Those parameters were subsequently hammered out through negotiations with the aforementioned BIR-DOF task force, resulting in December of that year in the promulgation BIR 13-98, the Tax Reform Act's implementing regulation concerning accreditation of NGOs and other non-stock, non-profit organizations for donee institution status.

The central PCNC roles set forth by BIR 13-98 are that it assesses applicants and informs BIR of those that it endorses for accreditation. The Bureau, in turn, automatically issues the qualifying organizations with certificates of registration as donee institutions. Donations to them are then tax deductible. BIR does not have discretion to refuse registration to those applicants approved by PCNC. Thus, in practice, PCNC decides which organizations receive certification/accreditation (with the terms used interchangeably), but the status is officially conferred by BIR.

As a compromise, the regulation intentionally does not stipulate that PCNC is the sole agency that can review NGOs for the purpose of establishing whether donations to them are tax deductible. As of this writing, however, it is the only organization designated by the Secretary of Finance to carry out that function. In addition, the wording of BIR 13-98 specifies that the 'Accrediting Entity' shall be 'composed of NGO networks' (Section 1-(d)), which may limit, though not eliminate the potential to establish alternative certification mechanisms.

THE CERTIFICATION PROCESS

Prior to BIR issuing the certification of registration, PCNC undertakes essentially a three-stage process in obtaining and reviewing NGO applications for donee institution status.

Written applications

- The prospective applicant first contacts PCNC in writing (either through email or a hard copy letter) to express its interest in applying;
- PCNC then provides the NGO with a Letter of Intent (to apply) form, which the applicant returns to the Council with a 1000 peso (approximately US$20) deposit toward an application fee.
- The applicant then receives and completes a Survey Form, which it returns, along with supporting documentation, to PCNC. The information requested for the Survey Form varies slightly, depending on whether the NGO has been operating for at least two years or less than two years (with the latter category including newly established organizations). In either event, the applicant must supply about 20 types of information/documentation. These include: a profile of the organization; its Securities and Exchange Commission registration with articles of incorporation (reflect-

ing the process by which the organization acquires formal legal status); a policy (signed by appropriate personnel) on conflict of interest; a list of current board members and officers; a list of key staff members; an organizational chart; an annual report/list of accomplishments for the past two years (if in existence that long), or a list of planned activities for the coming two years (if in existence for less than two years); and audited financial statements for the past two years (if in existence for that long).

- Based on the completed Survey Form and application, PCNC then decides whether the NGO is a realistic candidate for certification. If it is, the Council requires a 9000 peso (US$180) payment to complete the full application fee of 10,000 pesos (US$200) (including the 1000 peso deposit). This sum mainly goes towards the cost of a PCNC evaluation team visit, described below. To defray the costs of the visit and related expenses more completely, the Council is considering establishing a maximum fee of 20,000 pesos (US$400), with the fee for any given NGO established on a sliding scale based on the applicant's resources.

Evaluation visit

Upon completion of the first stage of the process, PCNC organizes and dispatches an evaluation team to undertake a two-day visit to the NGO. The team typically comprises two or three representatives of other NGOs that have already been certified as donee institutions and that therefore are PCNC members. They perform the evaluation function on a voluntary basis, the only compensation going to cover their expenses. The Council has selected and trained roughly 1200 evaluators.

On first meeting with the NGO, the evaluators provide further background on PCNC and the application process, hear an initial briefing on its work and finalize the schedule for their visit. Over the course of the two days, they meet with NGO staff and officers, review relevant documents (including financial records) and often visit project sites and representatives of partner populations. As explained on the PCNC website:

> *The following are the major criteria to guide the PCNC in evaluating requests for accreditation:*
> - Mission and Goals: *The mission and goals of the non-profit, non-stock corporation/NGO should justify its need for donee institution status. Statements of mission and goals shall serve as guideposts for its planning and operations and a framework for decision-making.*
> - Resources: *This criterion focuses on the adequacy of the resources and the effectiveness of the structure and systems of the applicant organization.*
> - Program Implementation and Evaluation: *The organization must demonstrate that it is effectively using its resources to accomplish the purposes for which it was created. Evaluation*

> *shall consider the program and projects implemented within the last two years and the presence of clearly-defined policies, systems, priorities, and guidelines in implementing the organization's programs and services.*

- Planning for the Future: *The organization must provide evidence that it has the capability to implement and monitor its programs and projects and to ensure organizational sustainability.*[5]

The most important single element in the evaluation pertains to financial management, which is weighted at 30 per cent of the overall assessment. The review of this aspect does not constitute an audit, however.

The team wraps up its visit with a meeting among the members, who discuss their individual and collective findings and decide what recommendation to submit to the PCNC Board. They do not reveal to the applicant their findings and recommendation. This is both to avoid uncomfortable situations and because the ultimate decision and responsibility rests with the Board and not with the team.

Board decision and resulting options

The Board reviews the evaluation team's report and findings:

- The PCNC Board endorses, defers, or denies certification of the applicant. (The Board comprises the PCNC Executive Director, a Corporate Secretary drawn from a leading accounting firm, a DOF-BIR official and Philippine NGO and foundation leaders.) As of 15 April 2004, 501 organizations had applied for donee institution status. Of those, 392 had been certified, 57 had been denied certification, 39 had received deferred certification and 13 applications were pending.
- The Board also decides the period of time for which an applicant is certified. This can be one (in the instance of some new applicants), three or five years. In selected cases certification may be conditional. In such instances, and if the applicant then decides to pursue standard certification, it undertakes certain tasks (regarding such matters as management or structure) during the period for which it is conditionally approved.
- Those NGOs whose certification is deferred may apply again six months later. Any applicant may request and receive follow-up advice from PCNC on how it can improve its management, operations or structure.

CURRENT PCNC ROLES

PCNC's role in NGO accountability

While there is no standard definition of accountability in general or even NGO accountability in particular, the latter often includes acting in an honest and responsible manner designed to advance its effectiveness in serving partner, client or beneficiary groups or organizations. Against the backdrop of this particular characterization, and taking into account other characterizations of the concept, does the PCNC certification process help increase or assure an NGO's accountability?

Yes, to at least a modest degree. Each facet of the process – the application, the preparation for evaluation, the evaluation itself, the feedback from the evaluation team and PCNC – may help an NGO think through its goals, operations and structure in ways that contribute to it performing in an honest and responsible manner designed to help it effectively serve relevant groups or organizations. The application also may make some NGOs think through the very concept of accountability. It may similarly encourage them to focus on whether and to what extent they are and should be accountable to various audiences.

And while the process is unlikely to make dishonest organizations or personnel trustworthy, being subject to a two-day review may modestly contribute to screening out (through a denial of certification) those NGOs that clearly are not forthcoming about their work. On occasion it may even help an NGO screen out dishonest staff members.

Alternatively, it is important to bear in mind PCNC's origins: it was not established as a vehicle for NGO accountability per se. The Council was launched because of the threat of BIR denying tax deductions to corporate donations to non-profits. At its core, PCNC provides assurance to the Philippine government that its loss of tax revenues is justified by the reasonable assumption that certified NGOs probably serve societal purposes. This is an important function that in and of itself justifies the Council's existence by facilitating funding for many NGOs.

Thus, while the Council serves an important role true to its original purpose, it is not a guarantee of NGO accountability – nor does it claim to be such. As a valuable byproduct of its tax function, the certification process helps make some organizations somewhat more accountable. It offers some assurance that an approved organization is somewhat likely to operate in an honest and responsible way. But there will inevitably be many certified NGOs whose operations do not benefit in this way and a smaller number for which the assurance proves false. This is not to fault PCNC. It simply represents recognition of the fact that NGOs – like businesses, governments and people – vary in quality and integrity, and even the best process does not always separate the wheat from the chaff.

PCNC's other roles

Quite correctly, the Council does not frame its work only in terms of account-ability or facilitating NGO funding. It adds value to the work of NGOs in other ways as well:

- *The opportunity to reflect* – one source of value involves the very process that an organization goes through in preparing for an evaluation visit. Certainly in the Philippines and to varying extents in other countries, NGOs may be so busy carrying out their activities that they lack the time or neglect the opportunity, to reflect on their work. The preparation process provides an opportunity to reflect and to place their organizational houses in order.
- *Sharing perspectives* – there is also value in the way that the evaluation process brings together NGOs with different orientations, areas of exper-tise and sectoral foci, indirectly enabling them to learn from each other's work. A particular problem plaguing the development arena (in some countries even more than the Philippines) is the sectoral barriers that divide organizations according to whether they work in education, natural resources, reproductive health, governance, microcredit or a host of other fields. The evaluation process sometimes helps break down those barriers by bringing together NGO personnel from different development disci-plines.
- *A source of advice* – added value can flow from the advice that PCNC provides applicants as a result of the certification process. This is particu-larly the case for those applicants that request consultations on their operations, management or procedures in the wake of the process. Such consultations most typically occur when their applications have been deferred for future consideration. But advice also is available to those who have been accorded or denied certification.
- *NGOs assessing NGOs* – a positive aspect of all of these Council roles is that its certification process involves NGOs evaluating NGOs. Although, as discussed below, this may be subject to challenge in some respects, it is certainly preferable to government personnel assessing whether an NGO passes muster. NGO personnel are far more likely to understand the challenges and constraints another organization faces. They are even more likely to offer practical perspectives and advice.

EMERGING ROLES AND ISSUES

Quality control

A basic challenge flows from PCNC's success to date: can PCNC maintain the timeliness and quality of its certification process as applications rise? The Caucus of Development NGO Networks (CODE-NGO, whose National Coordinator belongs to the Council's Board) aims to have as many as 2500 organizations belonging to its member networks certified by 2013 – although there are apparent exceptions to this rule.[6] CODE-NGO represents only a fraction of the NGO community in the Philippines. And NGOs represent only a fraction of the total number of non-stock, non-profit organizations in the country – as many as 60,000, according to PCNC's website.

Even allowing for the likelihood that most non-profits will not apply for certification, the potential workload for the Council represents a significant increase compared with the 501 applications considered from 1998 through 15 April 2004. In recognition of this, and as already noted, PCNC has trained 1200 personnel belonging to its own member NGOs to be evaluators. It may prove correct in its confidence that its evaluation teams can handle the increased numbers of NGO applicants. Nevertheless, this situation still presents challenges in terms of maintaining quality control, including not overloading its Board. Should PCNC find itself stretched too thin, it may find other civil society organizations actively seeking to launch independent certification mechanisms, or the government stepping back in to control the process.

The financial challenge

There is also a fundamental financial challenge, since the current fees that NGOs pay do not fully cover the certification process costs. One way of covering at least this aspect of the situation is to build a steeper sliding fee scale than the 10,000–20,000 peso (US$200–400) application fee range the Council is considering. This has merit, although in itself it could impose additional costs in terms of the staff time associated with determining which fees to charge. There also is the question of even a relatively low fee being unaffordable to new or small NGOs.

Another approach would be to charge funding agencies fees for evaluating NGOs that may apply to the agencies for support. This raises issues of whether and in what ways PCNC should evaluate NGOs for purposes other than donor tax deductions, an issue considered below.

A variation on this theme would be for PCNC to make donor support for its overall operations, rather than on a per-NGO fee basis, a key part of its fundraising strategy. If it becomes a sufficiently established part of the civil society landscape, it could make the case that such support leverages NGO accountability in a cost-effective manner. Whether donors would necessarily see PCNC this way is another matter, however.

Remaining apolitical and unbiased

An early challenge to PCNC emerged from some NGOs' suspicion of the role the Council would play in NGO regulation. The Philippine NGO community is characterized by diverse political perspectives. As PCNC was being launched and for a period afterwards, some organizations feared that its corporate genesis would bias the certification process or that the process would become a mechanism for frustrating, rather than facilitating, funding of civil society groups. Corporate foundations wisely sought to alleviate these concerns by involving major NGO networks, such as those belonging to CODE-NGO, from the outset. The networks' memberships include numerous organizations that do not receive corporate funding.

By broadening its base and building a positive image, PCNC has alleviated some suspicions that it is biased. Some NGOs, nevertheless, remain concerned that its process and approval potentially impose political or bureaucratic constraints on NGOs. Association of Foundations Executive Director Norman Jiao counters this concern, correctly pointing out that, 'PCNC looks at how an NGO is being run, not what it's doing'.[7] But there is the possibility that the former could blend into the latter.

Thus, to summarize a critique prepared by the Alternative Law Research and Development Center, Inc. (ALTERLAW), a Philippine NGO, there are concerns that BIR Revenue Regulation No. 13-98 is overbroad, granting the BIR (and PCNC) powers not authorized to it by law, regarding such matters as examining NGOs' policies, strategies, operations and internal documents; creates divisions between two classes of NGOs, those accredited and those not accredited, with the former being more attractive to the government and to funding organizations; permits subjective review and therefore potential abuse by PCNC, which can take the form of accrediting only NGOs sharing similar philosophies and work methods; and thereby allows PCNC to impose certain standards of 'good behaviour' and 'correct' strategies and methods of project implementation (ALTERLAW, undated).

ALTERLAW's critique seems to lie more in the realm of potential than actual action to date. But that certainly does not mean that the critique should be dismissed. The Philippines has gone through periods in which governments have been better or worse, more democratic or less so, and hostile or friendly to large segments of civil society. This raises the possibility that future governments could pressure the certification process. And the origins of PCNC as a product of corporate foundation efforts, coupled with the fact that those foundations retain substantial influence on its Board, suggests a possible corporate orientation on its part.

With these considerations in mind, one can see scenarios in which seemingly apolitical standards yield political consequences. PCNC of course would reject organizations engaging in criminal behaviour, as it was prepared to do in the Erap Muslim Youth Foundation case (discussed below).

But what of NGOs that engage in or assist partner populations in resisting arguably unjust laws? Regardless of whether such actions as land seizures by farmers, urban squatting and participation in banned demonstrations are right or wrong (or, for that matter, legal or illegal), they are tools through which the poor sometimes seek to affect political and economic imbalances of power in Philippine society, imbalances that build biases into the country's legal system. Should the PCNC deny or withdraw accreditation to organizations that promote such 'criminal' activity?

Even if the Council Board wishes to steer clear of such judgements, might government or business interests (including those represented in corporate foundations) pressure it to do otherwise? What, for example, if an NGO or its partner population (acting with the NGO's support) violates a court injunction against physically blocking construction of a power plant in which a given corporation has a large financial stake?

Alternatively, the very fact that NGOs control the process and that NGO personnel conduct evaluations insulates PCNC at least somewhat from the threat of outside pressure and abuse. The fact that many of the groups that launched PCNC have a corporate orientation could, in fact, contribute to building professional standards among successful applicants – many NGOs certainly could benefit from modern management practices. And the involvement of CODE-NGO and other NGO associations could provide a balance in the form of a network comprising many members with grassroots orientations.

Furthermore, a fundamental question to ask about PCNC is, 'Compared to what'? Even if not perfect, the organization and its process are preferable to a process controlled by the government. Concerns about potential bias are not unreasonable, but whether that potential will become a reality remains to be seen.

Influence on funding decisions

To what extent, if any, should PCNC play a role in funding agency decisions regarding whether to support an NGO? Of course, it already does so with respect to determining donee institution status, which can affect corporate donations. But what of the many foreign funders that need not be concerned with such status, since they are not taxed by the Philippine government? As the Council asserts, 'Certification by PCNC shall also be a "seal of good housekeeping" that funding partners and prospective donors may consider in their choice of organizations to support'. Should donors consider this in their funding decisions? If so, should PCNC certification merely add weight to an NGO's proposal or should it be an absolute prerequisite for funding?

As the Council statement indicates, this issue does not potentially loom over the horizon. It is materializing right now. PCNC reports that the World Bank will be requiring Council accreditation for any NGOs receiving contracts of US$50,000 or more. The Council aims to convince other donors to do the same.

Clearly the PCNC's intentions are good. And the benefits that could flow from donors requiring NGO accreditation include somewhat greater accountability and professionalism, as well as forestalling any possibility of the government taking over the accreditation process. But a shift toward donors requiring accreditation still stirs concern. The issue is not what the PCNC is now, but what it could become as it expands the scope of its operations. There is no reason to believe that it will forfeit its good intentions and professionalism, but most organizations take on greater bureaucratic characteristics as they scale up their work. This could impact the flexibility with which the accreditation process is administered.

This relates to ALTERLAW's alarm over Council-imposed standardization. An NGO may be unsophisticated in articulating its mission and goals, presenting a plan for the future, or otherwise satisfying PCNC criteria for accreditation, but may, nevertheless, possess the qualities or potential to justify funding. This could especially be the case where its leaders lack extensive formal education, yet understand and can address grassroots needs and realities far better than many college graduates or those with MBAs.

This potential requirement also should be considered in the context of other types of standardization that have swept through the development field in counterproductive ways, particularly for civil society. For instance, the indicator-driven approach to monitoring and evaluating performance arguably shackles donors and NGOs with meeting artificial goals rather than demonstrating and learning from real impact. Attempts to draft model laws, not least for NGO registration with governments, often backfire. Other attempts at promulgating so-called 'best practices' can impose boilerplate approaches on inevitably diverse societies, issues and organizations.

There are also situations in which requiring certification could run counter to donors' interests. Particularly, although not exclusively in the case of new NGOs, donors may base their funding decisions on the quality of the organization's personnel, ideas and endorsements, not on a formal checklist.

In this author's experience of funding Philippine NGOs for the Asia Foundation in the late 1980s, some of the best organizations to which the Foundation provided start-up support might not have been able to present the clearly defined missions, goals, policies, systems and plans required by the PCNC, except on a pro forma basis. Such groups, including the Philippine Center for Investigative Journalism and legal services NGOs that still operate today, defined their work through their post-funding experience rather than through pre-funding presentations. This is not to say that the highly sophisticated individuals staffing those groups could not have met the certification requirements – quite the contrary. But they likely would have done so in only a formal manner, rather than one that unrealistically hinged on thinking through issues and experiences they had not yet encountered.

Thus, a PCNC role in funding decisions could run counter to the ways some funding agencies (wisely) operate. Some donors undertake more extended and in-depth discussions than the certification process; others do not. In either event, many donors operate in ways that would not satisfy the formal requirements of the certification process, but that, nevertheless, effectively aid Philippine development.

A potential problem, then, could come where the funding of less sophisticated groups depends on clearing the PCNC bar. Conversely, in a society in which form sometimes substitutes for substance (and the Philippines certainly is not unique in this regard), an applicant organization can easily 'dot all the i's and cross all the t's' of the certification process, yet in reality lack clarity or dedication regarding its goals.

Another problematic aspect of requiring certification for funding is that good programming requires a degree of risk and failure. A donor that plays it safe may screen out the best ideas and initiatives even as it avoids those that will fall short. To illustrate this with highly successful examples the author has encountered in another country, Bangladesh, such a donor may miss the chance to support a young scientist starting an environmental NGO from his laptop and living room, a rural attorney seeking to mediate rather than litigate the problems of the poor, or a driven activist who begins organizing women in a conservative corner of the countryside.

The donor that depends on PCNC certification thus runs multiple risks, ironically by exercising too much caution. As in the examples drawn from the Philippines and Bangladesh, potential applicant organizations or the persons heading them may not pass muster, or may become discouraged by the application process, or may not afford the fees for that process, or may see it as adding another step to what may already be a lengthy donor approval process.

A final, fundamental risk is that the donor may abdicate responsibility by substituting PCNC judgement for its own.

The point in raising these concerns is not to raise doubts about the PCNC itself. As already emphasized, it carries out a number of valuable functions, including contributing to NGO accountability. Nor is it to suggest that donor and PCNC approval should be mutually exclusive – the latter could inform the former. And it could even be that requiring Council certification of NGOs could prove valuable for some funding organizations. But before taking that final step, it is important to consider the complexity and possible ramifications of such a requirement.

Inhibiting criminal and terrorist funding

A final challenge facing the Council is that posed by organizations pursuing criminal, violent or terrorist agendas. In fact, an early issue that confronted PCNC was the fear in some quarters that the Council might be used to attach a veneer of legitimacy to bogus NGOs that, by virtue of political connections, could exert great pressure for certification. During the 2000 impeachment hearings against then President Joseph Estrada, a representative of an organization he apparently founded for money-laundering purposes claimed that it had received PCNC certification. When the Council clarified that this was not the case, that the Erap (Estrada's nickname) Muslim Youth Foundation had not pursued an application and therefore had not been approved, it may well have bolstered PCNC's ongoing credibility.

In a related but even more dire vein, the international backdrop against which the Council today operates is a post-9/11 world concerned about the flow of funds for terrorism and the possibility that NGOs can facilitate that flow. This is salient in the Philippines, where there has been a small but threatening presence of individuals and groups with links to international terrorism networks. In addition, while the communist insurgency is far weaker than in its heyday of the late 1980s, it continues to operate partly through front organizations. In recognition of these realities, the first issue that PCNC President Victoria Gartchitorena highlights in her homepage statement on the PCNC website is how 'global terrorism has heightened the need for controls in the flows of funds in order to block the monetary lifelines of extremist groups'.[8]

It is unlikely that organizations engaging in terrorism or other forms of violence would seek certification. But if they did, PCNC would not necessarily determine their true nature. It is not an intelligence operation or a detective agency. Nevertheless, a potential issue for PCNC is the threat of having its credibility damaged if it mistakenly certifies a group linked to criminal or terrorist activity. There is no guarantee that such a group could not slip through the cracks of an evaluation process concerned with more mundane matters. This does not necessarily reflect poorly on PCNC, for its process can never be perfect. But it might want to portray any anti-terrorism role more modestly, rather than emphasizing that function, to avoid raising expectations about its contribution to such an effort.

NOTES

1   This chapter draws on document and website reviews and on interviews with Philippine NGO leaders, funding agency personnel and Council Executive Director Felicidad Soledad, to whom the author wishes to express particular appreciation. The author welcomes comments. They may be sent to him at Sjg49er@aol.com.

2   Philippine tax law's distinction between NGOs and other non-stock, non-profit organizations is a technical one of little relevance to this discussion of NGO accountability. It nevertheless should be noted because, despite its name, the Philippine Council for NGO Certification is authorized to certify not just NGOs, but also organizations falling within that latter, broader category (of which NGOs are a subset) (see BIR 13-98, Section 1(d)). Thus, while PCNC informally refers to all certified organizations as NGOs, other terms also apply to many of them. In addition to social welfare and development organizations, its list of certified organizations includes universities, other educational institutions, grant-making foundations, NGO networks and religious institutions. See List of Certified NGOs, www.pcnc.com.ph. Except in a few ways that such other organizations potentially pertain to the work of PCNC and NGO accountability, this chapter does not focus on them.

3   For further background on the PCNC, see Chamberlain, R. A. 'Regulating Civil Society', www.pcnc.com.ph.

4   In practical terms, however, the tax deduction is less likely to affect and influence salaried individuals whose taxes are taken out of their regular paychecks, as opposed to more affluent or self-employed persons who can more easily claim the deduction when filing their tax returns.

5   'Certification of Non-Stock, Non-Profit Corporations and Non-Government Organizations for Donee Institution Status: A Primer', www.pcnc.com.ph.

6   More specifically, although the matter needs to be clarified, this does not seem to include cooperatives and 'people's organizations', grassroots membership associations that many NGOs serve and with which they partner. Often known in other countries as community-based organizations (although in the Philippines people's organizations also can include unions and other groups that are not literally community-based), some people's organizations are relatively informal associations that do not necessarily have or seek formal status.

7   Interview with author, Manila, 28 May 2004.

8   On the Occasion of PCNC's 4th Annual Assembly, 'A Message from the President', www.pcnc.com.ph.

7

The Donor Accountability Agenda

Jem Bendell and Phyllida Cox

INTRODUCTION

Donors have the power to influence whether NGOs have the resources to do their work and how they can do it. Given the crucial role that donors play in shaping the NGO landscape, no consideration of NGO accountability would be complete without consideration of the accountability of the donors themselves. In this chapter we set out a new way of looking at donor accountability that places this issue within the context of achieving more democratically accountable decision-making in society as a whole. We put forth democratic accountability as an aspirational dimension to debates and initiatives on NGO accountability.

After describing some of the accountability issues arising from current donor practice, we outline four broad principles for a 'democratically accountable donor practice' that address how a donor generates funds, administers itself, disperses funds and influences other donors. For each of these areas of activity, donors should be clear about their purpose, seek greater transparency, identify their stakeholders and engage them, and create support mechanisms for complaints and enforcement. Given the diversity among donors, our discussion is fairly general and introductory, with further work on conceptual, practical and political levels required to develop and implement the agenda.

THE DONORS

Donors who give to NGOs come in a variety of shapes and forms and are accountable to very different constituencies. In this chapter we categorize them into three broad types: government, corporate and civil. The latter category refers to civil society, which can be understood as the realm of social participation by individuals or groups who seek neither governmental power, nor commercial power through that participation (Edwards, 1999).

Governments can provide funds to NGOs both at home and abroad. There are bilateral aid agencies like the Department for International Development UK (DFID), the United States Agency for International Development (USAID), the Swedish International Development Cooperation Agency (SIDA) and the Japan International Co-operation Agency (JICA). Government funds are also directed through multilateral organizations such as the World Bank or the United Nations. It is estimated that 15 per cent of total overseas development assistance is now channeled through NGOs (World Bank, 2001/2002).

In the civil sector, religious institutions have the longest history of philanthropy and now provide many millions of dollars to NGOs. Large NGOs in the global north also generate funds directly from their domestic populations and become major donors to other NGOs working in the south. Particularly wealthy individuals can be significant donors in their own right and constitute another important category of donors.

Some wealthy individuals establish charitable foundations, either as an ongoing legacy or in order to make their donations tax efficient. Some NGOs, religious institutions and corporations also establish foundations, so today there are various types of private, community and corporate foundations, each subject to variations in legal and fiscal environments from one nation to the next (European Foundation Center, 2004a). In the US alone there are over 70,000 foundations and a further 70,000 donor advised funds (DAFs) responsible for billions of dollars. The US indeed leads the world in terms of private philanthropy, a fact some attribute as much to its inadequate welfare policies and low income tax as to the actual wealth of its economy (OECD, 2003).

In 2000 there were around 62,000 foundations operating in the 'old' 15 European Union (EU) member states. Their size and scope relative to their US counterparts are generally constrained by higher taxation. Nevertheless, by 2004 there were approximately 16 foundations for every 100,000 people, which illustrates how donors may play a significant role within society (European Foundation Center, 2004a). This kind of charitable giving can be traced back to the Middle Ages across Europe but is on the rise. For example, over 40 per cent of German foundations were set up after 1990, 28 per cent in Belgium, and almost 50 per cent in Italy were created post-1999 (European Foundation Center, 2004b).

Until recently across Eastern Europe, the concept of the foundation had been foreign. It was only after the end of communism that foundations sprang up with the purpose of supporting the new wave of post-communist democracies (Volker and Timmer, 2002). Japanese foundations were first created in the 1920s, when the Zaibatsu elite fearing the rise of socialism in the wake of the Bolshevik revolution modeled foundations on the Rockefeller example. Rates of personal taxation preclude the amassing of personal fortunes in Japan, therefore most Japanese foundations are corporate. Unlike their US counterparts, however, Japanese foundations tend to avoid funding activities in their own business field, funding instead a broad range of social and cultural initiatives on similar lines to personal or family foundations in the US (OECD, 2003).

Corporations donate in a variety of ways, from tax exempt giving to foundations and employer money schemes. In 2001, US corporations donated 1.2 per cent of their pre-tax profits to charity, while Canadian corporations donated 1.3 per cent in 2000. Wal-Mart was the top US corporate funder in 2002, with total giving at around US$103 million (Foundation Centre, 2002). In the first three months of 2005, the US Chamber of Commerce reported corporate donations around US$500 million to various charities and foundations (Centre on Philanthropy, 2005). The top 60 largest US donors gave more than US$10 billion to charity in 2004 alone (Chronicle of Philanthropy, 2005).

WHY DONOR ACCOUNTABILITY?

Why should we concern ourselves with the accountability of organizations and people just described, who are choosing to give away their money? Is it not their right to give away their own money in the way they see fit? This seems a reasonable question. Our answer is no, for six reasons.

First, because much government aid is derived from tax revenue collected from citizens and organizations. Therefore, government aid through development and humanitarian assistance is a matter of public interest. A particular accountability concern is where aid ostensibly given to further the development of a country is really intended to serve the foreign policy or trade objectives of the donor. Another concern is that aid is often soaked up by others than the (supposedly) intended beneficiaries. This is so-called 'phantom aid', misdirected to highly paid international consultants, requiring purchases of products and services from donor countries and badly coordinated planning and excessive administration costs. It is estimated that 40 pence for every pound of UK aid is misdirected in this way, and 80 cents of every US dollar in aid returns to US companies through tied aid conditionality. Around 61 per cent of all donor assistance from G7 nations has been estimated to be phantom aid (ActionAid, 2005).

According to the British 1980 Overseas Development and Co-operation Act, aid can only be used for 'promoting the development or maintaining the economy of a country... or the welfare of its people'. With this law in mind, the British NGO World Development Movement (WDM) took the UK government to court believing government (and taxpayers') money was being used to finance the Pergau Dam in Malaysia in the hope of securing future arms deals (WDM, 2005). The Pergau case showed how aid budgets can be used to 'sweeten' trade and political agreements regardless of any developmental benefit.

A second issue arises because much private donor practice is augmented by public funds in the form of tax rebates from governments to individuals, corporations or charitable foundations. Therefore the question of what constitutes a charitable form of giving and funded activity is a well-established issue of public policy (Irvin, 2005). Tax breaks on corporate giving are premised on the understanding that their motives are supportive of the public good and so they should be rewarded and encouraged. However, this cannot account for instances where corporations are given tax breaks of public money when they donate to think tanks or research institutes that lobby governments or influence public perception on issues of public policy. This kind of 'deep lobbying' can influence a corporation's profit margins. In this sense tax breaks may constitute little more than the government subsidizing corporations (National Committee for Responsive Philanthropy, 2005). There are also questions about whether the governance and administration of foundations are suitable enough to receive tax advantages. Issues include the selection and salaries of officers, administrative overhead, the amount of funds dispersed every year and methods of auditing and filing tax returns (Baron, 2003).

A third issue has come to the fore in recent years due to growing concerns about the funding of international terrorism. Therefore, the challenge is to ensure that only non-violent activities are being funded by any donor, whether holding charitable status or not. In the wake of September 11, the US government has introduced a variety of measures to this effect, such as Executive Order 13224, related elements of the US Patriot Act and the voluntary Anti-Terrorist Financing guidelines for charities issued by the US Treasury in 2002. However, these measures sparked controversy over their potential for restricting beneficial international philanthropy. A group of US donor organizations drafted an alternative set of principles to the Treasury, arguing that the US charitable sector is already adequately governed by laws, regulations and IRS rulings that effectively prevent the diversion of funds for illegal purposes (Baron, 2004).

These two issues relate to a fourth reason for paying attention to donor accountability: the extent to which existing accountability demands placed on donors are dysfunctional, in the sense of impairing beneficial social change. Government accountability demands can be problematic in this regard (Irvin, 2005). The debate surrounding terrorism and the regulation of the philanthropic sector highlights this broader question of whether and how national governments can make donor organizations registered in their jurisdiction more accountable to a broader set of constituents than merely the government or the citizens of that state. This is because philanthropy often seeks to help those who are not benefiting from the policies of their own governments, or who live in another country, and therefore some independence from government is essential. Demands placed on philanthropic organizations from other constituencies, such as living donors or corporate sponsors, can also pose challenges for their ability to work effectively, especially if we regard accountability in terms of rights and democracy, as we discuss below.

A fifth reason for exploring the issue of donor accountability is because some donors themselves seek for their aid disbursements or grant-making to contribute to social justice and well-being. One's own accountability to intended beneficiaries can be regarded as a useful mechanism for improving the effectiveness of one's philanthropic interventions on a range of different issues, from poverty to environmental protection (Fowler, 1997). In addition, some regard the power asymmetries in society as a cause of social problems and therefore the greater accountability of powerful institutions and processes is a goal in itself (Goetz and Jenkins, 2002). With this in mind, some donors recognize their own power and seek to be more responsive in the development of their programmes of giving. One aspect to this is exploring how donors' demands for more upwards accountability from NGOs can complement greater downwards accountability from the donors to NGOs and from NGOs to their intended beneficiaries (Edwards and Hulme, 1995). It makes sense that donors would seek to integrate their espoused values and missions into their own internal activities, such as human resources, investments, procurement and supply, relations with applicants, grantees, the philanthropic community and the wider public. Across the US and Europe networks of philanthropic organizations fund research and engage in processes of shared learning to formulate best practices in effective philanthropy for foundations.

A sixth reason for questioning the accountability of donor practice is because the scale of publicly and privately donated funds has become large enough to have a significant impact on the nature of resource allocation, decision-making and public opinion in societies around the world. As citizens concerned about human rights and democracy, we should question how these funds translate the financial assets of already powerful people, organizations and governments into wider forms of social, cultural and political power. Although it may seem churlish to question the accountability of those who choose to give their money away, if we are interested in more democratically accountable societies as a whole, the accountability of those who exert more significant influence over that society is important. We believe this is a key reason for the importance of exploring donor accountability, which requires more attention by scholars, policy-makers and practitioners.

INTRODUCING DEMOCRATIC ACCOUNTABILITY

The idea that it is good for organizations and people to be more accountable is widespread in many societies, even if the word does not translate well into all languages (Lister, 2003). There is a wide variety of definitions of accountability used or assumed by people working on questions of organizational transparency, responsiveness, ethics, legitimacy and regulation, whether in relation to governments, corporations, NGOs or other organizations (Bakker, 2002). When we use the term accountability we can break it down into four questions: who is accountable, to whom, for what and how? If we look at how these questions have been answered by different organizations and individuals, immediately problems arise with the assumption that accountability is necessarily a good thing. 'I was just following orders' is an often heard refrain at war crimes trials from Nuremberg to present day scandals in Iraq and elsewhere. Repressive regimes often have very thorough systems of accountability. People's devotion to a specific group and its leaders and the unquestioning following of orders are all aspects of accountability that have facilitated some of the worst atrocities in the history of humankind. So accountability is not a good thing in itself and a lack of accountability is not necessarily a bad thing, particularly in societies that tend towards the centralization of power and autocracy. Is there a particular form of accountability that merits being regarded as desirable?

We argue that the answer to this question lies in a deep understanding of rights and democracy. The basic idea of *demos kratos*, or people rule, is that people govern themselves. In a democratically-governed society, a community of people ideally has meaningful participation in decisions and processes that affect them and is not systematically adversely affected by another group of people without being able to rectify the situation (Dahl, 1961; Isbister, 2001).

Organizations of all forms, not just governmental, influence people's lives. The concept of 'stakeholder' can be useful here as it groups together people on the basis of their being affected by an organization. Because the *demos* that make claims for the democratic control (directly or indirectly) of organizations are those affected by the organizations, this can be understood as 'stakeholder democracy'. Stakeholder democracy can be defined as an ideal system of governance of a society where all stakeholders in an organization or activity have the same opportunity to govern that organization or activity (Bendell, 2005).

With these concepts in mind, the ideal is a society where all decision-making is accountable to those affected by those decisions or indecisions. This ideal of democratic accountability is one that concerns the whole of society, not just a particular organization. However, for this principle to be workable for the management and regulation of organizations, our challenge is to identify a form of accountability for individual organizations that is constitutive of this broader societal democratic accountability.

The principle of democratic accountability means that a mining company should be more accountable to people poisoned downstream from one of its mines. It does not mean poisoned communities downstream from the mining company need be accountable to the mining company. This highlights how the accountability of individual organizations to those they affect is sometimes facilitative of the goal of more democratically accountable decision-making in society, but not always. If an NGO articulating the interests of the poisoned community had to be more accountable to the mining company, or perhaps a government that was strongly influenced by that company, this relationship would not necessarily increase the democratic accountability of decision-making in that context.

A real world example highlights this issue clearly. Recently there have been calls for advocacy NGOs to be accountable to those organizations they campaign on (Vibert, 2003). One NGO coalition called 'Fifty Years is Enough' criticizes the policies and programmes of the World Bank on behalf of its 200 member organizations. The World Bank manages over US$25 billion a year, with a paid staff of over 8000. 'Fifty Years is Enough' has three paid staff and a very tight budget. This NGO has an implicit accountability to the World Bank, in the sense that it would be quickly criticized if it made mistakes with its basic facts and figures and have to explain itself. Promoting greater organizational accountability of this small NGO to all those affected by its work, such as the World Bank, and with the resources this process would require, would not help promote the accountability of decision-making to those affected by decisions in the field it works on. Promoting organizational accountability as a whole may not promote the accountability of decision-making processes to the people whose lives they influence. The relative power of different organizations must be taken into account in our understanding of the accountability challenge.

This understanding of democratic accountability does not make the accountability of NGOs less important. Rather, it means that NGOs should be accountable to those they affect who have less power. To use the hypothetical mining example, if an NGO engaged with a community affected by a mine was successful in stopping the mining company from poisoning its river, but in doing so the company diverted its pollution towards other rivers and communities, the accountability of that NGO to the newly affected communities would become an issue.

The implication is that we need to consider social systems, rather than just organizational units within those systems. The accountability of one part of a system helps to create a more democratically accountable system if it is accountable to those parts affected by its decisions/actions that have less power and that are accountable to other parts of the system in the same way. Democratic accountability can be described by answering the four accountability questions as follows:

1 Who is accountable? The person or group that affects some relatively less powerful person or group.
2 To whom? To the person or group they are affecting.
3 For what? For the effect they have on them, particularly if it is negative.
4 How? In a way whereby the person or group affected can change the behaviour of the person or group affecting them (with the affected also becoming accountable to any third parties they affect when exerting this influence).

These are simple principles concerning individual organizational units in our infinitely complex and interconnected social system, and are therefore fallible and provide only a guide. The principles include recognition that ever wider circles of interconnection between organizations are crucial to whether the relationships between organizations at the centre of that circle are as constitutive of democracy as possible. The importance of the accountability of these wider relationships does not mean that an organization can claim it will not be accountable to a relatively less powerful organization unless that organization is itself accountable to other less powerful organizations or people. To continue with the hypothetical, the mining company should not require that an NGO working with a community affected by the mine be accountable to all other stakeholders before the company will be accountable to that NGO.

However, in recognizing the wider connections, it would be beneficial for the company to encourage that NGO to consider its own accountability to those it could influence by reaching agreement with the mining company.

A key issue that is raised by this definition of democratic accountability concerns how we know which organizations have more or less power. Power is a concept that has been explored in detail by sociologists for decades (Clegg, 1989), and although this work needs to inform policy and practice in this area, it is beyond the scope of this chapter. For our purposes, proxies for power can be found in property and force: those with more property are more powerful, as are those with more ability to use force, such as governments (who are meant to have a monopoly on the use of force in a society).

Many commentators on accountability emphasize 'placing a check on the authority of the powerful' to the extent that 'in common usage... "account-ability" is shorthand for democratic accountability – accountability to ordinary people and to the legal framework through which governance is affected' (Goetz and Jenkins, 2002). This is also implicit in the distinctions many people make between a people's or organization's upward accountabil-ity to donors or governments, or others with power over them, and downward accountability to those affected by them. By developing this implicit idea into an explicit concept of democratic accountability we seek to frame an agenda for donor accountability that supports the wider enjoyment of rights and the deepening of democracy.

In the following sections, we describe how different types of donors have important democratic accountability deficits within their current practice. We then outline a set of principles for democratic donor accountability, relate these to current initiatives on donor accountability and make recommendations for further work.

Democratic accountability deficits in current donor practice

Government donors

Government aid agencies that act as donors are accountable to the state they serve. Bilateral aid agencies have their overarching strategies and priorities developed by the politicians in government and must report back to often multiple arms of that government. The wholesale cutting back of the Danish bilateral aid agency after a change in government illustrates how this form of accountability is decisive. Intergovernmental donors (and lenders), such as the World Bank and the IMF, are primarily accountable to the governments that finance them. Consequently, the countries of Europe and North America have the most influence over these institutions. These forms of accountability can conflict with a broader conception of democratic accountability, where funders would be responsive to those in most need.

Historical and contemporary geopolitics mean government-to-government aid has not gone to those countries that need it most. Israel receives over US$2 billion a year in military aid and about US$600 million dollars in economic assistance from the US. In addition, much governmental aid is either explicitly tied or effectively allocated to companies based in the donor country. The same is true with NGOs, with governments often giving to those based in their own countries rather than directly to Southern organizations. Even emergency humanitarian aid has often been 'driven by political interests rather than according to need' (Harmer and Cotterrell, 2004). The tying of aid may also reflect other motivations such as religious values. The first administration of George W. Bush and its restrictive policy (popularly known as the Global Gag Rule) on giving to organizations providing resources or services linked to abortion is one such example (Centre for Reproductive Rights, 2003).

There are also accountability issues surrounding the influence that government donors (especially Northern ones) have through their funding of NGOs. Many governments in the global south are uneasy about their lack of control over organizations funded almost entirely by foreign interests. Some governmental concerns may arise from a desire to suppress democracy and centralize power, as has been suggested to be the government's aim in Colombia (War on Want, 2003). However, there is a significant issue about the influence of foreign-funded groups on domestic culture, economics and politics, especially where the concept of development is contested and hard to attain.

One controversial example of NGOs being used as subcontractors to fulfill a government donor foreign policy agenda comes from Iraq. In 2003, the Research Triangle Institute (RTI), an NGO involved in drug research, became heavily involved in the occupation of Iraq. RTI undertook a 'local governance' contract from the US government worth around US$466 million. 'It turns out that the town councils RTI has been setting up are the centerpiece of Washington's regional caucuses – a plan that has been so widely rejected in Iraq' (Klein, 2004). Under the friendly rubric of capacity building and local partnerships, Klein contends that RTI was playing its part in the creation of a US-appointed government that could then make or confirm a range of decisions on international agreements, privatization and IMF loans that would effectively handcuff future democratically elected governments. Therefore, it is not just the accountability of NGOs that can be questioned, but also the selectivity by which donors fund NGOs and the real commitment that donors have to increase citizens' participation through the medium of NGOs.

The lack of a commonly understood approach to international development assistance means that it is difficult to hold governments to account for their overseas aid programmes. Two key intergovernmental commitments provide something of a benchmark for assessing the accountability of government aid activities. The first concerns the amount of support. In the 1970s, donor-nation governments committed to contribute 0.7 per cent of their GDP to overseas aid (Bissio, 2003). In 2002, only 5 of the 22 reporting countries were meeting this target (German and Randell, 2004). The second concerns the intended development objectives of the donors. In 2000, countries agreed to the Millennium Development Goals (MDGs), which include a commitment to halve those living in poverty by 2015. While processes for monitoring developing countries commitments and progress have been institutionalized, systems for monitoring the performance of donors are only beginning to be put into place (UNDP, 2003). It is worth noting that the first goal, which sought gender equity in primary education, was already missed by some distance in 2005. No donors were held to account.

Tied aid, increasing levels of poverty and problems with the MDGs illustrate the challenge of establishing and then promoting an agenda for government donors to become more accountable to the people they claim to help.

Corporate donors

When corporations give away finance, products or staff time, they must do so in accordance with the governance of their organization. In the case of privately owned companies, the nature of corporate giving is dependent on the individual owners involved. For publicly traded companies, in most countries corporate law indicates that shareholders' interests must be paramount in the managers' considerations. Ultimately, reports to shareholders will encompass all corporate activities, including sponsorships and donations. The strength of these forms of accountability is questioned by some shareholder groups, who believe managers have too much freedom. This form of accountability is much more explicit than democratic accountability, which would encompass all those a corporation affects through the conduct of its business.

Corporate funding of NGOs has grown significantly in recent years (Common Dreams, 2003). Some of this is straightforward sponsorship aimed at very explicit marketing and advertising objectives. For example, in 1999, the tobacco multinational giant Philip Morris 'spent US$75 million on charitable contributions, and US$100 million to publicize these donations' (National Council on Responsive Philanthropy, 2005). Corporations sometimes donate money in order to influence public opinion in ways essential for brand confidence and loyalty. When health charity the Arthritis Foundation agreed to put its name to McNeil Consumer Products in exchange for a donation that totaled US$2 million, the company marketed aspirin and other common drugs under the Arthritis Foundation's name. McNeil was sued for a US$2 million settlement in 1996 for implying that the products were new medications created by the foundation. The Attorney General involved said 'when a nonprofit's credibility is sold for profit, the public has a right to know who's behind the name, what's inside the product, and where the money is going' (Centre for Science in the Public Interest, 2003).

The way that corporate donors may use their money to influence public perceptions is also an issue (Common Cause, 2005). But this goes deeper in ways firmly hidden from public view. For example, the US-based Society for Women's Health Research (SWHR) criticized the National Institutes of Health for publicizing a major study that found hormone replacement therapy (HRT) increased risks of breast cancer and heart attacks. What concerned citizens hearing of SWHR criticisms would not have known is that Wyeth, a company that markets the most widely used HRT drug is a major donor to SWHR (Centre for Science in the Public Interest, 2003).

Research institutes and think tanks have become key recipients of corporate funds and this has become a concern where they have significant reach and influence in arenas of policy-making. Public Interest Watch (PIW) is one of a new breed of conservative watchdog organizations whose purpose ostensibly centers on calling for more NGO accountability. PIW describes its mission as 'keeping an eye on the self-appointed guardians of the public interest' and lambastes non-profit hospitals in the US, saying they are grabbing huge amounts of public money that does not belong to them (PIW 2004). However, PIW is funded by companies including private healthcare providers whose interests are clearly manifest in PIW advocacy. The broader political interests of companies should also be remembered as factors that shape their philanthropy.

Many corporations establish foundations to organize their philanthropy. Funding for these can be raised by employee payroll giving schemes, or by donations from the corporate body itself. In most countries these foundations and the donations they receive are tax exempt. In return, the foundation is required to be operationally separate from the company (Common Dreams, 2003). However, in many cases the independence of these foundations can be questioned. The Shell Foundation, for example, is housed in the head offices of the oil company Shell, uses their information technology and administrative systems, has Shell employees on the board and secretariat and uses the same logo. Given this, it can be questioned why donations by these organizations often gain the same tax advantages as charitable gifts that do not enhance the position of a for-profit company.

Civil donors

We consider four broad categories of donors in the civil sector: religious organizations, highly wealthy individuals, large intermediary NGOs and charitable foundations.

Many religions inspire their followers to help other people, either directly or by providing funds. How that help is conceived depends on the particular religion, but it usually involves matters of basic welfare, such as food, clothing, shelter, healthcare and friendship, as well as the spiritual well-being of people. Concerns arise with the way religious beliefs may influence access to, or the nature of, any help provided. In addition, questions can be raised about the appropriateness of some forms of religious proselytizing, particularly in relation to contemporary notions of rights and democracy, as well as the political agendas that can be incorporated into spiritual messages. These concerns have become more acute in recent years as the nation state is less involved in providing welfare services and has started cofunding the provision of welfare by religious institutions.

Different religious institutions have different forms of governance and different freedoms or restrictions from the state, so the accountability issues they pose are diverse. Some religious institutions are democratically accountable to their followers, such as the Baha'i World Community, whereas others are more centralized, like the Catholic Church. The view that a religious community is ultimately accountable to a divine being, rather than the people it affects throughout their lives, may at first seem to challenge democratic accountability. However, most spiritual traditions explain that love for and service of others are the natural enactment of a spiritual consciousness, thus there need not be an inherent conflict at the level of principle. However, conflict at the level of practice is inevitable given the fallibility of any human and human institution, religious or otherwise.

Highly wealthy individuals are another category of civil sector donors with powerful influence over the work of those they fund. It may seem unnecessarily suspicious to question the accountability of a rich person only when they choose to dispose of their funds, but in a world where the 200 richest individuals have assets equivalent to the poorest half of humanity, the personal views of such donors can have a major impact on societies worldwide.

In recent years questions have been raised about the practices and accountability of charitable foundations, particularly in relation to issues like high salaries, controversial grant-making and inefficient monitoring. Susan Berresford, the President of the Ford Foundation, has urged foundations to make their sector more accountable: 'We have a clear problem of public accountability right now, but we have routes ahead that can help us' (Berresford, 2004).

Tax breaks are a major source of revenue for foundations. Estimates put the total percentage of US foundation funds earned through tax breaks at around 45 per cent, which is money that comes from the American public (National Council on Responsive Philanthropy, 2005). Even when funding is from independent charitable foundations, not overtly directed by corporations, reflecting on where the money actually came from provides different insights into the question of accountability. Many foundations are founded or funded by rich individuals, families or religious institutions and seek to give away money in the way that the founders request. A recipient of a donation from such a foundation may understandably feel some gratitude to the donor, and many recipients feel it is right to be accountable to that donor and to comply with the restrictions and expectations surrounding the donation. But we cannot ignore that the power of donors to be able to give comes from the endeavors and sometimes even the suffering of other people.

Consider the world's largest foundation. Its existence is a credit to the Gates benefactors, yet we should recognize how the funds originally came from Microsoft profits, which in turn came from the fact that employees of the firms in the global value chains making Microsoft products and services are paid less than those products and services are able to fetch, and that consumers of those products and services pay more than they cost to produce. This is not a specific criticism, since paying people less than the value of the products they produce is always how profit is derived. The value of a foundation is then maintained through its investments in other companies pursuing the same profit-motivated approach. Therefore, any money coming from a foundation arises through the efforts of millions of people.

This reminds us of the interconnections of endeavor and exploitation that generate the financial power that can then be reallocated through donations. Donors could consider themselves accountable to those who generated the revenues as much as they might expect NGOs to be accountable to them as recipients of these same accumulations of societal wealth. Whole societies are responsible for generating such wealth and so a donor can be said to owe a broad debt to society as a whole. Procedural approaches to accountability can not easily deal with this complexity. The implication is that our sense of inter-connectedness and the humanistic values this sense arises from and informs are as important to democratic accountability as management procedures or a financial audit. We can keep this difficulty in mind when considering what policies and initiatives on donor accountability might prove helpful in promoting democratic accountability more broadly.

CONTOURS OF AN EMERGING DEMOCRATIC DONOR ACCOUNTABILITY AGENDA

It is clear that there is a wide variety of donors that present a range of issues relating to rights, accountability and democracy. It is also apparent that various organizations are working on improving their own accountability, either as a procedural necessity due to pressures from governments or public criticism, or as a strategic mission-related goal that reflects an understanding of the centrality of accountability deficits in allowing social injustice. In support of this process, we offer an initial framework for conceptualizing a donor accountability agenda, arranged around four key principles: consideration of how a donor generates funds, administers itself, disperses funds and influences other donors.

Principle 1. Fund generation: Donors should seek to make their generation of funds both transparent and more democratically accountable to those affected by the activities involved

As discussed earlier, the financial assets that donor organizations are responsible for are generated by the efforts of employees, customers and suppliers, among others. The creation of that wealth involves economic activities that affect society, both now and in the past. A donor organization does not have the ability to affect what has passed. What we wish to focus on here is the way that fund generation affects people in the present and future. For governments, this is the economic policy that generates tax revenues that are allocated to overseas development assistance; for foundations, this is the way their invest-ments are managed; and for corporations, the way they conduct the business that generates the profits with which they can sponsor or make donations. Each area of fund generation raises important questions about how donor organizations are affecting democratic accountability in society.

The most important thing that a corporate donor could do to aspire to democratic accountability would be to ensure its normal business is more democratically accountable to those who are affected by its activities. However, the experience of more than a decade of leadership by companies on voluntary corporate responsibility suggests that not many companies can succeed if they internalize the loss of social and environmental costs, if their customers do not reward it, their competitors do not follow and their investors do not support it. The corporate accountability agenda must therefore be one where companies work together with others to influence the market and its governance (Bendell, 2004).

As with much donor practice, the funds not only come from the donor, but also from the government giving a tax break. We should recognize that most corporate giving must be rationalized in terms of how it will benefit the company, often through reputation enhancement. Corporate support of communities and causes can, in many cases, be welcomed. However, it is the primary role of governments to allocate resources for the public good. Corporations do not necessarily deserve to receive tax benefits for spending on activities that may have societal benefit, in particular, when they benefit from these expenditures themselves. This might not be welcomed by organizations that are increasingly or entirely dependent on corporate funds, yet given the growing and questionable influence of corporate-funded NGOs at local, national and intergovernmental levels, this is an important issue.

Civil donors generate much of their income from the interest paid on their investments. One of the most unaccountable impacts on society by civil donors is through the financial assets they hold. Many of these donors do not consider closely the types of companies and financial instruments they invest in, beyond financial performance. Given how fund managers usually maintain diverse portfolios, it would not be unusual to find civil donors funding peace work with money made from armaments companies, health work with money made from tobacco companies, labour rights work with money made from anti-union companies and environmental work with money made from companies with terrible pollution records. The problem is that many do not know, because they are removed from the day-to-day management of their assets and have not made the connections between their missions and their investments (Tasch and Viederman, 1995).

The principle of democratic accountability applied to fund generation suggests that donors should work towards ensuring the accountability of the financial assets they own. Some religious organizations have pioneered work on this issue. The Interfaith Center on Corporate Responsibility (ICCR) has for 30 years advanced environmental, human rights, diversity and other concerns by using their power as shareholders (ICCR, 2005; Viederman, 2002).

This discussion is also relevant to government donors, as their revenues arise from taxing companies and financial assets that they (de)regulate in ways that affect the espoused objectives of their aid agencies. Before one can 'make poverty history' one must stop making poverty through the normal course of trade and finance. A commitment to democratic accountability suggests that government donors, such as their bilateral development agencies, should increase their attention to the way other organs of their government undermine the accountability of trade and finance to those affected (WDM, 2005). Given the silos of different government ministries, this is no easy challenge.

Principle 2. Fund administration: Donors should seek to make the administration of their activities both transparent and more democratically accountable

There is a challenge for all donors to practice what they preach, to exhibit a reflexivity and integrity in their day-to-day functions of fund administration that mirror the espoused values of the organization. Our recommendations here apply to all donors, but particularly to large foundations, given their recent growth and the recognized need for greater oversight of their activities by regulators (National Council on Responsive Philanthropy, 2005).

A key issue is transparency. Donors should publish all accounts, sources of income, wages and funding decisions, unless posing a security risk for the individuals involved. All this information should be made available in a way that a wide range of people can access and understand, and with the facility for feedback to be recorded publicly.

The next issue is integrity: seeking that the espoused values and goals of the organization apply within its own walls. This includes assessments of human resources policies, governance, procurement and buildings management. Charity scandals concerning high salaries and lavish expenses have brought these issues into the media. Therefore, a broad responsible human resources policy is important, covering staff recruitment and remuneration, freedom of association and freedom from discrimination, among other issues.

On governance, donors need to move beyond a system that relies solely on the integrity of senior management and trustees. Key here is to ensure a separation between the day-to-day running of the donor organization and the highest level of governance of that organization. A separate board of trustees, with clear criteria for nominations, selection or election and roles, combined with transparent processes for regulating the secretariat, including the disciplining or firing of personnel, is essential for foundations and a useful system to consider for government donors.

Improved governance, environmental performance, labour rights and equitable wages, low overhead and ethical purchasing are all important for an organization aspiring to democratic accountability, even if these specific issues are not covered by the organization's mandate, as they involve the way the organization impacts on others. In many ways, the democratic accountability agenda of donors in this regard mirrors accountability demands by donors on the governance of NGOs who receive money from them.

Principle 3. Fund provision: Donors should enhance the transparency and democratic accountability of their grant-making decisions and of the activities they fund

One of the most significant influences a donor has is through decisions on who or what to fund. The first challenge is to improve the transparency of the donors' decisions and their responsiveness to feedback in a way that influences and improves future grant-making. Key to transparency is to have clear goals by which a donor's performance can be evaluated. For government donors, the MDGs are a useful start, as are the Millennium Declaration and the 20/20 Initiative. The latter is an agreement between donor and recipient countries that an average of 20 per cent of donor aid and 20 per cent of Southern government spending should be for basic social services, such as water, sanitation and education. Currently these commitments do not have appropriate systems of monitoring, reporting or evaluation. Donor progress on the 20/20 Initiative is meant to be reported through the 21-member Development Assistance Committee (DAC) of the OECD and via the UNDP Development Cooperation reports. However, a consensus on the importance of 20/20 or ways to implement it between governments has not been reached. Overall systems for reporting on aid flows need to be improved, enabling both civil society and intergovernmental bodies to evaluate donor practice.

For foundations, the communication of goals and strategies was identified as one of the top three issues considered to be important by grantees, according to a survey by the Centre for Effective Philanthropy (CEP, 2004). In addition to setting clear goals for donor practice, information about specific grants is important for democratic accountability. For instance, donors could publicly register applications, along with their reasons for or against making a funding decision, as well as the opportunity for a publicly recorded response from the applicant. Initiatives such as www.guidestar.org, which provides online information on the grant activities of grant-makers as well as grantees in the US, could be expanded to cover forms of reporting as described above.

A second key challenge for donors in enhancing the democratic accountability of their fund provision is to ensure that those they fund are themselves organizations or persons who understand and take the issue of their own accountability seriously. Donors could do this by requiring recipient organizations to adopt the same type of commitment to democratic accountability that the donor seeks to exhibit. The issues for fund administration described above could form part of this requirement. These could include a request for recipient organizations to have management systems that adhere to local laws and relevant international human rights standards. It could also include requesting that systems are established for affected community consultations and the possibility to lodge complaints. Donors could also collaborate to develop independent mechanisms of complaint and enforcement regarding a recipient's adherence to these principles.

The third challenge for the democratic accountability of fund provision is simply that the donors are in charge. If the donor uses its power in the way just described, then this power can be instrumental in delivering more accountable societies. However, as discussed earlier in this chapter, many donors give aid for political reasons, with strings attached to influence decision-making in their own interests. This is unjustifiable. It is clear that the most 'donative' or giving approach is to give something and not stipulate what is to be done, apart from basic principles about the type of organization and type of activity to be funded that would ensure both are increasingly accountable to those influenced. Therefore, once it is established that potential recipients are aspiring to democratic accountability themselves, they then should be eligible for more untied funds. Untying bilateral aid in conjunction with more recipient country ownership of the aid process would theoretically allow more of it to be used for the purpose of sustainable human development. This principle is enshrined in the Monterrey consensus on the MDGs and is therefore a key guideline for their accountable implementation (Cidse, 2005).

Principle 4. Fund frameworks: Donors should take steps to influence the regulatory and social environment for donors in order to ensure support for democratic accountability

It was discussed at the outset that democratic accountability reflects an ideal state of society. Given complex interactions and power relations in society, one individual organization can never reach a state of democratic accountability, but should rather aspire to help move society towards that ideal. This suggests that donors should themselves work towards frameworks of governance that make all donors more supportive of democratically accountable societies.

How might such change among the broader donor community occur? Individual donors can take a lead in implementing processes that accord with a commitment to democratic accountability. Doing so would certainly encourage some other donors to follow by demonstrating that it is possible. However, other donors, such as some conservative foundations and unilateralist governments, may continue their current practices that actively undermine democratic accountability. Some donors pioneering new ways of working that address their own accountability could be undermined, or have less influence on society than those that pursue unaccountable approaches. There is a need for all donors that aspire to democratic accountability to engage in efforts to shift the regulations and social pressures on donors for all to act in more accountable ways.

The ability of foundations to affect public policy was identified as a key role by many grantees in one survey (CEP, 2004). Donors should engage in research, dialogue, communication, advocacy, political lobbying and collective self-regulatory initiatives to improve the frameworks within which all donors operate. For corporate and charitable foundations, this ultimately means that national regulations should encourage different aspects of the donor account-ability agenda described in this chapter. For government and multilateral donors and lenders, this means that more processes of scrutiny need to be created, including intergovernmental oversight of commitments they make. Ultimately, it also means looking at new ways of generating funds for global public needs that overcome the problems of national interest.

CONCLUSION

The issue of donor accountability is receiving more attention, particularly as private philanthropy increases its influence on social welfare, culture and polit-ical discourse. In 2005 the European Foundation Centre and the US Council of Foundations established a Joint Working Group on Accountability in International Giving. This initiative aims to develop a set of stewardship princi-ples and guidelines for accountable international grant-making and operating activities that are relevant to their respective memberships (European Foundation Center, 2005). Although some participants in such initiatives may have been pushed to engage due to concerns about public criticism or growing governmental oversight, there is an opportunity to engage in a broader accountability agenda that could enhance the progressive role of philanthropy in the world today. There is an opportunity to embrace an agenda beyond fund administration and consider issues such as fund generation and provision, and the social and regulatory frameworks outlined in this chapter. More impor-tantly, there is the opportunity to move beyond the procedural and explore the mission-related importance of accountability. We hope that such an explo-ration may lead to wider understanding and support for approaching organizational accountability in terms of encouraging more democratically accountable societies as a whole. It is an opportunity for people who work on very different issues to recognize the common cause that is their motivation to help promote the flourishing of people in harmony with others. For this oppor-tunity not to be lost will require leadership to articulate and then mobilize a common approach to democratic donor accountability.

In attempting to describe this potential agenda we have really been talking about what constitutes the responsible use of power. The challenge remains therefore to understand further the nature of power and the nature of its responsible use. In doing this we should remember that this task will never be complete, as democratic accountability is a total concept, an ideal for human-ity.

Section III

THE BENEFITS OF EMBRACING ACCOUNTABILITY

8

NGO Governance in China: Achievements and Dilemmas

Kang Xiaoguang and Feng Li

INTRODUCTION

The last 20-year period of reform and opening up in China has led to an 'explosive growth' of NGOs. They have not only grown in number but also in their variety, scope of activities, capacity and roles. However, compared with their counterparts in other countries, China's NGOs must still be characterized as being far from well developed. Some NGOs make mistakes or even become instruments for crime, against the expectations of society. At the same time, the general public, donors, beneficiaries and the mass media, that is, the NGO stakeholders, have gradually matured, with greater awareness of their respective rights and of the responsibilities of NGOs. They have also begun to exercise their rights consciously. Some of them have started to condemn and protest against various unlawful and immoral acts. Obligations, responsibility and accountability have become issues that NGOs in China need to address.

In 2002, two headline-making events occurred in China. The China Youth Development Foundation, a famous government-organized NGO (GONGO), and Lijiang Mothers Association, a famous private NGO, were both sharply criticized by the media. The public criticism of NGOs was a symbolic event in the development of Chinese NGOs, which indicated that the improvement of NGO accountability had become an urgent and serious practical question in China.

NGO accountability refers to the set of internal and external mechanisms that provides a framework for NGOs to pursue their objectives in line with their mission and goals and offers an analytical approach to study their situation and development. For our analysis, we divide the accountability mechanisms for NGOs into internal and external. The internal accountability mechanisms include the organizational mission, culture, board and the general internal management system. External accountability mechanisms can be both positive and negative. The positive include the administration by the Ministry of Civil Affairs departments, control by the professional supervisory organizations, government audits, independent audits, supervision by donors or stakeholders, public supervision, sector self-regulation, supervision by specialized NGOs, publication of periodic financial reports, surveys of public opinion and so forth. The negative includes such things as 'cessation of cooperation' from society, which implies a loss of 'social legitimacy'. This refers to legitimacy gained because of consistency with cultural traditions, social customs and other non-governmental (civil society) standards (Gao Bingzhong, 2001).

If we want NGOs to play their roles, they must be given corresponding rights. If they enjoy certain rights, they must also uphold corresponding obligations or responsibilities. This requires mechanisms that allow stakeholders such as the government, international organizations, donors (multinational companies, domestic enterprises and individuals), the beneficiaries, research groups, the media and the general public to judge whether the behaviour of an NGO is in line with public interest and on that basis to award or punish the NGO concerned. In this respect, rights, obligations, responsibilities and accountability constitute the core concepts of NGO governance.

This chapter focuses on NGO accountability. The first section defines NGOs in China. The second section touches on the responsibilities and obligations of NGOs. The third looks into the internal governance of NGOs and whether it can ensure fulfilment of their responsibilities, while the fourth is about external supervision and regulation. We discuss whether there is an external mechanism that enables stakeholders to supervise effectively the behaviour of NGOs and hold them accountable. The fifth section explores the environment for the existence of NGOs and, in terms of the broad economic, social and political background, seeks to find the sources of NGO governance. Finally, there is a brief note of the key steps needed to improve NGO governance. China in this chapter refers to the mainland of China. The regions of Taiwan, Hong Kong and Macao are not covered.

WHAT IS AN NGO IN CHINA?

The Chinese government divides civil society organizations into three categories: social organizations, foundations and private non-enterprise entities. A private non-enterprise entity is roughly equivalent to a not-for-profit organization (NPO) and the other two types are equivalent to NGOs. The 2002 Statistics and Report on Civil Affairs Activities, issued by the Ministry of Civil Affairs, included the following figures: at the end of 2002, there were 133,000 registered social organizations in China, among which 1712 were engaged in activities throughout the country or across provinces, 20,069 were active within a single province, 52,386 existed within prefectures and 15 were foreign chambers of commerce. There were 1268 foundations and 111,000 private non-enterprise entities registered with the civil affairs authorities. Apart from the above-mentioned organizations that have undergone formal registration, a large number of informal organizations exist. According to a report by Tan Ailing, an official at the Ministry of Civil Affairs, 'some social organizations are not registered with the Ministry of Civil Affairs' and 'it is estimated that registered NGOs only account for one fifth of the total number of such organizations' (Tan Ailing, 2003).

The NGOs discussed in this chapter refer to those social organizations that have a formal organizational structure and engage in public welfare activities, regardless of whether they are independent of the government or whether they have legal status as a social organization. This is because in the mainland of China there are almost no NGOs defined according to Western standards. GONGOs are NGOs with an official background. That means that for GONGOs the government is the initiator, the supervisor or the provider of various resources. Independent NGOs do not have an official background. They have neither support nor limitations from government. They are sometimes registered as enterprises. Chinese NGOs are either lacking in independence and under strict government control, or are not formal organizations. They do not have legal person status or the status of a legal social organization. Sometimes they engage in for-profit activities without paying taxes according to the law.

Current opportunities and constraints in the role and function of NGOs in China have to be seen in the broader context of ongoing economic and political change. More than 20 years of reform and opening up have made today's China enormously different from that of the Mao Zedong era. A market economy is replacing a planned one. Authoritarianism has replaced totalitarianism, with political control relaxing and greater diversity of thinking emerging. With economic autonomy and the private life of citizens no longer controlled by the government, there is basic autonomy in the 'private sphere'. However, the state still has the desire and ability to exercise strict control over the public sphere. Consequently, what is replacing the old state-dominant system is not social autonomy but rather a new state-dominant system, which can be called a 'structure of control by category'.

The ability of different types of organizations to challenge the political power of the state varies. If we conceive of them as a series of concentric circles, with the organizations that have the strongest capacity to challenge the political power of the state at the center, then political opposition organizations would be at the core. The functional organizations such as the labour unions, the women's federation, the Communist Youth League and the Association of Industry and Commerce would be next. The next circles would be the important social service organizations that provide social services needed by both the government and the population, such as trade associations, research societies, charity organizations and religious organizations. Less important social service organizations that provide services needed by the public include environmental protection organizations, hometown associations, alumni organizations and campus interest groups.

The government adopts different strategies towards these different organizations according to its political relations with them. It firmly bans political opposition organizations, integrates the functional organizations into its own organizational structure, exercises indirect control (the dual management system) over important social service organizations, while allowing the existence of small independent groups of this type, and conducts very relaxed management of less important social service providers. In general, the social structural change of the Chinese mainland since reform and opening up can be seen as part of a process for the state to establish this 'structure of control by category', that is, a process through which the state has reshaped its mechanisms of social control. To be exact, it is now a structure of comprehensive social control by the state using non-governmental ways in the new economic environment. It is fair to say that Chinese NGOs are non-governmental organizations under the leadership of the government.

The limited areas of NGO activities reflect the impact of the structure of control by category. At present, NGOs are very active in education, public health, environmental protection, legal assistance and support for vulnerable groups. They also make some contribution to research, exploration, advocacy, conceptual change and institutional innovations. They have forcefully promoted opening up to the outside world. Environmental protection, women's rights and industry associations are very active in international exchanges. However, some areas have always been shut to NGOs and the government adopts a rather utilitarian attitude towards them. On the one hand, it hopes to see them play a complementary role. On the other hand, it restricts activities that it is not happy with. In this regard, all NGOs observe an iron law: they must not offend the strong government. NGOs know very well that if the government is offended they will achieve nothing, the organizations may be banned and the leaders may be jailed. In this sense, all NGOs are very self-disciplined.

STAKEHOLDER EXPECTATIONS AND THE CALL FOR ACCOUNTABILITY

NGOs' social function – the provision of public goods – directly determines their responsibilities and obligations. An NGO must cooperate with other social organizations or individuals to realize its social functions. Consequently, it has to satisfy the expectation or demand of these stakeholders. NGO responsibilities and obligations are defined by its social functions and its stakeholders.

In China, NGOs have a large number of stakeholders and the most influential among them are still the government, international organizations, multinational corporations, big domestic enterprises, experts and the mass media. It is usually their requirements and expectations that define an NGO's responsibilities and obligations. Therefore, we have focused our research on the expectations and requirements of these specific stakeholders. Since an

NGO's recognition of its own responsibilities also has a direct bearing on its behaviour, we have also investigated this dimension.

Government expectations are embodied in a series of laws, regulations, rules and policies such as the Regulations on the Registration Management of Social Organizations, the Regulations on the Management of Foundations, the Law on Welfare Donations and the Law on Trusts. The Law on Welfare Donations provides that NGOs must use the donations they receive to finance activities and undertakings that are consistent with their purposes, manage and use donations according to the wish of the donors, regularly report to competent government departments about the usage and management of donations for the purpose of supervision by the government, and make public the receipt, management and usage of donations for supervision by the general public. The law also provides that an NGO has to accept the corresponding legal responsibilities if it arbitrarily changes the nature and usage of a donation or diverts, misappropriates or embezzles donations. When collecting donations, an NGO must truthfully tell the donors about the purpose and mission of the organization, the purpose of the collection and the performance of the organization. It has to provide a legal and valid receipt for each donation. An NGO has to give truthful replies to the donors' enquiries about the usage and management of donations. The newly released Regulations on the Management of Foundations (March 2004) provide that a public donation foundation must use no less than 70 per cent of its total income of the previous year for public welfare undertakings identified in its charter, and the proportion for a non-public donation foundation is no less than 8 per cent of the balance of the fund of the previous year. Staff salaries and the running costs of a foundation shall not exceed 10 per cent of the total expenditure of the year.

According to international organizations, a second major stakeholder, the activities and influence of NGOs should not be restrained to a narrow social field, such as satisfying people's need for social services and defending the interests of vulnerable groups. NGOs can influence the whole of society by advocating new views, exploring new directions, affecting the legislative, administrative and decision-making work of government, establishing political legitimacy, cultivating ways of life for citizens, laying down foundations for democracy and providing a basis and supportive functions for the role of the market. Furthermore, through NGOs the government can provide more public services and benefits while reducing costs. Therefore, international organizations hope to see NGOs active in the areas of human rights, democracy, environmental protection and poverty alleviation. At the same time, they want them to be accountable to society, transparent to the public and with greater depth and width of public involvement. According to international organizations, NGOs' being responsible, transparent and participatory is something that should be directed towards all stakeholders and not only to government authorities.

Multinational corporations and domestic enterprises, a third important donor-related stakeholder, realize that they and NGOs are strong in different areas. They hope to improve their corporate image, enhance their reputation, facilitate relations with the government, develop a corporate culture and strengthen corporate cohesion through cooperation with famous NGOs. Many enterprises regard charitable undertakings as effective soft advertisement. Between 9 and 11 November 2003, more than a dozen of the most influential public welfare organizations, together with United Way International (UWI) and the US-China Business Council, organized a high-level forum in Beijing on multinational corporations and welfare activities. Participants were from multinational companies, international institutions, domestic civil society organizations, government departments and the media. A proposal signed by the delegates urged domestic civil society organizations to give a positive response to the call for an accountability mechanism, stronger governance and enhanced transparency, so as to obtain public trust and support and to build up their capacity through increased exchanges, dialogue and cooperation with enterprises. At the meeting, the World Bank delegate, Austin Hu, pointed out that 'non-governmental public welfare organizations need to strengthen insti-tutional and capacity building, to establish a complete financial management system and to increase transparency and public trust before they can lay down a basis for trust and cooperation with enterprises' (Austin Hu, 2003).

In order to compete for scarce resources and satisfy the expectations or requirements of the above stakeholders, Chinese NGOs have begun to explore accountability concepts, moral standards, self-disciplinary mechanisms and the culture of the NGO sector. In October 2001, the China Foundation for Poverty Alleviation organized an International Conference on NGO Poverty Reduction Policy. Participants from NGOs and academic circles exchanged views on self-discipline and peer supervision among Chinese public welfare organizations, on institutional ways to build up social trust for Chinese NPOs through self-discipline and social accountability, external controls and legal regulation of NGOs and other relevant topics. The 'Beijing Joint Declaration on Poverty Alleviation by Chinese NGOs' issued at the meeting put forward principles such as not abusing social trust and hope, increasing transparency, gradually forming an NGO sector culture and code of conduct, establishing self-disciplinary mechanisms, exercising self-governance and maintaining industry integrity.

Two months later in December 2001, the China NPO Network organized a forum on the self-discipline of NPOs. Participants were from NPOs, acade-mia, government, international organizations and the media. They explored ways for Chinese NPOs to realize self-discipline on the basis of their practical experience, existing legislation and the social environment. The forum put forward 'Nine Principles of Self-Discipline for Chinese NPOs' and encouraged participants to sign to reflect their adherence to the principles. Most partici-pants responded positively to the principles (Shang Yusheng and Cui Yu, 2003).

In November 2003, more than a dozen NGO leaders placed their signa-tures on a 'Letter of Appeal for Accountability and Self-Discipline among Chinese NPOs'. The document clearly stated the following:

> NPOs for public welfare purposes undertake the mission of
> realizing social justice and equality and eliminating poverty and
> play an important role in communicating information and
> promoting exchanges between donors and beneficiaries.
> Therefore, the accountability of these organizations and the
> relevant projects is the focus of government, enterprise and public
> attention. Chinese NPO leaders are determined to promote the
> development of NPO accountability and self-discipline mecha-
> nisms. We strongly call upon the formulation of accountability
> standards and a charter of self-discipline among Chinese NPOs.
> We hope domestic and foreign NPOs will join our effort in this
> regard. (Yan Mingfu et al, 2003)

Issued at the same time was the 'Accountability Standards for Chinese NPOs'.
This document stressed the non-religious, non-political and non-profit nature
of NPOs, emphasized avoidance of conflicts of interest by not promoting the
private interests of stakeholders and urged NPOs to share information and
resources, to cooperate with, consult with, support and assist one another and
to set up necessary mechanisms. It also stressed that 'the information and
materials provided in fund-raising activities should be truthful, reliable, not
misleading and consistent with the stated mission of the organization'. The
document emphasized the need for open, transparent, just and reasonable
project assessment and autonomy. It recommended fiscal transparency, respect
of donors' wishes, acceptance of independent audits and the publishing of
annual reports and true, accurate and timely financial statements for public
supervision and enquiry. It stressed the need for release of information and
urged NPOs to answer openly public inquiries. The idea of moral accountability was also raised, calling for the formulation of moral standards such as a
clean and honest performance, whole-heartedly serving the public interest and
the maintenance of due professionalism and expertise by professionals and
volunteers (Public Trust Standards for Chinese NPOs, 2003).

REGULATORY STRUCTURE AND INTERNAL
ACCOUNTABILITY MECHANISMS

Since the internal governance structure of GONGOs is markedly different from
that of independent NGOs, the chapter will discuss them separately. It has to
be made clear that within both GONGOs and independent NGOs huge differences exist, with a small number of good performers and a majority of
mediocre ones. However, the small number of well-performing NGOs has
attracted enormous attention, resulting in a misunderstanding by the public of
the overall situation. They are not representative of all the NGOs. What we
are going to discuss here is the general situation.

In the West, the most important internal governance mechanism of an
NGO is the board. The board represents social interests and holds decision-

making power, thus holding the NGO responsible to the society. However, the situation in China is different. Generally speaking, a board in its real sense does not exist, neither in GONGOs, nor independent NGOs. This phenomenon is a reflection of the unique NGO administration system in China.

The Regulations on the Registration Management of Social Organizations issued on 25 October 1989 and the Regulations on the Management of Foundations effective as of 27 September 1988 established a dual administration system for NGOs.[1] In 1998, the government issued new Regulations on the Registration Management of Social Organizations and Regulations on the Registration Management of Private Non-Enterprise Units. Both entered into force on 25 October 1998. New Regulations on the Management of Foundations were published on 19 March 2004 and have been effective as of 1 June 2004. However, these new regulations did not change the old administrative framework. They only divided social organizations into social organizations and private non-enterprise units.

The dual administration system delegates major power to professional supervisory units. Furthermore, it provides that only Party or government departments or their authorized institutions can act as professional supervisory units, thereby placing all formal social organizations under direct government control. According to the Regulations on the Registration Management of Social Organizations, the professional supervisory units should exercise a series of supervisory and administrative functions. They include the following:

- Reviewing preparations and applications for the establishment of social organizations, including the registration upon establishment, changes and de-registration;
- Supervising and guiding social organizations to abide by the Constitution, laws, regulations and national policies and to conduct activities according to their charters; carrying out a preliminary review for the annual examination of social organizations; assisting registration authorities and other departments in investigating and dealing with unlawful acts;
- Together with other relevant departments, guiding NGOs in clearing up their accounts.

As a matter of fact, the functions of professional supervisory units are not limited to the above list. The Regulations are very tactical in holding back some statements on the power of the authorities. The Ministry of Civil Affairs authorities are more straightforward in this respect. According to *Shetuan Guanli Gongzuo* (Administration of Social Organizations), a book edited by officials from the Ministry of Civil Affairs, the professional supervisory units administer the daily running of registered social organizations. They carry out regular education of leaders and staff of social organizations about the general situation and their tasks, making them familiar and compliant with national laws and policies. They review the elections of organizational leaders, Party work within the organization and changes in the posts and salary of staff. They carry out reviews and administration over major activities including the holding of seminars, financial activities, receipt of donations and foreign-related activities. They review and provide opinions on the internal organizational changes and urge the organization to go through change or deregistration procedures at the original department of registration. They also help social organizations to clear their equities and debts, provide certificates of debt repayment completion and deal with other related matters (Wu Zhongze and Chen Jinluo, 1996).

In short, the professional supervisory units of NGOs hold all the powers of NGO boards in other countries. As a result, the boards of these GONGOs exist only in name. Such a governance structure is abnormal and cannot ensure GONGOs are serving social interests. In theory, a GONGO should be responsible to its professional supervisory unit. In reality, they are often responsible only to the personal interests of the competent officials of the authority and the managers of the organization. Within such a governance structure, the managers are often appointed by the professional supervisory units. The management team, as a result, is usually lacking in a sense of mission or capabilities and often acts arbitrarily. Since most managers come from government departments and there is a lack of a sense of responsibility and enthusiasm, the organizational culture of GONGOs is more or less like that of a traditional *yamen* (local government office), in which there is a strict hierarchy and it is difficult to formulate the organization's mission and objectives on a consensus basis. However, in order to survive and develop and in the face of market competition, GONGOs can respond to social needs, but only within the scope encouraged, allowed or at least acquiesced to by the government. The project design and implementation process is often tarred by departmental or even individual interests. The secretary-generals usually dictate the activities of GONGOs with no transparency both within and outside the organizations, and with even less of a sense of responsibility to society.

Independent NGOs are in a rather different situation. Although unable to get favourable treatment from the government, they escape strict government control. The Regulations on the Registration Management of Social Organizations provide that the establishment of a social organization must be reviewed and approved by its professional supervisory unit before it can apply to the registration department. That is to say, a social organization can be founded only when there is a certain professional supervisory unit that is willing to act in that capacity. The same regulations also provide that there should not be more than one organization with the same functions in any one locality and that a social organization should not set up branches. As a matter of fact, through a 'conspiracy of power and law' the NGOs that the government is not happy with cannot even register legally as social organizations or foundations. In general, only GONGOs are able to obtain the green light for registration and it is almost impossible for independent NGOs to register. Consequently, independent NGOs have to register as legal enterprises, affiliate with other formal social organizations, or conduct activities without registration. In fact, at the same time as failing to prevent independent NGOs from obtaining legal person status, the existing laws also create troubles for NGOs and hidden perils for the development of the third sector as a whole. In effect, they create a 'legal gap', because the civil affairs departments, which should be responsible, cannot assume their responsibility because these organizations are not registered with them, while the industrial and commercial authorities cannot be responsible because it is not relevant to them, resulting in an administrative vacuum and dislocation (Xie Lihua, 2002).

Because of difficulties in registering legally as social organizations, many independent NGOs have had to register as enterprises and thereby face a number of special difficulties. Xie Lihua's organization is a typical example. In 1996, Xie Lihua created the Migrant Women's Club but was not successful in getting registration as a social organization. The Club had to exist as an affiliated agency of the Rural Women Knowing All Magazine. It was then integrated into the Cultural Development Center for Rural Women when that was established in 2001. According to Xie Lihua:

> *the Cultural Development Center for Rural Women is an NGO. Having not been able to register with the civil affairs department, it had to copy the practice of other NGOs and register with the Industrial and Commercial Bureau. For a non-profit organization to register with the Industrial and Commercial Bureau creates numerous embarrassments and difficulties in our operation.* (Xie Lihua, 2002)

The Center actually has two constitutions, one as a shareholding enterprise used for the Industry and Commerce registration and another as an NGO for the implementation of the actual work. This creates a lack of consistency. The constitution used for the registration includes provisions about the board and the organizational structure, but these are only nominal for the Center, even though they have legal force. The real board and organizational structure established according to the constitution of an NGO are not in actual practice protected by law, implying hidden legal problems.

Another problem is that independent NGOs that register as industrial and commercial entities cannot possibly enjoy preferential tax treatment. According to current tax laws, the Cultural Development Center for Rural Women must pay business taxes, income taxes, real estate taxes, vehicle taxes, education supplements and urban construction taxes. Xie Lihua (2002) argues 'the problems that we have encountered are the same problems that all NGOs that have registered with the industrial and commercial authorities have encountered. The problems of registration with the industrial and commercial authorities simply must be solved'. Lihua does not touch on a more serious issue: if an NGO registers as an enterprise, legally the assets of the NGO belong to the shareholders when actually they should not. Thus, there is a moral risk. On the one hand, donors worry about moral risks and feel reluctant to give large donations. On the other, an enterprise constitution delegates too much power to the founder of the enterprise, allowing him or her the legal right to assume all powers within the organization, which is against the ideas and principles of an NGO.

In practice, independent NGOs in China are usually founded, organized and led by a leader who has worked overseas, has been employed by an international organization, has certain overseas connections, or is an idealist with a high sense of responsibility and action. These independent NGOs have clear missions, well understood within their organizations. The organizational culture is usually rather pure. They are able to make timely responses to the needs of society, but their scope of activity is very much influenced by their financial capacity. Due to a lack of legitimacy, independent NGOs do not have much local fundraising ability. Overseas companies do not support them either, since they are not welcomed by the government. In this connection, almost all independent NGOs rely fully on funds from overseas NGOs, which consequently have a decisive bearing on the NGOs' project choices and even their survival and development. This is why successful NGOs and their leaders usually have an overseas background. Since the supporting overseas NGOs place high requirements on their grantees, independent NGOs are relatively more responsible and transparent and thereby enjoy high legitimacy and public trust among overseas NGOs.

EXTERNAL SUPERVISION AND ACCOUNTABILITY MECHANISMS

An NGO's internal governance structure is related to whether it is accountable, which means not deceiving others and taking the initiative to fulfil its due responsibilities or obligations. Being responsible is an intentional pursuit of NGOs. The external supervision of NGOs relates to accountability, which stresses the rights and mechanisms for stakeholders to hold NGOs accountable. There are two types of accountability: positive and negative. The former refers to after-the-fact investigation and punishment. The latter refers to non-cooperation by stakeholders.

In China, existing positive external accountability measures include management by the civil affairs departments, control by the professional supervisory units, government audits, independent audits, supervision by donors, beneficiaries, media and the general public, self-discipline, supervision by specialized NGOs, regular issuance of financial statements and surveys of public opinion. Generally speaking, management or administration by the civil affairs departments or professional supervisory units is either too relaxed or too strict. Auditing by the government or by independent agencies is usually a formality. Due to a lack of professionalism on the part of independent auditing agencies, annual reports published by NGOs are not very trustworthy. Beneficiaries are usually not able to supervise the activities of the NGOs. A self-disciplinary mechanism among NGOs does not exist and there are no NGOs specialized in consultancy, review and supervision. In recent years, the media, and the internet in particular, have played a more and more powerful supervisory role. It is also notable that the judicial departments have begun supervising the activities of NGOs.

Three headline-making events illustrate this. First, a former staff member of the China Youth Development Foundation (CYDF) accused the organization of making losses in investments, non-compliance with its constitution and corruption among its leaders. Second, the American Mothers, Inc., sued the Lijiang Mothers Association for using donations against the wishes of donors and falsifying financial records. Third, victims of fraud accused Dong Yuge, Headmistress of Shandong Huanghe Orphanage.

The reputation of the CYDF suffered severely under the intense coverage and attack from the mass media, and especially from the internet. The judiciary also played a role. On 29 October 2002, a final verdict was issued by the Yunnan Provincial High Court that the Lijiang Mothers Association should return to the American Mothers, Inc., the RMB907,890 (around US$110,000) that had not been used according to the wishes of the donor. On 5 April 2002, the Mudan District People's Court, Heze, Shandong Province, sentenced Dong Yuge to 11 years in prison and a fine of RMB50,000 (US$6,58) and ordered the return of the RMB334,800 (US$40,564) in illegal gains (Don Xueqing, 2000). In the CYDF case, the judiciary did not intervene but the State Audit Administration and the Disciplinary Committee for Departments directly under the Party Central Committee carried out strict scrutiny and investigation. After that, the CYDF conducted a comprehensive and systematic reform of its governance structure and management system. Important reform measures included the establishment of a real board.

The three cases revealed that the annual examination by the civil affairs departments, regulation by the professional supervisory unit and government and independent audits play little or no preventive roles. As a matter of fact, in China most NGOs can do anything they want. They enjoy privileges without undertaking any social responsibilities. At junctures critical to their survival, the professional supervisory units of GONGOs may even use administrative power to prevent supervision from the outside, since to protect their GONGO is to protect themselves.

The three cases also reveal a basic model of successful external supervision under the present circumstances, that is, whistle-blowing by insiders, media coverage, government or judicial intervention, with perpetrators being held accountable either by losing their reputation or by being punished by law. Although NGOs have been in frequent conflict with their stakeholders, only a few of these conflicts are made public and even fewer brought to court. Most of the conflicts ended with a 'termination of cooperation'. However, that does not mean that NGOs can easily escape punishment. They have to pay heavily in terms of social legitimacy. In the intensely competitive market of public welfare, the loss of social legitimacy is tantamount to the loss of resources for survival and development. In today's China, competition for donations constitutes a major mechanism of negative accountability.

NGOs in the form of an enterprise can also survive without legal or administrative legitimacy, as long as they have social legitimacy and do not infringe on any political taboos. They have to be positive and upright in improving their services and delivery ability so as to get donations. GONGOs all need social legitimacy if they want to obtain resources from outside the government. Project Hope, the school development programme for poor rural areas run by the CYDF, is an example here. Independent NGOs that register as industrial or commercial entities have two bases for social legitimacy purposes. Usually the founders of such organizations are already famous activists before their organizations were created and are acknowledged by their peers and international organizations. Their reputation constitutes the initial social legitimacy of the newly created organization. The performance of the NGO, if consistent with the expectation of the stakeholders, will consolidate and enhance the social legitimacy of the organization and thereby facilitate it gaining further support to sustain its development.

Since the government does not provide any financial resources, legitimacy in the legal sense is only a protective resource. Financial resources for further development can only be found by asking for funds from the public. Therefore, independent NGOs as well as a majority of GONGOs have to gain social recognition and legitimacy in order to survive. In short, they have no way to escape from negative accountability.

BACKGROUND OR MACRO ENVIRONMENT

NGOs do not exist in a vacuum. The national polity, legal framework, relevant policies, public demand and available resources, as well as overseas funds, knowledge and personnel exchanges all have strong influences on NGO accountability. Thus, in order to understand the governance situation of NGOs in China, one must understand the economic, social and political conditions of China and the meanings of reform and opening up.

The reform has broken the original mechanism of supply of public goods. The new mechanism is not yet in place, while the demand for public goods is sharply increasing. Given this big gap between supply and demand, there is a dire need for NGOs. However, available local resources are very limited, and this is magnified by the public's lack of knowledge of NGOs. Few individuals and enterprises are ready to provide financial support for NGOs, there is no culture supportive of NGOs and there is an extreme shortage of professionals and volunteers. Meanwhile the mass media, which are needed to mobilize communities, are in the hands of the government. There are also not enough management professionals for such organizations, nor is there adequate supervision.

Before 1989, the West had placed its hope for China's democratization on reformists within the Chinese government. The hope was broken by the Tiananmen incident. Some people then turned to the idea of 'civil society resisting the state', reflecting on the drastic changes in Eastern Europe and the Tiananmen incident, which brought them new hope. As a result, the West started to expect bottom-up changes, the best tools of which are NGOs. In the eyes of Western governments and international organizations dominated by developed countries, NGOs are the main tools to promote democracy, human rights, market mechanisms and bottom-up peaceful evolution.

It must be pointed out that the facts are not what some researchers conclude or expect – that NGOs can be a positive force to disintegrate dictatorship and promote democracy and that civil society resists the state. In China, NGOs play a dual role: maintaining government authority and enhancing the autonomous capacity of citizens at the same time. Undoubtedly, the development of NGOs will exert a positive influence on Chinese society. It is, however, impractical to expect NGOs to change the Chinese political and social structure in the near term. In today's China, it is political evolution that determines the fate of NGOs rather than NGO development that influences political development.

The opening-up policy has exposed China to overseas influence, which is significant for the development of Chinese NGOs. Without enormous influence from abroad, the NGOs would not be what they are today. Overseas NGOs are directly involved in activities in China and provide a driving force, opportunities, pressure and resources. At the beginning, the establishment of many GONGOs was intended to facilitate exchanges with organizations outside China. The establishment of NGOs by government was also the result of learning from foreign experience. For the Chinese public, government, enterprises and the NGOs themselves, knowledge of NGOs, including their value, functions, governance structure, mode of management, project operation, fundraising, sense of responsibility, organizational culture, supervision, review, training, consultancy and research methods, have come from overseas. Even personnel in this area are from overseas. Because of this continuous and pervasive influence of overseas NGOs, a great majority of Chinese NGOs do not manage to become fully independent organizations.

In the past two decades, overseas influence has been increasing with each passing day. It will further strengthen. Andrew Watson points out the opportunities and challenges for NGOs brought about by China's accession to the WTO (Watson, 2002): first, a change of government functions will produce corresponding changes on the part of the NGOs; second, more and more enterprises coming to China and developing their own charitable undertakings will both provide opportunities for Chinese NGOs and bring higher requirements for their work ability, management system, sense of social responsibility and transparency; third, international NGOs and NPOs will also develop in China, providing cooperation opportunities for Chinese NGOs and intensifying competition for talented people in particular; fourth, with economic growth and increased competition, workers have to face employment risks and farmers have to adjust their production structure and some have to migrate to the cities for completely new lives – the government and the NGOs must address all of these issues together; and fifth, Chinese NGOs need a more rational and improved legal framework, which requires joint efforts by Chinese NGOs and other organizations to achieve. As various NGOs and NPOs are playing more and more roles in the world, Chinese NGOs must think over what role they are going to play in the international arena.

BASIC STRATEGIES TO IMPROVE GOVERNANCE MECHANISMS

How to improve the governance of Chinese NGOs is a very important question. If the question is to be answered, the starting point must be based on reality rather than on empty idealism or prescriptions based on misuse of Western social experience. While recognizing that serious problems exist and huge improvement is urgently needed in almost all aspects of NGO governance, what we want to address here are the most important and most urgent questions.

The most serious problem is the lack of a rational legal framework. As a result, citizens and vulnerable groups in particular, are not able to realize their rights of association fully, and some other rights provided by law (such as preferential tax treatment) are absent.[2] A further consequence is that NGOs do not have sound internal governance. GONGOs lack autonomy and are heavily dependent on their professional supervisory units. Independent NGOs cannot obtain proper legal person status and exist as enterprise legal persons, which leads to a conflict between legal legitimacy and social legitimacy. An additional consequence also includes irrational government intervention, rendering effective external supervision impossible. Good governance of NGOs requires boards responsible to public interests, effective external supervision and a sound legal environment. However, the question of the legal environment cannot be addressed in a short time or by the NGOs themselves. The fate of NGOs is closely linked to the macro political environment, and the direction and results of political reform are dependent on many other factors.

Nonetheless, NGOs should not wait passively for the external environment to improve. They should, on the one hand, cooperate with other players to facilitate improvement of the legal environment and, on the other hand, improve their own internal governance. Consensus building should be the primary task. What are NGOs? What purposes do they serve? Where does their legitimacy come from? To whom are they responsible? What responsibilities do they have towards the stakeholders? What aspects of their behaviour must be accounted for and how? How should NGOs respond to criticisms? NGOs need to reflect on these questions and form a consensus on the answers. NGOs must have ideals and objectives and demonstrate sympathy, a sense of responsibility, humanism and altruism. An NGO's projects and activities should be based on good values, which are embodied in the vision, mission and strategic objectives of the organization. NGOs must not stop at following the chosen values and moral principles but should take a step further to extend the values and moral principles to all stakeholders.

It is also important to establish a social consultation mechanism through meetings, discussions, the internet, magazines and other media so as to build a common understanding of the good governance of NGOs and to take concrete and effective measures on that basis. To address the registration problem, specific programmes and agencies can be developed to carry out identification and accountability assessment. They can also help introduce common moral standards, supervise their implementation and serve as an important force to develop industry culture and self-discipline. To this end, it is necessary for organizations of nationwide influence to promote the development of moral standards and to conduct extensive international cooperation.

Finally, it is necessary to set up a mechanism of extensive participation. NGOs not only need recognition by law but also need the support of all stakeholders and, at the very least, of the donors. NGOs must pay attention to their social legitimacy and thus need to increase their transparency and open up their decision-making processes so that stakeholders can really take part in the making of important decisions. Public opinion surveys are another way of involving the public. In short, donors, beneficiaries, collaborators, the media, the general public, independent auditors and the government all need to be involved in the governance of NGOs. Such participatory mechanisms constitute supervision of NGO activities. Experience also suggests that self-discipline alone is not enough and without effective external supervision it is not possible for NGOs to develop healthily. Unswerving and strict external supervision can effectively promote NGOs to fulfil their roles.

NOTES

1   The so-called 'dual administration system' refers to registration of NGOs with registration management authorities under the Ministry of Civil Affairs and with a professional supervisory unit responsible for oversight of their professional work.
2   The Provisional Regulations on Enterprise Income Tax (1994) provide that 'the amount of donations by a taxpayer to public welfare or disaster relief can be deducted from taxable income at a level equal to or less than 3 per cent of the taxpayer's taxable income of a specific year'. The Regulations on Implementation of the Law on Personal Income Tax (1994) provide that the amount donated by an individual to education and other public welfare undertakings should be deducted from that individual's taxable income up to the level of 30 per cent of the tax to be paid. The Individual Income Tax Law (1999) stipulates that 'according to relevant orders of the State Council, donations to educational causes and public welfare can be deducted from the tax payable'. The Welfare Donations Law (1999) provides preferential tax treatments for donors:

> Corporate donors to public welfare may according to law enjoy preferential treatment for enterprise income tax. Natural persons and self-employed people, if donating to public welfare undertakings, may enjoy preferential treatment in personal income tax. Overseas in-kind donations to public welfare or non-profitable organizations for public welfare purposes may enjoy reduction or exemption of import tax and

import VAT. Projects supported by donations should be assisted and favourably treated by the relevant local governments.

However, the above-mentioned preferential tax treatments for NGOs provided by laws and regulations are not always realized. A donor's demand for tax exemption using a receipt issued by NGOs is usually ignored by the tax authorities, which will agree to a reduction or exemption only when the donor's demand is supported by special consideration from authorities with real power. Generally speaking, the current practice is review and approval on a case-by-case basis. Ironically, NGOs existing in the form of enterprise legal person are always able to avoid or evade tax by claiming zero profit or by asking for special favours through advocating their missions to the tax collectors.

9

NGO Governance and Accountability in Indonesia: Challenges in a Newly Democratizing Country

Hans Antlöv, Rustam Ibrahim and Peter van Tuijl

INTRODUCTION

The collapse of President Soeharto's authoritarian New Order regime in 1998 and the ensuing transition towards democracy has brought about many changes in Indonesia, including a tremendous growth in civil society. The number of civil society organizations, including NGOs, throughout Indonesia has increased substantially. It is no exaggeration to describe the recent developments as the rising era of civil society in Indonesia. The global spread of democracy has opened up new opportunities for Indonesian civil society groups to participate in establishing rights, institutions and mechanisms of accountability in a society where citizen involvement not very long ago was discouraged.

With the basic freedoms of expression and association upheld, the civil society sector has grown rapidly and intensely. Myriads of new and old organizations are trying to make their voices heard in the public sphere. Several trends exemplify this. It is almost impossible to capture the diversity of the non-profit sector in Indonesia. There are tens of thousands of civil society organizations in Indonesia today, including religious organizations, mass-based membership organizations, unions, ethnic-based organizations, community organizations, NGOs, professional associations and politically affiliated organizations.[1] Prior to 1998, there was only one labour organization and one farmer union acknowledged (and controlled) by the government; now there are no less than 40 national labour organizations and 300 local labour unions, more than 10,000 labour associations at the corporate level and hundreds of peasant organizations. Social-religious groups, research institutions, study groups and think tanks have also grown in numbers.

Despite the growth of the NGO sector, now as a part of a broader civil society in Indonesia, it is important to realize that the impact of a prolonged experience of repression is still very significant. During more than three decades of authoritarian rule, civil society in Indonesia was seen as a part of the problem, not as the solution. Civil society was there to be controlled, not to be listened to or as a partner to work with. The implication is that while after 1998 civil society was expected to contribute to democracy and good governance, it actually had to rethink its strategies and reform and adjust itself as well, quite fundamentally and dramatically, in order to rise up to the challenges and opportunities of a new situation. This process is still ongoing.

The uncertainty in the position and strategies of civil society in Indonesia is compounded by the increasing call for accountability. Right at the moment when there is a lack of confidence among civil actors about what they are actually able to achieve and how to achieve it, both the internal governance of civil society organizations (CSOs), as well as their external performance in the public domain are becoming subject greater scrutiny. Yet, a number of initiatives to improve CSO governance and accountability have been taken and are beginning to solidify. This chapter will focus in particular on NGOs, as an important subsection of civil society, and their role in developing the governance of the non-profit sector in Indonesia.

THE PERMITTED GROWTH OF THE NGO SECTOR AND ITS IMPACT

There is a long history of civic associations in Indonesia. A rich texture of social groups and movements has existed: religious societies, private schools, credit associations, mutual assistance self-help groups, neighbourhood organizations, water-user associations and many others. These were mainly ascriptive and not voluntary. It was only with the rise of liberalism and modernity that such organizations in Indonesia developed into an emergent and self-sustaining public sphere during a decade of political awakening, 1915–1925. Hundreds, if not thousands, of popular, mass-based organizations were established, based on religion, ethnicity, political affiliation and other joint concerns.

NGOs[2] began to be recognized in Indonesia in the early 1970s in line with the development activities carried out by the Soeharto government.[3] Although the government was able to maintain high economic growth of 8 per cent per annum, widespread poverty and lack of community participation in development activities created room for NGOs to play a role in community-based social and economic activities. These NGOs (often indicated as 'development NGOs') were involved in a wide variety of fields, either as a complementary provider or as an agent of government programmes that could not reach the lowest strata of society. Their programmes covered health services, nutrition, clean water and sanitation, family planning, non-formal education, applied technology, microcredit, small enterprises, informal sector joint ventures, cooperatives and others.

The growth of the NGO sector in Indonesia in the 1980s was caused by both international and domestic concerns. Internationally, more and more donors were realizing that in order to achieve their social goals, they needed to cooperate more closely with various NGOs. And as the cold war came to an end, the democratization agenda became more significant. Critical in this was the growth of civil society and therefore the support of NGOs became important not only for programmatic concerns, but also in itself, as the actors that strengthen civil society.

By the early 1980s, even for Soeharto's government it had become clear that the state alone could not bear the full costs of development and therefore needed the participation of communities. The state opened up to NGOs to become a player in development. But the approach to the NGOs by the Indonesian authorities was predominantly instrumental and certainly not supported by the language of 'democracy building' that the donors were using to support NGOs. As a matter of fact, the Indonesian regime increasingly orchestrated other types of organizations outside government and limited their number.

Towards the end of the 1980s, 'civil society' in Indonesia consisted of a series of single-issue or single group-oriented umbrella organizations for farmers, workers, women, sailors, officials and many other groups, all effectively controlled by the government. The number of political parties was limited to three. Equally, Indonesian civil society was purposely trimmed into a well-managed miniature. This process has been aptly called the 'bonsaification' of Indonesian civil society.[4] Limited room for a more politically oriented function in civil society was left only for a few large mass-based Islamic organizations and for NGOs. The Islamic organizations could maintain some space as they benefited from the clout granted by the sheer numbers of their membership, strong community roots and skillful leadership. Room for NGOs was left by the regime because of their contribution to delivering services to communities and because of international support, politically and financially.

It is important to understand how the growth of Indonesian NGOs for at least two decades took place in a context of a civil society that was deliberately dysfunctional in its political features. It made NGOs almost synonymous with 'civil society' in the eyes of donors as well as in terms of self-perception, and it cloaked NGOs as a virtual political opposition. Donors' support for NGOs was similarly portrayed as support for civil society and democratization. In fact, the one-sided support of development NGOs, rather than other associations within civil society, did not contribute to a broad based civil society growth and is one of the causes for the present weaknesses of NGOs: elitism and a lack of effective grassroots participation. To the excuse of donors, the Soeharto government did not give them much choice in supporting anything else.

Within this limited space, NGOs active in human rights and in environmental protection and preservation began to emerge, in line with global trends. These NGOs started to carry out advocacy activities in support of those whose rights were violated by the regime, such as indigenous communities, women and workers. Or they became active with regard to areas of environmental degradation, such as the pollution of air, sea and land, and the destruction of forests and other natural resources due to development and industrialization, rapid population growth and poorly planned transmigration programmes.

During the 1990s, more NGOs started advocacy divisions, moving beyond the framework of community development. The impetus for these changes was the increasingly tense relationship between community development NGOs and the more politically oriented activists. This friction between NGOs culminated with a critical attack on the established NGOs by a group of smaller organizations in Central Java (Johnson, 1990), followed in December 1990 by the announcement of a 'no-confidence motion' of the whole NGO sector in a larger advocacy meeting in Bali (Eldridge, 1995). NGOs in Indonesia, according to the advocacy oriented activists, had merely become the extended arm and implementing agencies of the authoritarian government and had lost their commitment towards change. They were criticized for hierarchy, bureaucracy, co-optation and lack of internal accountability.

It is fair to say that NGOs and the leadership that grew up in the NGO sector subsequently played a significant role in the transition to democracy. Had it not been for the voluntarism and commitment among NGOs and some of the remaining relatively autonomous organizations in Indonesian civil society, the transition towards democracy would have taken longer and the road would have been bumpier. The advocacy groups established in the 1980s were a building block for the democracy movement. They formed an important element in the aggressive public pressure on the Soeharto government that emerged in the mid-1990s. At the time, many of these groups had only limited, if any, political influence, but could, nevertheless, contribute to the loose pro-democracy movement that eventually forced Soeharto to resign. With the growth of a professional and more critical middle class, a reassured urban working class and sensitized political parties, the necessary preconditions and the right constellation of actors for a political transition were in place. The Asian economic crisis that started in 1997 provided the trigger.

The fall of the Soeharto regime and the ensuing democratization process in Indonesia led to the emergence of a discourse on good governance, accountability and transparency of public institutions. NGOs that were active in monitoring the activities of state and other political institutions emerged and became known as watchdog organizations. Starting with the heavy involvement of NGOs in the 1999 election, nowadays almost all aspects of state institutions are being watched by NGOs. The Indonesian public recognizes various organizations such as Indonesian Corruption Watch (ICW), Parliament/legislative watch (DRP-Watch), Government Watch (GOWA), Police Watch (PolWatch) and budget watch (FITRA).

To engage more effectively in promoting just public policies, Indonesian NGOs have also grouped themselves in a number of coalitions to carry out advocacy to change, influence and/or draft new laws. Examples of such coalitions are the NGO Coalition for the Foundation Law, the NGO Coalition for the Public Freedom to Information Law, the NGO Coalition for a New Constitution and the NGO Coalition for the Participatory Law-Making Bill. However, alliance building among Indonesian NGOs has so far never reached the level of a nationwide coalition, such as in many other countries. What is still missing is an organization that monitors the NGOs themselves, or at least a professional association of NGOs.

Seven years into what is known as *reformasi*, citizens in Indonesia are in a myriad of ways making their voices heard, filling spaces opened up by democratization and decentralization, and are in the process of building a new relationship with the state. Since the fall of Soeharto, it has been truly possible for Indonesian citizens to express their voices in public and speak out about what they feel important in life. Despite continued corruption and power abuse, civil society grows and is strong. There remains today a flowering of new ideas and social actors, as people who had been denied participation for a long time seek to get involved. There is a momentum for negotiating and reformulating the balance of power between the state and its citizens. NGOs have an important role to play in this. This has been made possible by the continued freedom of assembly and freedom of the press. Newspapers are free to write what they want and are often very brave in doing so. There are dozens of television talk shows discussing in a very open and inclusive manner the problems of government and society.[5] We will now review the present situation and perceptions of Indonesian NGOs in more detail, starting with a brief overview of changes in the regulatory framework for NGOs.

CURRENT REGULATION OF NGOS

In Indonesia, there are two kinds of legal entities for non-profit organizations: foundations (*yayasan*) and associations (*perkumpulan*). *Yayasan* was first recognized as a legal entity during the Dutch colonial era (1870) to designate non-membership organizations. Most *yayasan* were established under the European legal system, while some adhered to other legal systems such as *wakaf* (donations or grants under Islamic law).

For many years, all forms of *yayasan* were based solely on societal norms and Supreme Court jurisprudence. The *yayasan* form is actually derived from the agreements and aspirations of the founders and then developed into legal practice. The purpose and agreement for establishing a *yayasan* is then authenticated by a public notary act, registered in the district court and announced in the State Gazette.

In general, the objective of a *yayasan* is social, religious, educational or humanitarian in nature. Unfortunately, however, there was no limitation to the activities that a *yayasan* could implement, so many *yayasans* were used as profit-making entities or even for money laundering purposes by the founders. Many of the major military business groups during the Soeharto era had a *yayasan* as their legal basis and were consequently unregulated (Robison and Hadiz, 2004). There were also *yayasans* founded by Soeharto to obtain donations from conglomerates; *yayasans* established by the military to shelter their businesses; and hospitals and universities that raise public funds for the benefit of their founders.

In line with the demand for good governance after the fall of President Soeharto and in response to pressure from the IMF to regulate military and state-based *yayasans*, the government of Indonesia submitted a draft *yayasan* law to the parliament in 2000, ratified as Law 16/2001.

The basic aim of the new Law 16/2001 is to promote transparency and accountability in *yayasan* governance. The preamble states that:

> *Facts indicate the tendency of some members of society to estab-lish* yayasan *to take shelter behind the legal status of* yayasan *which are used not only to develop social, religious, humanitarian activities but also to accumulate wealth for the founders, board members and supervisors. Along with this tendency, a number of problems have emerged in relation to* yayasan *activities that are not in line with the purpose and objectives stipulated in its Articles of Association and the suspicion that* yayasans *have been used to accommodate illegally gotten wealth of founders or other parties.*

This law can be considered an important breakthrough for the good governance of the non-profit sector in Indonesia, as it provided assurance and legal certainty, as well as restored the *yayasans'* function as a non-profit institution with social, religious and humanitarian goals. On the accountability and transparency of a *yayasan*, the main regulations are as follows:

- The *yayasan* is obliged to issue an annual programme and financial reports, by at least placing an announcement in the notice board of the *yayasan*'s office (Article 52 Clause 1).
- A *yayasan* receiving funding from the state, overseas donors or other parties in the amount of Rp500 million (approximately US$50,000) or more, or having assets of more than Rp20 billion (approximately US$2 million) is obligated to publish its financial report in an Indonesian language newspaper (Article 52 Clause 2).
- A *yayasan* receiving funding equal to or more than Rp500 million, or having assets amounting to Rp20 billion must be audited by a public accountant (Article 52 Clause 3).
- Annual financial reports of a *yayasan* must be prepared based on the Indonesian Standard of Accountancy (Article 52 Clause 5).

The other legal form used by NGOs is the *perkumpulan* (association), which is established by a number of people to serve the interests of its members or the public. Different from a *yayasan*, which is a non-membership organization, a *perkumpulan* is established on the basis of membership or a group of people with a common social service objective and not-for-profit making purposes. The legal title of association is obtained through approval from the Minister of Justice and is published in the appendix of the State Gazette.

With the promulgation of Law 16/2001, a number of NGOs – particularly organizations active in social movements and dependent on a broad membership base – have begun to reconsider their legal status, that is, whether to remain a *yayasan* or become a *perkumpulan*. This has been the case with NGOs involved in the women's movement, consumer protection, the environment and human rights. The reason is that membership-based organizations are seen as more accountable and less prone to authoritarian governance tendencies, different from *yayasan* where the founders control everything. We will return to this issue below.

PERCEPTIONS AND WEAKNESSES OF NGOs IN THE REFORM ERA[6]

Government perceptions

In line with the ongoing democratization process in Indonesia, perceptions of the government, the private sector and donors about the existence and role of civil society in general and NGOs in particular have also changed. Except for some vocal NGOs working on human rights and environmental issues, the government seldom intervenes directly in NGO activities anymore.[7] There are indications of increasing appreciation of the role of NGOs, for example, in the post-tsunami disaster and relief operations in Aceh. The government begins to see the need to create a new division of roles among stakeholders (government, private sector and NGOs) by giving opportunities to independent community initiatives, as well as encouraging them to participate actively in government programmes. According to government statements, it is hoped that a stronger, more democratic and more dynamic community will emerge through improved community capacity to solve their own problems (Tulung, 2002).

However, the government still has difficulties in developing effective partnerships with NGOs. This is particularly due to the fact that the rapid growth of NGOs has not been accompanied by the creation of an umbrella organization to represent NGO interests in dealing with the government. For the government, therefore, it is difficult to obtain inputs or to develop accords widely supported by the NGO community in a more formal sense.

There is also among state actors a lingering hesitation towards limiting state power as advocated by some NGOs. We can see this for instance in the statement of then president Megawati Soekarnoputri in 2002 warning of the 'ultra democracy' of NGOs, media and political parties that were only thinking of their own advantages (*Jakarta Post*, 26 November 2002). This is connected to nostalgia and romanticism of the stability and efficiency of the Soeharto regime.

Many people within the government believe that in the present transition to democracy, the NGO community should consolidate internally to strengthen its own capacity, because both the government and NGOs have equal potential to be corrupt and lose focus in the absence of a code of ethics, accountability mechanisms and transparent control. That is why the government appreciates NGO efforts in promoting good non-profit governance, and in improving professionalism, transparency and accountability. The government also sees the need for a forum of NGOs to create NGO accountability in carrying out their functions.

Private sector perceptions

In the past, relations between the private sector and civil society were often full of conflicts, but due to the changes in the political climate and NGO pressures, the private sector's perception towards NGOs has been undergoing some change. Companies are more willing to collaborate with civil society organizations in community development projects. A number of multinational corporations, directly or indirectly, through their community relations department or corporate foundations have begun to provide assistance for communities surrounding the locations of their business, through programmes in community health, clean water and sanitation, agriculture and the development of small-scale enterprises, all in collaboration with NGOs. These kinds of relationships were almost unheard of in the past.

There is also an emerging constituency in Indonesia for corporate social responsibility (CSR) and philanthropy. Several networks have been established, including Indonesia Business Link (for CSR) and the KEHATI-led Initiative on Strengthening Philanthropy. There is an emerging convergence between the 'supply' and 'demand' side of civil society, between the philanthropic sector providing funds for charitable activities and the non-profit organizations that work with end-users in providing actual development programmes. Recent collaborations in the tsunami-hit province of Aceh point towards further improvements in the relationship between these two sectors, where trust is beginning to be built.

Donor perceptions

Meanwhile, donor agencies mainly have continued to view NGOs as alternative institutions with the ability to provide public services and at the same time exercise some control over government power. Since the changes in the political regime, many of the obstacles for NGOs to contribute to democratization and policy change have been removed. Having said that, while during the previous authoritarian regime NGOs were often seen as the *anak mas* ('favourite child') of donors, today there is more criticism, also among donors. Three donor reports funded by USAID (Holloway and Anggoro, 2000), the

United Nations Support Facility for Indonesian Recovery (UNSFIR) (Feulner, 2001) and the World Bank (McCarthy, 2002), plus a study by the international NGO Mercy Corps (Damayanti, 2002) and two MA theses (Sudarbo, 2002; Hidayat, 2003) provide a good picture of the complexity of donor–NGO relations in Indonesia.

Donors see that there are at least four important areas for improvement among Indonesian NGOs. First and foremost is internal governance. This includes decision-making processes, division of roles between the board and executive, establishment of accountability mechanisms to constituents, as well as issues related to the establishment of a clear vision, mission and objectives. The second area to be addressed is accountability, both to the government and to the public. So far, NGOs mainly attempt to be accountable to donor agencies in the form of narrative and financial reports on projects. Third, NGOs need to improve external relations with other NGOs and with the public or its beneficiaries. If an NGO is working directly with the underprivileged then it needs to understand how it can really empower them so that they are stronger and more critical. For advocacy NGOs, networking and alliance building with other NGOs are important tools so that activities at the community level can be promoted at the national level. The fourth area needing improvement is NGO management, including strategic planning, programme development and financial and human resources management.

Donors will eventually evaluate NGOs based on the four factors above, that is, technical capability, legitimacy, accountability and transparency. Furthermore, a majority of NGOs do not have any criteria or parameters to track programme achievements. Outcomes become the indicator for success (an indicator of success for a training session is thus often that '30 persons were trained'), without any real substantive way of measuring the medium- and long-term impact of the activities.

Summary of NGO weaknesses

A recent series of academic studies of the civil society sector, NGOs and the pro-democracy movement in Indonesia complements the picture (Wacana, 1999; Ibrahim, 2002; PIRAC, 2002; Hadiwinata, 2003; Stanley et al, 2003; Sidel, 2004). Below is a summary of some key characteristics of NGOs today. They are, by necessity, brief and to some extent caricaturized. But the issues and problems these groups have encountered, we believe, are real, although not to the same extent for all NGOs:

- *Centralized and urban* – most NGOs are based in larger cities in Java and in Jakarta, even though they might be working in the outer islands. Many of the larger development NGOs have regional branches with limited autonomy, but this is slowly changing.
- *Elitist and middle-class* – the foundation (*yayasan*) form of NGOs often encourages a powerful role for the director of the institution, who usually is the founder. This may lead to a situation in which most decisions are

taken by the top layer of the organization's leadership without involving field staff. The leadership is often (aspiring) middle class with university degrees but little knowledge of grassroots mobilization (Sidel, 2004). There have been cases of great distance between NGOs and the communities they were working for, geographically, culturally, socially and economically.

- *Free-floating* – recent research by DEMOS on the pro-democracy movement has shown the detachment of many NGOs from the everyday reality of common people. Very few NGOs are mass-based or based in the countryside. Neither do they have political impact upwards. They are thus floating in-between the state and the community (Stanley et al, 2003).
- *Sectoral and fragmented* – many NGOs are focused on sectoral programmes. There has been a lack of coordination between NGOs.
- *Lack of managerial and advocacy skills* – since NGOs are micro-oriented and elitist, they often have weak organizational skills.
- *Lacking focus and ideology* – NGOs efforts have often diffused into a variety of activities without necessarily having any skills in that field. Environmental groups are election monitors, research institutions manage development programmes, anti-corruption groups deliver emergency assistance, and so on. Many groups go where the problem or the money is, the 'flavour of the month'.
- *Lacking accountability* – there are few mechanisms through which NGOs can be held accountable to communities, further reinforcing the social distance and lack of impact. The general public, the media, as well as state actors are increasingly complaining about the lack of accountability of NGOs and other civil society organizations.

The above list of weaknesses and problems is framed by the continuous reliance on assistance from foreign donors. This does not help generate public trust towards NGOs in developing legitimacy, accountability and transparency. These challenges are probably best illustrated through the case related to the Indonesian Legal Aid Foundation (YLBHI). YLBHI has been one of the outstanding NGOs in the fields of law, democracy and human rights for the past 30 years. However, this organization is now in the middle of a severe financial crisis after two major donors stopped their assistance. The decision has had a huge impact on YLBHI and they have decided to reduce their activities and to rationalize the number of staff. The reasons for the cessation of aid to YLBHI are related to management quality and internal governance issues, particularly the conflicts between the board of trustees and the executive office during the last couple of years.

The above illustration provides an example of the financial reality of Indonesian NGOs. When donor support is stopped, it affects programmes and even the NGO's own existence. This suggests the need for Indonesian NGOs to raise their funds from domestic sources, from the public, the government or the private sector. In order to gain public trust, however, Indonesian NGOs need to improve their governance first, especially in relation to the issues of legitimacy and accountability. It is important for NGOs to prove their capacity to deliver intended services to the community so that their existence can be socially recognized and supported.

RESPONSES AND INNOVATIONS FROM NGOS

The rapid growth of civil society and the increasing discourse on good governance have caused anxiety among the NGO community in Indonesia and critiques of NGOs have increasingly entered the media and public discourse. Although it has had positive impacts on the democratization process, it is now more generally understood that the explosive growth of new NGOs during the last five years has also created problems of quantity versus quality. Some even question the growth as 'too much, too fast' (McCarthy, 2002). Many organizations that were established after the fall of Soeharto and call themselves NGOs have questionable objectives and some of them have been involved in malpractice, and have thus affected the reputation of NGOs in general (Ganie-Rochman, 2000). These include NGOs that sold subsidized rice destined for the poor, NGOs established just for the purpose of gaining access to development projects, NGOs established by political party activists to mobilize funds and support to gain political power, as well as NGOs acting as debt collectors or specializing in mobilizing mobs for hire. There have been newspaper articles about the 'Billion rupiah business of NGO' (*Bisnin Milyaran LSM*) and allegations of corruption and misuse.

As already mentioned, there is no umbrella organization for NGOs in Indonesia yet. In other countries, such umbrellas can function as a key conduit for promoting the existence and the interests of NGOs to outside parties and serve internal capacity building purposes for its members. The absence of such an organization may be related to the traumatic history of Indonesian NGOs, who always tried to avoid unity to avoid being co-opted by the Soeharto authoritarian regime or used as a political vehicle by opportunistic NGO leaders. During the last few years, however, a number of influential NGOs have begun to take new and sometimes quite innovative steps to address the issue of NGO governance. We will briefly present some of these efforts.

Preparation of an NGO code of ethics

Since 2002, the Agency for Research, Education, Economic and Social Development (LP3ES), a national NGO, has taken the initiative to prepare and implement a code of ethics and to establish an NGO association or umbrella organization, particularly for NGOs that are working in community-based social and economic development. The preparation of the code of ethics and the establishment of the NGO association have been carried out through a number of meetings, seminars and workshops with the NGO community and stakeholders, such as the government and the private sector. The programme has been organized in provincial capitals, involving at least 500 local NGOs.

The programme eventually managed to formulate a written code of ethics. The code, signed by 252 NGOs from 8 provinces, contains matters related to integrity, accountability and transparency, independence, anti-violence, gender equality and financial management, including accountability to external parties such as beneficiaries, government, donors, other NGOs and the public at large. There are a number of points in the code of ethics that may be considered important to improve NGOs' accountability and transparency as non-profit organizations, including: first, an NGO is not established for the purpose of profit-making for its founders; second, an NGO is not established in the interests of its founders but is intended to serve the people and humanity; third, all information related to its mission, membership, activities and financing are basically of a public nature and is therefore available to the public; and fourth, an NGO utilizes bookkeeping and financial systems that are in accordance with acceptable accounting standards.

The NGOs participating in formulating the code of ethics also agreed to establish regional associations of NGOs, which are responsible for the implementation of the code, and to help NGOs in their capacity building. Future challenges for the NGOs that have accepted the code of ethics are how to apply it consistently in each organization and sanction those in violation, so it will not become merely an on-paper agreement.

NGO certification programme

Satunama, a Yogyakarta-based NGO that is active in education, training and management consultancy, has launched a programme called 'Certification of Indonesian NGOs'. The programme is intended to improve NGO public accountability and management performance in order to strengthen partners' trust in NGOs and to make NGOs capable of serving their advocated groups well (Satunama Foundation, 2002).

The programme began with a national seminar in Yogyakarta in November 2002, attended by 50 NGOs, all with 5 or more years of experience and from various provinces in Indonesia. The workshop produced a task force consisting of 12 NGO leaders to formulate future work programmes and prepare instruments required for a certification programme. During the preparation of the instruments, the programme received valuable input from the Philippine Council for NGO Certification (see Golub, Chapter 6).

The task force has formulated a programme vision and mission statement and is presently (2005) conducting a series of activities that include: the establishment of solid instruments, procedures and certification standards; a public campaign for NGO certification; the establishment of an NGO Certification Agency; advocacy campaigns for tax law reform and laws for the non-profit sector; and a programme designed for NGO capacity building and implementation of various types of technical assistance. It is recognized that the future central issue of the programme will be NGO accountability and transparency, with certification being one of the instruments that will be developed.

Civil Society Index

YAPPIKA, a national NGO alliance for civil society and democracy, implemented a programme starting in 2000 to assess the health of Indonesian civil society using the CIVICUS Index on Civil Society (www.civicus.org). The objectives of the assessment included increasing the knowledge and understanding of the status of civil society in Indonesia, empowering civil society stakeholders through dialogue and networking, and providing civil society with tools to analyse sector-wide strengths and weaknesses, as well as to develop strategies to foster positive social change (YAPPIKA, 2002; Suryaningati, 2003).

YAPPIKA organized participatory dialogues involving a wide spectrum of civil society organizations, as well as a number of key stakeholders, such as government officials, local parliament members and representatives from the private sector. The dialogue was conducted through a number of workshops in several provinces and involved more than 400 CSOs from all over Indonesia. The definition of civil society was debated, the CIVICUS analytical tools were reviewed and a number of indicators were formulated and analysed by participants to assess the level of CSO health. Five dimensions were analysed: first, the political and socio-economic context as the external environment in which civil society operates; second, the scope of CSOs, including the breadth and depth of citizen participation within civil society, its inter-relations and resources; third, values, norms and behaviours being promoted by CSOs; fourth, the relations of CSOs with the state and the market; and fifth, CSO contributions to the solutions of social, political and economic issues confronted by the nation. The results of the provincial Civil Society Index exercises were then discussed in a national seminar, resulting in a report on the status of Indonesian civil society and common strategies to increase CSO performance over the next five to ten years (Abidin and Rukmini, 2004).

HAPSARI women's association: From foundation to association

In 1990, four women from Sukasari Village, Kabupaten Deli Serdang, 60km from Medan (North Sumatra) established a working group called 'Village Women Working Group'. Each individual in the group began to interact with individuals and groups of women in their village and with groups from other villages to develop jointly a women's organization to strive for gender justice and equality. The method of work was through 'critical education' in the form of discussions to break the silence and to build awareness. Ideas about gender justice were disseminated to village communities through agriculture programmes managed by women or through the community radio station (Zailani, 2003).

In 1997, in order to obtain legal formal legitimacy, especially in relation to the government and to enable them to gain access to donor assistance, this working group transformed itself into a *yayasan*, a foundation. They invited a number of outsiders (men and women) who were concerned about gender equality to sit on the Board of Trustees.

In 1998 the HAPSARI Foundation carried out strategic planning to formulate the vision, mission and goals of the organization. Fifteen persons attended from the Board of Trustees, Executive Board, representatives from its beneficiaries and a number of NGOs that had working relations with HAPSARI. With its status as a foundation, HAPSARI obtained its formal legal legitimacy to move more freely within village communities and began to receive assistance from donor agencies.

But the leadership was, nevertheless, concerned about the top-driven character of the *yayasan* and the lack of a membership-based constituency. Like many other foundations in Indonesia after 1998, HAPSARI began to explore the possibility of establishing a mass-based organization. In due course, the women's groups nurtured by HAPSARI established an independent women's organization. In 1999 a Free Women's Association (Serikan Perempuan Independen) was founded in North Sumatra with 721 individual women members from the lower strata of the community, such as farm workers, plantation workers, fisherwomen and small vendors. Serikan Perempuan Independen was then divided into five districts/*Kabupaten* based working areas in North Sumatra. The function of the HAPSARI Foundation changed into providing funds, technical and moral support to these local Serikan Perempuan Independen branches to function effectively.

In September 2001, Serikan Perempuan Independen organized its first congress. The congress is the highest institution that formulates the vision and mission for the organization, as well as acts as an accountability and reflection mechanism for its members. It was agreed at this congress that each *Kabupaten* level organization was allowed to have its own structure and management, relatively independent of one another.

In November 2002, the HAPSARI Foundation produced a new organizational design and structure in response to the continuing changes in its working relationships with Serikan Perempuan Independen. All the local Serikan Perempuan Independen organizations came together and decided that HAPSARI should dissolve itself and become the secretariat for a Federation of Independent Women of North Sumatra. This federation functions as an umbrella organization of the local women's organizations mentioned before. The HAPSARI experience may become an example of how a non-membership NGO in the form of a *yayasan* can dissolve itself to become a broad-based membership organization and obtain better social legitimacy.

The Consortium for the Development of Civil Society

When Indonesia's first democratic elections were held in 1999, the country was literally flooded by funds and organizations supporting voters' education and election monitoring. With lots of energy and enthusiasm, thousands of NGOs entered into this field. While the majority did a good job making sure that the elections were free and fair, there were unfortunately also organizations that misused funds or were created only for the purpose of accessing donor funding.

Things were no different in the province of West Sumatra, where an estimated 50 NGOs were created simply to be able to get a share of the funds. A year after the elections, a dozen established regional NGOs came together in the provincial capital of Padang to try to address the lack of accountability among civil society organizations in the province. They created the Consortium for the Development of Civil Society (Konsorsium Pengembangan Masyarakat Madani or KPMM). During the past years, KPMM has developed a code of ethics and standard operational procedures for its membership organizations. But the struggle of KPMM is also a good measure of how difficult it is to promote issues of internal good governance among NGOs. Of the 12 organizations who founded KPMM in the year 2000, three have left the consortium since they felt that the code of ethics was too strict (such as a proposed ban on polygamy for NGO activists). And few new organizations have joined.

CHALLENGES FOR INDONESIAN NGOS

Indonesian NGOs are coming from a politically marginalized position, burdened with overblown expectations. While the number of NGOs has grown significantly since 1998 as part of a broader development in which Indonesian civil society is 'coming out of the closet', most NGOs have little experience in positively engaging with government, the corporate sector or other stakeholders. The *reformasi* period has established a new strategic environment for NGOs, considerably more complex and difficult to navigate than the simple pro- or contra Soeharto dichotomy that set the framework during the previous decades. Moreover, even though the new environment for civil society and NGOs is certainly more open in terms of access to information and possibilities to organize civil life, this is no guarantee for a welcome reception of NGO contributions to public and political discourse.

Several challenges remain that must be confronted by Indonesian NGOs for them to be an effective part of civil society. At the top of the list is a reformulation of NGO positions vis-à-vis the state (government) and various other sectors in society. With the emergence of democracy, power is no longer centralized but distributed among new power centers such as parliament, political parties and judicial institutions. The critical stance taken by some NGOs that consider themselves watchdog organizations towards all state institutions has been a tendency to disregard the real progress in the decentralization of power and democratization that has taken place. New local governments and local parliaments also need time to learn how to do their job. By the same token, NGOs are in a process of learning how their watchdog function is part of an equation in a process of creating checks and balances, and no longer suggests a self-standing political agenda. In addition, the role of public watchdog is no longer monopolized by NGOs, but is shared – and has to be shared – with other actors, foremost the media, but also academia and other civil society organizations.

Accusations against the political aspect in the NGO role remain, but are now made by political parties instead of the government. NGOs are still branded as agents of foreign interests and traders of poverty, especially due to the fact that there have been corrupt practices among NGOs themselves. Politicians have started to ask questions regarding NGO legitimacy and how much they really represent the interests of their constituents.

The situation seems to be unfavourable for the immediate future of the NGOs without a breakthrough in relations and interactions with the government and other sectors in society. There is a need for a genuine two-way dialogue with the government and the private sector to develop trust, as well as a common cause. This change from protest politics to developing strategies of engagement means bringing changes towards a better Indonesia through the process of lobbying and negotiations.

It is still early in the day, but there are indications that the positive role of NGOs in delivering emergency assistance in Aceh after the tsunami of December 2004 is opening some of these avenues for a more productive relationship between Indonesian NGOs and other actors. The necessary focus on quality of management and speed of delivery, yet in a difficult political context calling for close consultation and participation of local communities, is shared by NGOs and government in post-tsunami Aceh.

However, even if advocacy and watchdog functions are better balanced with effective service delivery, building a healthy NGO sector is not an easy task in a country with a strong predatory state and a weak and unaccountable civil society. Some of the lessons from the Indonesian case are the dangers of project- and donor-driven NGO development. Since donors have a tendency to work with articulate, efficient, centrally-located groups, rural mass-based movements are often out of the picture. There are very few alternative sources of income for the civil society sector today.

In order for the accountability and responsibility of NGOs to take root in Indonesia, there are a couple of preconditions. One is that funding agencies begin to realize that accountability is not only accounting; donors need to hold grantees to high standards of public accountability. It is also important that the philanthropic sector expands in Indonesia, so that civil society organizations in Indonesia become less dependent on foreign funds and in that process start to relate increasingly directly to Indonesian stakeholders, becoming more responsive to local developments.

NOTES

1   It is impossible to estimate the exact number of NGOs in Indonesia, since only those NGOs that are legal entities (normally foundations or *yayasan*) need to report their existence to the authorities.

2   During Soeharto's rule, Indonesian NGOs began to use the name *Lembaga Swadaya Masyarakat* (LSM) which means 'self-reliant community development institution'. The English term NGO was often interpreted as 'anti-government

institution'. This was especially related to the Soeharto regime's policy not to give room for any opposition. LSM is still commonly used, although some have changed to *Organisasi Non-Pemerintah* or ORNOP, which is the literal translation of 'NGO'.

3   There are a handful of good analytic studies of the NGO sector during the 1980s and 1990s. See, for example, Eldridge, 1995; Fakih, 1991; Uhlin, 1997; Hadiwinata, 2003.

4   The term has been coined in informal discourse among Indonesian NGO activists in the late 1980s, but to the best of our knowledge never made it into the academic literature.

5   However, we also need to recognize the ultimate lack of political impact of many civil society organizations. See the studies by Hadiz, 2003; Stanley et al, 2003.

6   Part of this section is based on opinions as expressed in a series of seminars on 'Developing Strong, Healthy, Democratic, Transparent and Accountable NGOs' held in eight provincial capitals in Indonesia from May to July 2002. Speakers from the government, private sector and donor agencies were invited to present their views on NGO roles. The seminars were organized by LP3ES, a national NGO based in Jakarta.

7   The disturbing exception has been the killing of Munir, Indonesia's foremost human rights activist, in September 2004. There are strong suspicions, but as yet no proof, of structured government involvement in ordering the assassination.

Section IV

INNOVATIONS: EXPANDING THE ACCOUNTABILITY FRONTIER

10

Chameleons and Accountability: Linking Learning with Increasing Accountability in ActionAid International Uganda and the Ugandan Land Alliance

Sarah Okwaare and Jennifer Chapman

In Kupsabiny, a kanunbut *(chameleon), with its distinctive rocking motion and swivelling eyes, is said to learn as it moves along.*

INTRODUCTION

Accountability has become a big issue in Uganda for both the government and civil society. Much of this debate centers around public policy where it focuses on tracking and eliminating corruption, ensuring transparent, effective and efficient use of public resources, promoting good governance and building systems of ethics and integrity in public life, as well as monitoring the implementation of Uganda's responsibilities under international laws and conventions.

Both the government and NGOs are seen to have roles in ensuring public sector accountability. The Ministry of Finance, Planning and Economic Development handles financial accountability, the Directorate of Ethics and Integrity works on anti-corruption, the Inspector General of Government looks at social accountability and the Ministry of Labour, Gender and Development looks at compliance by local government. Meanwhile, civil society is seen as having a watchdog role to complement all these other efforts. For example, the Ugandan Land Alliance (ULA) is monitoring the implementation of the Land Act at the community level and the Ugandan Debt Network is attempting to mobilize communities to participate in monitoring public expenditure and reject substandard public works. At the national level NGOs such as FIDA Uganda, Legal Aid Uganda, Uganda Human Rights Network and Uganda Women's Network are linking with bodies such as the Directorate of Ethics and Integrity and the Inspector General of Government to inform policy and anti-corruption activities. While public accountability remains problematic, these developments are going some way to promote public sector accountability in Uganda.

An area that in the past has received less attention is the accountability of NGOs themselves. NGOs in Uganda are strong, yet some would claim they exert power without responsibility – that their accountability to Ugandans in general is weak, and, in particular they lack accountability and transparency to the poor communities they claim as the reason for their existence.

Some organizations, such as ActionAid International Uganda (AAIU) have been trying to address this issue, but as this chapter shows it is not an easy path to follow.[1] Really working to strengthen NGO accountability to all stakeholders means also having to address difficult questions of power within and between organizations, financial dependency, working styles, organizational culture and leadership.

CHANGE IN ACTIONAID UGANDA

Background

ActionAid International Uganda started work in the 1980s at the end of the dictatorial regime of president Idi Amin Dada. Over time, the organization has undergone major changes, moving from a post-war welfare agency to an organization delivering services to poor communities in specific geographical areas, and later to an organization working within a rights framework where policy and advocacy are central strategies and work is increasingly carried out with and through partners spread over a much larger area of Uganda.

AAIU also operates in a wider context, both the changing context of the rest of ActionAid, an international NGO, and the changing political environment in Uganda. Events and trends in both contexts have affected the changes that took place in AAIU. The trend within ActionAid internationally has been from delivering needed services to marginalized communities to a rights-based approach that emphasizes working with partners on policy advocacy. This was captured in the 1999–2005 Strategy, 'Fighting Poverty Together' (ActionAid, 1999).

This coincided with changes within Uganda that provided a conducive environment for this new kind of work. It included opening up democratic space for NGOs to do policy and advocacy work under the regime of President Museveni[2] and the support of donors for advocacy work. In addition, the growth and development of local NGOs and CBOs had been going on for several years, making it possible for AAIU to find potential partners both at the national and local levels, such as the ULA, which was established in 1995 and which will form the focus of the case study later in this chapter.

The introduction of a decentralized system of governance by the regime of President Museveni led to district level planning and budgeting and opened up more participative ways of working within Uganda, creating opportunities for AAIU to build on at the district level. Processes such as the Uganda Participatory Poverty Assessment Project (a Poverty Reduction Strategy Paper (PRSP) initiative) opened up forums for poverty analysis and listening to the voices of the poor, claiming to ensure inclusion of the poor people's perspectives in policy processes for accountability, although some have questioned the value of civil society involvement in the PRSP process (Ocaya and Roden, 2004).

The main driver of change in AAIU was the new country director, who had experience of working with ActionAid and a good grasp of new developments within ActionAid International. She took advantage of the need to develop a new country strategy paper to manage the change process to make significant differences in the way AAIU worked.

The Accountability, Learning and Planning System[3]

At the same time as introducing 'Fighting Poverty Together', ActionAid introduced new internal systems intended to free up time and energy for learning and to strengthen accountability. In the past, ActionAid International, like many large NGOs, had rigid accountability and reporting systems characterized by central control and bureaucracy. The system was designed to meet upward accountability to managers, donors and sponsors, for which plans and budgets provided the framework. It did not facilitate accountability to partner and poor communities. Information was generated from the community, processed by the fieldworkers and then sent to the managers, who eventually sent it to donors and sponsors. Despite the fact that staff had much knowledge to share, the reporting system did not foster learning and there was no space to reflect, interact and share with one another. Instead, there was a lot of emphasis on written information in limited copies, and the mode of communication was written English, which could not be easily accessed by partners and communities. Poor communities, the reason for the work, never got to discuss, learn or contribute to discussion and reports on issues that affected their lives.

A long process of internal dialogue and discussion, drawing on many years of experience from different country programmes[4] led to the design of a new system – the ActionAid Accountability, Learning and Planning System (ALPS) (ActionAid Uganda, 1999):

> *ALPS recognizes that social development, rights or social justice cannot be planned for, managed and delivered in a linear fashion. It recognizes that the principles and attitudes and the ways in*

GUIDING PRINCIPLES OF **ALPS**

- ALPS strengthens ActionAid's main accountability, which is to the poor and marginalized women, men, boys and girls, and our partners with whom we and they work.
- ALPS work to strengthen ActionAid's commitment to gender equity.
- ALPS applies to the whole organization at all levels and covers horizontal and downward relationships.
- ALPS information must be relevant and useful to the people who produce it, receive it and who need it to make decisions. It should be written in the language spoken by the majority of the users and translated, usually in summary form, where necessary. It must be approved, in most cases, only one level up line management.
- ALPS requires that the information provider must receive feedback. Approvals should be given in a non-bureaucratic manner.
- ALPS aims to make best use of staff time by cutting down on the amount of written information needed. It also promotes learning, which in turn improves skills and programme quality.
- ALPS recognizes the need to relate financial expenditure to programme quality.
- ALPS promotes critical reflection that enables us to learn not only from our successes but also our failures.
- It recognizes that procedures are important but so is discretion, sensibly exercised and properly and openly communicated.

Source: ActionAid (2000)

---

which we do things are more important than plans and reports. To carry out ActionAid's new strategy space needed to be created for ActionAid staff to reflect and work in a different way with their partners and poor people. Attitudes, behaviours and principles were therefore fundamental to ALPS. (Chapman et al, 2004)

ALPS makes it clear that ActionAid's primary stakeholders are the poor people we are trying to help, and that as an organization we need to put more effort into ensuring balanced accountability to them as well as donors. In order to do this, ALPS opens up space for community and partners to be more involved in planning, monitoring and reviewing programs and learning about the value of our work. Transparency is also seen as a key element of becoming more accountable to the communities with which we work. It requires ActionAid to begin sharing information more openly and encourages us to move towards a time when the community groups with whom we work are actively involved in planning, budgeting, assessing the value of our interventions and participating in the recruitment of front line staff.

The organizational development process[5]

The end of the 1990s was a turning point for AAIU as an organization and for its staff as individuals. The new country director, Meenu Vadera, faced the task of leading an organization needing to come to terms with a parent organization that was changing fast and that was making new demands and expecting new types of work, combined with a quickly changing Ugandan context. She was keen to restructure and refocus AAIU to ensure that it became a flexible organization, able to work in new ways and meet these new challenges. Meenu initiated an organizational development process that aimed to address the need for change and enable staff to see change as normal and part of the growth of an organization, rather than a threat to be resisted.

The country director rooted the process in a leadership team that shared a common vision and represented all aspects of the organization, hence from the start the work was carried out with a large group of AAIU leaders. The process was supported by an organizational development specialist who facilitated discussions with key staff on how to proceed. The specialist emphasized the need for a new vision, for developing strategic approaches to work and for finding ways to reflect and deepen understanding of the way the organization worked. He addressed issues of leadership and the need to develop capacity for continuous learning. The issues were less about what structures to set up and more about relationships, leadership styles and ways of working.

The staff were supported to analyse what they did in the field and what was and was not working well. They were also supported to explore relations with ActionAid beyond Uganda. The process involved extended discussions in different teams – the field team, the thematic and the enabling teams around the same set of issues, to give people room to express different views and opinions, and to allow disagreement and questioning. Some staff found the questioning difficult and expressed feelings of disempowerment and confusion, but this approach signalled the start of a critical process of identifying issues and areas of agreement and shared thinking, as well as areas of conflict that form an essential element of change.

One thing that emerged clearly from this initial stage was that AAIU:

> *had a highly skilled, perceptive and well trained staff, yet they were not fulfilling their potential. The organization was hierarchical and fragmented, with staff working in tight teams with little horizontal communication, relying on instructions and memos to do their work. There was little questioning or discussion about ways of working; these were driven by extensive systems of top down management, accounting and reporting.*
> (Wallace and Kaplan, 2003)

It was clear that this culture of working was not going to allow strengthened accountability to communities and partners.

A change process was then began with some initial structural changes:

> *designed to breakdown the separate hierarchies and draw the organization into one functioning whole. A major shift was to understand all the functions of AAIU as inter-related, represented by an overlapping structure of three circles, each representing a different team. The work of the field, thematic and enabling teams was clearly seen as inter-related and complementary, not separate and in competition. The over-arching focus for these changes was to improve the quality of AAIU's work on the ground; regionalization was started with discussions focusing on the roles and responsibilities of leaders and teams within the new three-circle structure.* (Wallace and Kaplan, 2003)

Regionalization led to the devolution of decision-making and resources to the lower level to enable AAIU to serve the community better.

Country programme ten-year review[6]

All ActionAid country programmes are required to undertake periodic reviews involving external input. The Uganda Country Programme Review took place in 1999 and was carefully planned to complement the organizational development process that had already started. The country director sourced a consultant whose skills she felt would complement the organizational development work, and who could challenge staff and deepen their analysis in learning from the past to manage a change process. The review looked at how far AAIU had achieved its goals and whether these goals, which had been set five years earlier, were still relevant in the fast changing context of Uganda. The core review team was made up of three AAIU staff and the consultant acting as trainer, facilitator and outside questioner, and was carried out in a participatory manner. The emphasis was on asking the organization hard questions and on opening the organization up for critique by others.

According to the report, 'it was a challenging and exciting experience for everyone involved. The internal team drew lessons from each other, from their field visits, and from discussions with an external person; they developed critical questioning skills during the process. For the consultant it was informative to work with people who had a deep understanding of the programmes' (Wallace, 2001).

The internal members of the review team found it difficult at times to undergo the extensive questioning of their own and their team's work. However, as a result of this methodology the review was in touch with local realities and rooted in AAIU. In addition, the team developed their understanding of issues and changes needed in the organization, and an ability to undertake critical analysis and ask difficult questions. Unfortunately, only one person from the team remains with AAIU at the time of writing.

A key reason for designing the review in this manner was that the country director did not want AAIU to follow directives from outside the country unthinkingly (for example, the wider ActionAid strategy, 'Fighting Poverty Together') or concepts drawn from other contexts, but for staff to develop their own analysis and understanding of the need for change. Although many of the findings were very challenging to AAIU staff, they eventually accepted them because they came from their peers and a participatory process in which they were all involved.

The review did not make recommendations, but it presented the challenges facing AAIU and provided opportunities to discuss them during the subsequent strategic planning process. Critical issues raised included that while AAIU had done much interesting and innovative work, there was little cross learning between the older, more established work in defined geographical areas (development areas) and the newer thematic work. New initiatives were often undertaken with little coordination leading to work being fragmented, work overload and a lack of clear focus. As a result, staff were very activity focused, paying little attention to learning or understanding changes in the external context. AAIU paid little attention to other development work in Uganda and did not review or update the Country Strategy Paper.

Staff tended to work in their local areas, but little value was given to their local knowledge, which was often overridden by organization policies and procedures. Staff followed orders and were not empowered to take independent decisions or challenge approaches even where they knew work was not locally relevant.

AAIU road to change

At the end of both exercises a forum was organized for all staff to hear feedback from both consultants. This meeting was characterized by heated arguments. Some found it very difficult to hear their work criticized, particularly as the critique was endorsed by their peers. Some were angry that despite their conviction that they were doing useful work, things were being changed. Others were hostile towards the leadership that suddenly expected them to make bigger decisions and take on new responsibilities. Working with partners was the biggest challenge and frustration to AAIU staff.

In the words of Allan Kaplan, one critical moment was when people were asked to perform a role-play of how they saw their roles in the organization. Many strong images of being subservient, followers, unquestioning doers were presented, the most memorable being the image of AAIU staff as 'African cows following their leader in and out of the homestead every day, unquestioning, uncomplaining and obedient' (Wallace and Kaplan, 2003).

The task was immense: 'moving an organizational culture from one able and willing to do what was asked of it, to carry out orders, to undertake myriad and multiple activities without asking questions to a responsive, questioning, thinking and learning organization' (Wallace and Kaplan, 2003).

Nevertheless, some agreed parameters were outlined for the next strategic plan signaling major changes for AAIU.

Changes involved scaling down service delivery and scaling up rights-based, policy and advocacy work, and working in partnerships as clearly spelled out in the new country strategy paper. This new strategic direction echoed many of the changes being undertaken at the global level, but represented a huge shift for AAIU, one rooted in learning from their own past work and their own analysis of causes and symptoms of poverty in Uganda.

Kanambut: AAIU's accountability, learning and planning system

ALPS provides an overall framework and general principles for ActionAid International to follow in planning, learning and accountability. However, just as AAIU felt it necessary to develop their own country strategy rooted in their own experience and reflection, they also wanted to develop their own version of ALPS that would be owned by their staff, rather than unquestioningly follow systems developed elsewhere. Thus Kanambut is a localized version of ALPS. It arose from realization that AAIU's prior planning and reporting system, rather than helping to achieve its mission, on many occasions acted as a constraint. As remarked by one staff member: 'We prefer being busy rather than reflecting', unlike our partners in Kapchorwa who refer in their Kupsabiny language to a kanambut (a chameleon), as an animal which is said to learn as it moves along.

The changes and new developments that were taking place in AAIU quickened the process of developing Kanambut because of the accountability and learning issues that emerged. Kanambut was thus meant to foster learning, trust and self-confidence, rather than accountability towards hierarchical superiors; to foster multiple accountability and to ensure that AAIU systems were in tune with our principles and policies, such as the gender policy (ActionAid Uganda, 2002a).

Principles in Kanambut promoting change in AAIU

The following principles underpin Kanambut (ActionAid Uganda, 2002a):

- *Learning* – should be central to the process. This might include issues of best practice, challenges, failures and measuring change, both qualitative and quantitative.
- *Confidence-building and not extracting* – the system should foster participation, creativity and feedback, and be empowering to users.
- *Horizontal and vertical relationships* – vertical and horizontal (for instance between colleagues) information collection, analysis, use and sharing should be encouraged to ensure efficiency, effectiveness and openness.
- *Trust* – information, whether written or oral, should foster trust. It is also important to collect and share information that is reliable to avoid

mistrust. Similarly, information collection and dissemination should be done in an ethical manner.

- *Explicit gender perspective* – it is important to be specific as to how the information collected, used and shared clearly relates to the lives of women, boys, girls and men.
- *'Downward' and 'outward' accountability* – the information collected should be such that it can flow back to the community who has contributed to it. Partners should be able to identify with and understand this information.
- *Really needed and relevant* – to avoid information overload, information should only be collected and shared if deemed necessary to the intended users.
- *Accessible* (simple, retrievable, user-friendly) information that satisfies intended customers/clients – the information collected should be user-friendly to women and men across all generations and poverty categories. It should take into account the educational and conceptual levels of the various categories of intended users. We should therefore avoid jargon and language that might marginalize users. This might mean using different languages and different media to communicate.
- *Cost effective/time effective* – information should be collected in the shortest possible time so that action can be taken as soon as possible. Simple procedures help to reduce costs and are generally more effective.
- *Adequately processed at each level* – analysis and feedback should take place at the very levels where information is needed. It needs to be presented in a way that these levels can manage.

Changes brought by Kanambut

Since 2001 when Kanambut was introduced, modest but significant changes have been made. Perhaps the most important change has been the acceptance and internalization of Kanambut and what it stands for. Along with the then ActionAid global strategy 'Fighting Poverty Together' and ALPS, Kanambut came to be seen as a key reference document throughout AAIU. It is something that AAIU staff aspire to achieve, particularly its principles.

Kanambut creates space for people's striving to learn. It offers teams the possibility to challenge themselves to improve the quality of their work. It brought a lot of innovative learning approaches, including Participatory Review and Reflection Processes (PRRPs), learning diaries, mentors, intranet, working groups and quarterly reporting. PRRPs stood out as the most popular learning approach and were widely translated into action in both the organization and among partners. They therefore form the main discussion in this section.

Each unit of AAIU, together with partners and stakeholders, engages in annual reflection, learning and planning through a PRRP. These annual review exercises use participatory and other relevant techniques to ensure that the learning points represent the views of all our stakeholders. Quarterly fora and reporting also feed into this annual process. Annual learning and reporting focus on an assessment and sharing of learning from progress made against the annual plans and the country strategy to increase our accountability to stakeholders. Lessons learned from our achievements and failures facilitate and feed into the development of plans for the following years.

The introduction of PRRPs has led to a marked shift in the way ActionAid documents its work. Previously ActionAid programme reports concentrated on activities. Currently, reports are more concise and give more emphasis to the changes AAIU and its partners have brought about in people's lives. This is reinforced by the involvement of stakeholders in many review processes, which led to the refocusing of analysis on what is important in people's lives and learning from the community how best to address their needs and tell them the kinds of changes we are making. PRRP learning forms the bulk of the information for plans and budget reviews.

The introduction of Kanambut has created a much greater degree of self-questioning and openness about difficult development issues, which is evident in almost every report presented. Staff are no longer simply reporting on activities, but delve into what they do, question why and how much their work is appreciated, understood or seen as relevant by those they are working with. Furthermore, through the different meeting foras, the system has encouraged greater participation, improved our analysis of power and gender, enhanced a culture of transparency and openness, and increased our accountability to poor people, partners and other stakeholders. The following is an excerpt from an AAIU PRRPs report, the 2004 Partner Review Forum:

> *A national partners' forum was convened and most of the Development Initiative partners, partners at the regions, and national level partners and government representatives came together for a two-day meeting. The partners discussed the quality of support from AAIU, and their perspectives of the outcomes of their rights-based advocacy and policy work in partnership with AAIU. The partners discussed relationship between them and AAIU, discussed their limited understanding of rights-based and advocacy work and the need for capacity building with support from AAIU. They particularly said that AAIU should carry out needs assessment in the different organizations to assess the magnitude of the capacity support needed. This time round, key issues mentioned by partners were lack of support by the frontline officers who were reported that they visited partners sometimes only once a year. They also mentioned that AAIU in many cases emphasised results and forgot to attach value to process outcomes. They complained of lack of communication and explanation on budget cuts. The problems caused by delays in the disbursement of funds were also emphasized. Some of the issues were news to the AAIU leadership team who took serious note of the concerns. Action points were jointly*

developed to minimize the problems and responsibility attached to either the partners or AAI. In this forum, partners are holding the AAIU staff accountable. (ActionAid Uganda, 2004)

Kanambut emphasizes accountability to poor people and communities. When working through partners, this may imply making additional demands on partners. In some cases, ActionAid's motivation for this has been mistrusted. Initially many of the NGO partners showed resistance towards this mode of review involving the community (ActionAid Uganda, 2002b). They perceived it as a form of policing/inspecting by ActionAid stemming from the international level. Some of the partners even accused AAIU of not having trust in their report and hence involving the community in the review process. However, slowly the partners are beginning to appreciate the learning events because they are increasingly demanding them.

Financial transparency

Despite financial transparency being particularly challenging, AAIU has started work towards increasing downward accountability and transparency through greater involvement of finance staff in participatory review processes. AAIU Development Initiative annual PRRPs include partners and other stakeholders we work with, such as local government councilors and district government officials from various departments, especially education and health. At these meetings ActionAid staff share annual reports, plans and budgets for the different sectors. Participants are given space to ask ActionAid staff necessary questions. Events have led to AAIU building capacities of its staff in participatory planning with the local government. In some cases government officials have started to demand serious accountability and transparency from AAIU partners and other NGOs working in the districts.

The chapter so far has looked at changes in AAIU in both culture and systems. However, one of the key differences in our work now is that the majority of it is done through partners. Kanambut both challenges us to increase our accountability to these partners, but also, in turn, to support them in becoming more open, accountable and reflective organizations. The final section of this chapter looks at what this has meant in practice within the partnership between AAIU and the Ugandan Land Alliance.

INCREASING ACCOUNTABILITY
IN PARTNERSHIP WITH THE ULA

Background

The ULA was set up in January 1995 and is a consortium of 67 NGOs (including AAIU) and 10 individuals. ULA's mission is to ensure that land policies and laws address the land rights of the poor and protect access to land for vulnerable and disadvantaged groups and individuals. They are involved in advocacy, public dialogue, awareness-raising, research, documentation and monitoring of the implementation of policies and structures. A key approach is to ensure that the voices of the marginalized are central to their advocacy.

Equitable access and ownership of land is a key challenge in Uganda because more than 80 per cent of the country's population is involved in agriculture and other land-based activities. By far the most significant recent event in the country with respect to land has been the enactment of the Land Act in 1998, on which the ULA had an influence. This gave some security of tenure to the people of Uganda, by putting in place a system that catered for individual land rights. For example, squatters who had lived unchallenged on land for over 12 years automatically became its bona fide occupants.

But changing laws is a very different thing from ensuring they are implemented, especially when they run counter to traditional ways of doing things. It was clear to the ULA that the Land Act in itself was not going to make much difference to most poor or marginalized men and women in remote areas of Uganda who were unlikely ever to hear about it. Informing rural communities of their new rights and helping the marginalized claim these rights thus became a new focus of work for the ULA.

ULA, in partnership with its members, established a number of land rights information centers at the district level as the nearest information points to the poor men, women and children at the grassroots level, and recruited two volunteers (paralegals) per sub-county to act as agents of change in the community.

The concept of paralegals is embedded in the idea of 'barefoot lawyers'. In this model, paralegals are teams of people, both men and women, selected and recommended by the community and trained in land related laws, in particular the Land Act of 1998, human rights issues, mediation skills, planning, monitoring and evaluation and gender analysis. If a land dispute arises in the community, either party can approach a paralegal of their choice, who will then attempt to reach an agreement between the parties by mediation. If the matter cannot be resolved or the case is beyond their jurisdiction or knowledge, they refer it to the Land Rights Information Centres. In many cases paralegals are successful in resolving disputes on site. The community play an important role during the mediation process by acting as witnesses, observing and monitoring the case, seeing how certain local traditions run counter to the law and learning how the law might apply to other cases in the local area. Individual cases thus have the potential to lead to a multiplier effect.

At the same time the community also has the opportunity to monitor the quality of the work being done by paralegals, thus acting as an incentive for them to perform better. If the community feels the paralegal is not working well, they can bypass her and take their case straight to the Land Rights Information Centre, who would then demand an explanation from the paralegal who should have handled the case.

The Land Rights Centres, supported by the paralegals, also disseminate information on land related laws and educate the community on their land rights, empowering them to demand and defend their rights as well as challenge issues from an informed point of view. This is achieved through parish and village meetings. The Centres also monitor the implementation of the Land Act of 1998, identifying gaps and emerging issues. For example, information from them has led the ULA to realize that the clause they are promoting on the co-ownership of land may not benefit the majority of rural women who have a customary marriage and live under the customary land tenure system. Members of the Alliance are now carrying out research to ascertain the relevance of the clause.

Accountability and learning processes introduced

Between 2001 and 2005, ActionAid and the ULA undertook action research to improve the accountability, learning and planning systems of the ULA.[7] During this time the two organizations worked intensively with the Kapchorwa Land Rights Centre in Eastern Uganda.

An initial activity was an orientation workshop at the Land Rights Centre that brought together staff from the ULA, AAIU and the Land Rights Centre, along with paralegals and others working on land issues at the grassroots. This explored the paralegals' work and potential entry points for better understanding and increasing accountability. This was a new approach because previous meetings had focused on training the paralegals or telling them how their role would work. This was the first time that the focus had shifted to listening to the way they viewed their work and their preoccupations and concerns.

One of the main concerns raised by the paralegals at this initial workshop was that they did not have a good idea as to how their work was viewed by the local communities. The paralegals demanded that AAIU/ULA go to the community to learn how the community view their work in terms of their roles, skills and quality. They also urged the development of monitoring indicators with the community to gain insights into the longevity of the land settlements reached by paralegals.

Community view of paralegal work

Community reviews were subsequently carried out on a pilot basis in three sub-counties. Each team included the Land Rights Centre desk officer, the programme officer from the ULA, an AAIU programme officer and two paralegals drawn from a different sub-county. The aim was to allow some element of peer review, while at the same time allowing for a capacity building exercise for the paralegals involved.

For the first time communities had an opportunity to comment directly on what they thought of the paralegals and ensure that the emerging issues were taken into account by ULA/AAIU. The community was able to say whether they appreciated the paralegals and how their service could improve.

The overwhelming conclusion was that those who had witnessed and benefited from paralegal work appreciated their role, especially their skills and manner of handling cases. Community members preferred the service of the paralegals to other avenues open for resolving land disputes. They said that paralegals objectively investigated land cases and used the law fairly to resolve most of them. Many poor men, women and children had benefited from the services through the interpretation of land laws, empowering them on their land rights through education. Poor women in the community, especially widows, specifically said they preferred support from paralegals over taking their cases to the local council courts (the government administrative unit at village level) and the clan leaders because the paralegals handled cases with due regard to their rights as women.[8] They said that the clan leaders were not objective because they resolved cases depending on one's status and tended to favour the rich. According to the community, clan leaders used the tradition to exploit the poor and the vulnerable. The categories most affected in communities were the widows and the orphans because traditionally they are not entitled to own land:

> *My children and I were helpless upon the death of my dear husband. My in-laws sold off our land without our knowledge and we only realized this when the buyer came to evict us. However, with paralegal support, we were able to get back our land and are now more confident and sure of how to defend our property.* (Felitus Kures, widow)

The community indicated that the situation was worse with the local councils because they are politically elected in office and, as such, tend to serve the interest of their supporters against those who opposed them during the elections. In addition, there is a heavy court fee of USh5000 (US$2.50) for a file to be opened. The reviews revealed that the poor at times forwent their rights to land because they were unable to raise the court fee. One woman was quoted to have said, 'let the land go' because she could not raise the court fee. Because of this the free service offered by the paralegals is very much appreciated: 'The paralegals are our saviour especially for us who cannot afford the local council 1 court fees of USh5000' (Tongo, a middle-aged man).

Because of the good services the paralegals were offering, the community clearly expressed their desire for more paralegals to promote the rights of the poor, stating that in most cases there were not enough paralegals to cover all the villages. In one community visited, the respondents complained of lack of support from a particular paralegal and therefore recommended that a new active and capable person be identified to replace her.

Paralegal review and reflection forum

After the community review, the paralegals who took part requested ULA to organize a forum where all paralegals from the Kapchorwa Land Rights Centre could meet, share experiences, learn and forge a way forward. They also wanted an opportunity to air the challenges they encounter in the process of doing their work at all levels. Concern was expressed that some of the land cases mediated by them are not honored, due to lack of recognition, while some paralegals felt they had inadequate skills. During the review and reflection process the following were suggested:

- quarterly refresher courses for paralegals in, for example, alternative dispute resolution skills, the Land Act, report writing;
- an official launch of paralegal activities in their respective sub-counties to ensure communities and authorities know about their role;
- joint workshops, seminars, meetings among the paralegals, district land board and tribunals, police, magistrates and other stakeholders like Local Councils, chiefs, clan leaders, opinion leaders, and so on; and
- regular follow-up and monitoring of paralegal work by the Land Rights Desk officer.

Most of the issues raised were incorporated in the AAIU/ ULA work plan and some of them have already been implemented, such as training on report writing.

CONCLUSIONS

During the action research a number of innovations were introduced by the ULA with support from AAIU to increase the ULA's own accountability to its stakeholders, particularly the paralegals and the communities in which they work. This work has begun to show interesting results in terms of giving both communities and paralegals a meaningful voice within the ULA. However, it has been very demanding of staff time, calling for a lot of hands on work and facilitation.

This kind of opening up of the work of the paralegals to questioning and challenge by the communities, and the exposure of the joint work of the ULA and AAIU to questioning and challenge by both the paralegals and communities, would not have been possible in the hierarchical organization that AAIU used to be. AAIU has come a long way, but challenges remain.

There remain power issues in relationships where one partner is a conduit for funding to the other. Full openness and accountability in this situation is difficult. We still have further to go in fully sharing information about plans, expenditures and budgets with our partners and the poor and marginalized groups, and further to go in ensuring that poor and marginalized groups and the paralegals have a say in the performance appraisal and training of ULA and AAIU field staff, not just in commenting on the performance and training of the paralegals.

It is clear also that this sort of change in culture needs strong supportive leadership from the top and a clear indication that accountability and learning are taken seriously. After this work started, there was a long gap between one country director leaving and another one being recruited, and many senior staff left AAIU leading to a gap in leadership for a while and much of the progress made was lost. Similarly, within ULA there has been a knowledge gap in the innovations within the organization as a result of changes in leadership. This has to some extent, created negative repercussions in terms of relationships between AAIU and its partners.

The Kanambut system within AAIU catalyzed by the country review, organizational development process and action research project has created space for participation and questioning in AAIU and its partners. The staff and partners have the space to challenge themselves to improve the quality of their work. There is notable improvement in terms of communication, transparency and accountability around our work.

However, we still have the challenge of implementing and making ALPS and Kanambut work fully. Ensuring that participation is meaningful and useful remains challenging. The question of power issues between AAIU and the partners we work with, considering that we are donors to most of them, makes the level of transparency, accountability and participation limited and questionable. We still have a long way to go in learning how to share financial information in an empowering manner with communities. At the same time, ActionAid needs to deal with the reporting requirements of donors that may contradict the spirit of ALPS and Kanambut.

Overall, there have been signs of progress and elements of success. AAIU needs to put in more effort in building staff capacity in order to change their rigid attitude from the old ways of thinking in monitoring and evaluation towards having open minds, being ready to provide space and lend a listening ear to communities and partners, as well as donors.

NOTES

1   For the majority of this case study ActionAid Uganda was a country programme of ActionAid. Since 2004, ActionAid has joined with other linked organizations to form ActionAid International, which is the term used in this chapter.

2   This chapter was written in 2004 and therefore does not take into account recent political developments in Uganda.

3   A full description of ALPS can be found in Chapman (2003).

4   A full description of this process can be found in Scott-Villiers (2002).

5   This section draws heavily on Kaplan (2001) and Wallace and Kaplan (2003).

6   This section draws heavily on Wallace and Kaplan (2003) and Wallace (2001).

7   The work in Uganda was part of a larger action research to develop systems for planning, learning and accountability in rights-based advocacy work. The resource pack developed can be downloaded from www.actionaid.org/index.asp?page_id=773.

8   In Uganda in most cultures women are traditionally not supposed to inherit property such as land. The constitution of Uganda and the Land Act provide for equality: everyone has a right to own/inherit property. However, the traditional ways of doing things have been internalized by communities, especially men.

11

NGO Accountability and the Humanitarian Accountability Partnership: Towards a Transformative Agenda

Agnès Callamard

INTRODUCTION

The pilot phase of the Humanitarian Accountability Project International (HAP) was launched at the beginning of 2001 by a number of humanitarian agencies concerned with the lack of accountability towards crisis-affected communities. HAP was the last one of a series of initiatives within the humanitarian community that, spread over the 1990s, sought to address collectively the accountability changes and challenges faced by the sector. Their birth came about as a result of a major human disaster: the genocide in Rwanda, which placed a harsh light on certain humanitarian practices and highlighted the weaknesses and shortcomings of a system almost solely regulated through and by the good intentions of its actors.

The Joint Evaluation of the International Response to the Genocide in Rwanda is often seen as a turning point in the increased awareness of accountability and quality within the humanitarian sector (Steering Committee of the Joint Evaluation of Emergency Assistance to Rwanda, 1996). Shortly after its publication, a number of humanitarian organizations came together and initiated various joint projects, aiming to implement one or several recommendations from the Rwanda evaluation. Responses were diverse and rich, ranging from improving evaluations to the development of humanitarian standards, better management practices and a stronger commitment to accountability, including to donors and to a lesser extent to the beneficiaries of humanitarian assistance. The responses included the Sphere project, focusing on collective standard-setting for the sector; People in Aid, aiming at strengthening people's management through a code of conduct and rigorous monitoring; and the establishment of the Active Learning Network for Accountability and Performance in Humanitarian Action (ALNAP), which spearheaded the improvements in evaluation standards of the 1990s through innovative research and lesson sharing.

Attempts were also made to implement the accountability-related recommendations and to establish an independent humanitarian accountability mechanism. The recommendation was carried forward in the United Kingdom, initially as the Humanitarian Ombudsman Project. At an international conference in Geneva in March 2000 it was realized that an international ombudsman was not the way forward, but that there was a genuine interest in some form of an institutionalized accountability mechanism. Thus, the Humanitarian Accountability Project was born, its aim to identify, test and recommend a variety of accountability approaches.

The attacks of September 11, 2001 in the US and the resulting so-called 'war on terror' have added another layer of complexity and challenges to the search for stronger accountability in the context of humanitarian assistance. One may even argue that it is the very existence of the humanitarian project as we have known it (maybe the humanitarian project of the first generation) that is now being challenged, rather than certain practices. Indeed, the interventions in Afghanistan and Iraq have resulted in the further appropriation of the 'humanitarian' concept and work by actors that had been perceived until then as acting at the periphery of humanitarian actions, including armies, politicians and the private sector.

The initiatives and projects created in the late 20th century aimed to challenge certain humanitarian practices. From this standpoint, they had a 'betterment' objective. What may be required now, in view of the new context, is a transformative agenda. Over the first three years of its existence, HAP-I contributed in many ways towards the betterment objective and in a smaller fashion towards a transformative agenda.[1]

HAP DEFINITION OF ACCOUNTABILITY AND DUTY-BEARERS

HAP's first contribution to the betterment objective consisted in moving away from a definition of accountability privileging a technical and self-referential reading of accountability to one that encompasses affected populations. Traditionally, accountability has been defined as the duty to provide an account. According to Edwards and Hulme, 'accountability is generally defined as the means by which individuals and organizations report to a recognized authority, or authorities, and are held responsible for their actions' (Edwards and Hulme, 1995). Another operational framework of accountability includes an added dimension. This dimension suggests that to enable power-holders or duty-holders to account for their actions, there must be preliminary steps undertaken that allow citizens, staff, service users and others to ask questions or report complaints (Callamard, 2001). Therefore, the definition of accountability adopted by HAP includes two sets of principles: individuals, organizations and states must account for their actions and be held responsible for them; and individuals, organizations and states must be able, safely and legitimately, to report concerns, complaints and abuses, and get redress where appropriate.

The operationalization of these principles was summarized through a framework with five main elements:

1   *Who is accountable?* Duty-bearers with a responsibility towards crisis-affected populations. These include: governments, armed forces, NGOs, the International Red Cross/Red Crescent Movement and United Nations agencies.
2   *To whom?* Duty-bearers are accountable, first and foremost, to the populations and individuals affected by disaster and conflict. They are also accountable to their staff and donors.
3   *For what?* To meet responsibilities as defined by international legal standards, ethical principles, and professional, agency or inter-agency codes, standards or guidelines.
4   *How?* Through establishing mechanisms of accountability at field, headquarters and inter-agency levels. These include: setting standards and indicators, monitoring activities, investigating complaints, reporting to stakeholders and identifying duty-holders.
5   *For what outcomes?* Changes in programmes and operations, sanctions, recognition, awards and redress.

One evident consequence of the definition and framework adopted is that while HAP recognized that governments remain the primary duty-bearers in humanitarian operations, it also considers that other actors, including humanitarian organizations, carry a set of responsibilities too.

Traditionally, public international law has focused almost exclusively on the actions of states or state agents. However, there have been instances where non-state actors have also been included. Examples of this include the international treaties to end slavery, which prohibit the actions of individuals, in particular slave traders (International Council on Human Rights Policy, 2002). Interpretations of international human rights law have also held governments responsible for their failure to act with due diligence vis-à-vis the actions of private individuals or institutions (Amnesty International, 2000; 2001). In these instances they have also been found directly responsible for the activities carried out by these non-state actors when they have contracted out or delegated activities to these actors.[2]

The Committee on the Rights of the Child in its 2002 discussion on the private sector as service providers insisted on the primary responsibility of the state for compliance with the provisions of the Convention on the Rights of the Child.[3] In particular, states were deemed to have an obligation to set standards in conformity with the Convention and ensure compliance through the implementation of appropriate monitoring of institutions, services and facilities of both public and private actors. But the Committee also called on all non-state providers to respect the principles and provisions of the Convention. It encourages non-state service providers to ensure that service provision is carried out in accordance with international standards, especially to the Convention. It further encourages non-state service providers to develop self-regulation mechanisms, which would include a system of checks and balances. Non-state actors have also been found to be directly responsible, including under international human rights law (International Council on Human Rights Policy, 2002). Hence, the activities of multinational corporations and other businesses have been assessed for their compatibility with human rights.

AFFECTED COMMUNITIES AT THE CENTRE FOR THE HUMANITARIAN ETHOS

HAP's second contribution to the betterment objective is that it has placed accountability to affected communities at the centre of its concern. As highlighted above, within the disaster relief and humanitarian sectors the questions regarding the legal and ethical responsibilities of organizations vis-à-vis affected populations have tended to be overlooked or overshadowed by another set of relationships, namely, between the humanitarian organization, on the one hand and donors and the host state, on the other hand.

HAP argued that the dominant and unquestioned message of the heroic Western intervener saving the lives of hapless (non-Western) victims is both problematic and inappropriate to address the present and future challenges confronted by humanitarian agencies. It sustains images, jargon and practices that borrow heavily from the military sector (while the blurring has been made worse by the increasing insecurity, it did not originate there). Most importantly, HAP argued, the message is exclusively self-referential. The humanitarian ethos cannot remain defined through and by one single actor (the intervener), but must take its moral cue from those suffering and surviving crisis situations (Slim, 1997).

HAP trial field operations in Sierra Leone, Afghanistan and Cambodia sought to place the affected communities squarely at the centre of its work and approaches. How it was done varied from one trial effort to the next. The differences were all based on the commitment and decision to build the next model on the basis of the evaluation and learning from the previous one. From this standpoint, the thorough evaluation and critical assessment by the various HAP teams were essential in ensuring that HAP learned from its experiences and moved from one approach to another. On the basis of its findings and evaluations, the humanitarian accountability project progressively moved from being and testing the accountability mechanism (the constable in Sierra Leone) to supporting agencies in setting up or strengthening their own accountability mechanisms (Cambodia). The Afghanistan trial served as the connection or transition between the two approaches.

THE HAP MODEL TESTED IN THREE COUNTRIES

Sierra Leone (December 2001–May 2002)

HAP was composed of nine international and national staff and consultants. The team tested a constable or trouble-shooter model out of Port Loko (Christoplos, 2002a). It investigated a number of accountability issues and sought to provide rapid redress to humanitarian claimants by approaching possible field-based duty-bearers. The HAP team worked mostly at field level, rather than at the level of the capital city and its main level of engagement was with fieldworkers.

On the positive side, HAP was welcomed in Sierra Leone. By raising day-to-day accountability issues, HAP efforts provided some redress to affected communities, while the majority of fieldworkers found the existence of HAP 'eyes and ears' useful and helpful. It was also found that the HAP constable could stimulate local-level changes and learning. The limited involvement with agencies at capital level and at managerial level meant that the learning and change process was limited. There was no institutionalization and therefore no sustainability. Managerial accountability was not sufficiently considered and articulated. It was also felt that HAP should build on and complement existing efforts to improve accountability among agencies. This approach would be more cost-effective and allow for better sustainability (Van Brabant, 2002).

Afghanistan (May–July 2002)

HAP operated out of Herat. The team was composed of 26 international and national staff. As part of its facilitation role, HAP conducted workshops and two agency surveys, provided regular reports of its research findings and held regular bilateral and inter-agency meetings to discuss these findings (Christoplos, 2002b). Monitoring included following accountability issues raised by agencies, monitoring an information campaign and directly investigating accountability issues in camps of internally displaced people (IDP). This required the recruitment and training of a team of ten male and ten female Afghan researchers (Featherstone and Routley, 2002).

HAP's facilitation role was appreciated, but agencies would have also welcomed technical and strategic accountability support. Monitoring allowed HAP to build its credibility and legitimacy and to raise its profile by bringing up cases or issues. It provided HAP with an independent way of assessing humanitarian actions. HAP monitoring work also illustrated the importance of methodological rigour in order to be seen as credible when challenging agencies. It was found that it would be difficult to extend the Herat accountability mechanism beyond fairly restricted boundaries. The mechanism was cost-efficient but probably not so if implemented on the scale of a whole country. Lack of sustainability remained a challenge. Some of the factors were external to the model tested, in particular, the very high staff turnover in Herat at the time of HAP operations. It was decided that HAP Cambodia would seek to address primarily the question of sustainability of HAP accountability work.

Cambodia (August 2002–February 2003)

The team was composed of 22 international and national staff. It also worked in partnership with two local agencies specializing in training and capacity building. HAP sought to assist and support selected agencies in improving their own internal capacity for accountability and in developing a collective and permanent mechanism of accountability (Kahn, 2003; Rahman, 2003). The approach adopted had four main components: first, beneficiary-based accountability action research – an action research of agency accountability practices and beneficiaries' views, with the objective of agreeing to immediate actions and improving practices; second, organizational self-assessment of accountability practices, aiming at defining and measuring performance against a number of accountability indicators; third, development and testing of accountability training; and fourth, creation of an accountability advisory board that accompanied the progress of the HAP field trial, served as a forum for debate and discussion on accountability, and identified recommendations for a more permanent accountability mechanism in Cambodia.

The Cambodia field trial demonstrated the added value of the monitoring and technical support model and its potential for sustainability. Agencies welcomed HAP monitoring work, coupled with active learning, and took steps to implement accountability recommendations. The Cambodia trial also confirmed the rights-based approach adopted throughout. Following the completion of the trial, agencies that had worked with HAP and others agreed to establish a new network, the Humanitarian Accountability Network (HANet, with a Khmer abbreviated name ANet). Four international and three national organizations were selected for the executive committee: Oxfam, CARE Cambodia, World Vision Cambodia, Concern Worldwide, Cambodia Red Cross, the Urban Sector Group and Neak Akphihat Sahakum (NAS). Oxfam GB is temporarily hosting HANet, which is supported in this early stage by HAP International through the donation of its field trial equipment. HANet seeks to promote and strengthen accountability among agencies engaged in humanitarian action in Cambodia.

Taken together, the three HAP field trials provided many findings and learning. We will highlight only a few results. There were plenty of examples in all three trials indicating systematic patterns, in many cases, or anecdotal instances, in a few, of a lack of accountability. The most often-cited concerns by crisis-affected individuals included: lack of information regarding relief entitlements and their future; the inability to recognize and identify who is who; the impossibility of raising issues or asking questions; misunderstanding, misinformation or disinformation regarding relief entitlement; security, ranging from cars driving too fast to human rights abuses; and corruption.

These problems appeared especially acute as far as the poorest, women-headed households, children and the disabled were concerned.

Sexual violence and exploitation constitute the most dramatic illustrations of abuse of humanitarian power and of the failure of humanitarian actors to meet their responsibilities, namely, to contribute to protecting crisis-affected populations against abuses of their rights and, in particular, the rights of the most vulnerable among them, children and women, and to be accountable to those with and for whom they are working. HAP research work has shown that to be accountable to beneficiaries, agencies should inform, listen, monitor, respond to concerns and report back. In particular, agencies should be encouraged to set up mechanisms allowing them to listen to complaints from beneficiaries and respond to them.

The model of an external monitoring and accountability body will work best within a self-contained environment (for example, a camp). For this approach to work in a different humanitarian context, such as among a large number of disaster-affected communities spread over a large region, an equally large number of monitoring and redress teams will be required to ensure full coverage. A more cost-effective and sustainable way of ensuring accountability to beneficiaries is therefore to work through existing operational agencies and ensure that individually, but preferably collectively, they implement strong accountability mechanisms.

Operational actors are best positioned to ensure and strengthen accountability to beneficiaries. This requires setting up accountability mechanisms within operations, as well as strengthening managerial accountability and responsibilities. Accountability to beneficiaries will not be sustainable and institutionalized unless more efforts are made towards better and stronger self-regulation at both agency and inter-agency levels. No independent body, as effective and large as it may be, will suffice to ensure that the millions of humanitarian claimants have, for instance, access to avenues of recourse if and when they have legitimate complaints or concerns.

HAP has sought to place disaster-affected populations at the core of the accountability principles it developed or insisted on. Primarily based on the above findings in the field, but further informed by HAP research into accountability mechanisms in other organizations, codes of conduct, quality standards and policies concerned with improving performances, HAP established a set of core accountability principles that requires agencies to:

- respect and promote the rights of disaster-affected populations;
- establish and apply quality standards in humanitarian assistance;
- inform crisis-affected populations about the standards and their rights to a say;
- involve crisis-affected populations in project planning, implementation, evaluation and reporting;
- demonstrate compliance with their quality standards through monitoring and reporting;

- enable crisis-affected populations and staff to report any complaints and to seek redress effectively; and
- implement these principles when working through partner agencies.

MEANINGFUL SELF-REGULATION

HAP's third contribution to the betterment objective has consisted in proposing a definition and model of self-regulation that insisted on monitoring and performance assessment, complaints mechanisms and compliance. In January 2003, 15 humanitarian agencies moved HAP from its pilot phase and initiated the Humanitarian Accountability Partnership International (HAP-I), an organization whose mission is to uphold the highest standards of accountability through collective self-regulation. Its vision is of a humanitarian sector with a trusted, transparent and accessible accountability mechanism.

This decision was not meant to contend that an external accountability mechanism, for example, in the shape of a watchdog, would not be necessary. In fact, this author has insisted that an independent humanitarian watchdog will play a major role in ensuring that concerns are heard and addressed. However, it was not felt to be the best instrument at this stage for HAP-I to focus on and develop. The day-to-day, operational and global dimension of humanitarian assistance, the multiplicity of sites of action, the relative good will among the main actors mandated a different HAP-I approach. Further, if affected populations were to be at the centre of accountability, a watchdog would not necessarily bring them further and closer to the centre of action and decisions.

Under self-regulation, rules are developed, administered and enforced by those whose behaviour is to be governed, with the ultimate aim of improving the services offered to claimants. A self-regulatory scheme may be developed by a single organization, but is more frequently developed at inter-organizational or sector level (Callamard, 2001). As HAP-I research notes, good practice in self-regulatory schemes includes, among other things, transparency and participation by those whose interests the standards, rules or code are designed to protect.

Meaningful self-regulation also insists on both individual and organizational responsibilities; while individuals are to perform according to a set of agreed standards and rules, the development of accountability at both field and headquarter levels requires an examination of how the organization guides and influences the conduct of its fieldworkers. Through listening and responding to disaster-affected populations, changes in practices at the field level require broader transformations.

Existing experiences with self-regulatory bodies tend to indicate many similar shortcomings or pitfalls, primarily their tendency to become a membership club whose sole mandate is the protection of members' interests. Critiques and evaluations have made a number of recommendations to address this problem, including the introduction of service-user representation in self-regulatory (and regulatory) agencies, the strengthening of transparency through public reporting, the independence of the panels or members responsible for investigating complaints, and the obligation placed on these panels to initiate inquiries.

HAP-I has sought to implement these recommendations to the extent possible in the context of lengthy negotiations. Four out of the twelve board members are independent, that is, they have not been a staff, board, consultant or trustee for any member agency for at least three years, and two of them have personally experienced a humanitarian crisis. Further, HAP-I will report annually on its activities and findings, including with regard to the complaints review and the monitoring of agencies' accountability work plans. HAP-I General Assembly, during its first meeting in December 2003, insisted that transparency should not be the victim of confidentiality. Members of the General Assembly strengthened the organization's reporting capacity at the conclusion of a complaint review. Should the matter become public at anytime, HAP-I Board shall issue a public statement about the procedures followed and the status and/or the outcome of the complaint review (HAP-I, 2003b).

PERFORMANCE ASSESSMENT OF HAP-I MEMBERS

HAP-I insisted that meaningful self-regulation for the humanitarian sector requires moving away from a passive commitment to codes of conduct and standards towards an active demonstration of their implementation. HAP-I membership requirements state that within three months of joining, each new member is required to produce an accountability work plan based on minimum requirements established by HAP-I. This enables the agency to show how it will work towards implementing HAP-I accountability principles and to secure and demonstrate ownership of humanitarian accountability. Each member agency develops and reports on its own accountability work plan that also serves as the basis for external monitoring and performance assessment (HAP-I, 2003a). For the first years of its existence, the Secretariat of HAP-I is responsible for the external monitoring, but in the future, nothing prevents the organization and its member agencies from outsourcing the external monitoring to independent certification bodies, possibly accredited by HAP-I.

THE UNFINISHED COMMITMENT
TO THE AUTONOMOUS OTHER:
MEDICAL ETHICS AND COMPLAINTS

HAP had sought to insist, with mitigated success, that the call for reclaiming humanitarianism must be associated with the beneficiaries of humanitarian assistance or the crisis-affected communities, as *subjects* of the humanitarian universe. For this to happen, affected communities and individuals must be (seen as) autonomous Others, free to receive and reject, demand and question. This is a difficult call. Under any circumstance, individuals, societies and governments find it difficult to see the relativity of their own perspectives by taking into account those of others. This is particularly challenging in crisis situations, where the 'others' are so clearly in need; under this extreme power imbalance we have it all, while the other is frail to the extreme.

HAP-I laid the ground for increased awareness about the autonomy question through a focus on medical ethics.[4] Discussions and a workshop were organized, bringing together ethicists, medical practitioners and relief workers. The preliminary findings were greatly relevant to the strengthening or the building of a humanitarian ethos. These, however, were a very first step. Much remains to be done to translate medical principles and obligations into human-itarian principles and praxis.

When looking across history and cultures, there are some universal tradi-tions, principles or presumptions that could be used to guide the thinking process to address dilemmas and/or hard choices. These principles should be used in a transparent, structured dialogue between the relevant stakeholders to come to a consensus on what could best be done given the circumstances. They can also assist agencies in explaining why and how they have arrived at a certain conclusion and difficult choice. These principles are:

- the primacy of the patient/population;
- self-determination of the patient/population;
- confidentiality;
- non-discrimination;
- informed consent;
- standards of care;
- do no harm;
- risk and benefit ratio; and
- resource allocation and distributive justice.

In addition, there are three obligations that fall on the medical practitioners, their employers and the medical sector as a whole. History has shown that good intentions from well-educated people are not always enough to warrant the trust that they will do the right things:

1   The professional obligation of the individual medical practitioners to maintain knowledge, to train and teach and to tell the truth.
2   The obligations of the organization to maintain an adequate monitoring system on the character and the knowledge of the people being recruited.
3   The obligation of self-regulation. Central to medical care is the trust that patients have in doctors. This trust is essential but comes with high levels of responsibility for doctors. Systems of self-regulation are the public acceptance of these responsibilities and can be seen as a privilege. Peer review constitutes a particularly important mechanism of quality (HAP-I and WHO, 2003).

From its inception, HAP-I strongly advocated a rights-based approach, in particular, for the right of disaster-affected populations to raise complaints and concerns and the obligation placed on humanitarian actors to listen and respond to legitimate complaints.[5] On joining HAP-I, member agencies commit to establish complaint referral systems within their own agencies and programmes. HAP-I can assist them in doing this. Moreover, HAP-I itself is an avenue for handling complaints. For this purpose, a Standing Complaints Committee has been set up. It accepts complaints against agencies that, in the course of providing humanitarian assistance, allegedly have failed to apply, enforce or otherwise implement HAP-I accountability principles. The capacity of HAP-I to initiate complaints investigations remains limited, in that the first responsibility for investigation remains with the operational actors. However, the space for reviewing complaints, including those against non-member agencies, is there. Practice will tell the extent to which and how this space will be utilized.

CONCLUSION: ACCOUNTABILITY'S LAST FRONTIER?

Building and institutionalizing accountability towards disaster-affected populations shares many similarities with other transformative processes at social or organizational levels. Much work remains to be done, by HAP International and others, to identify the mechanisms and tools that will allow for this transformative process. The managerial accountability instruments referred to in the first part of this chapter may be of use, provided they are somewhat 'subverted' to fulfil a greater good. An essential requirement for true accountability must be met: the creation and implementation of arenas or spaces aimed at listening, responding and providing redress to disaster-affected populations.

Accountability aims to ensure that humanitarian power is exercised within a framework of fairness, respect and justice; crisis-affected populations are not a number on a ration card, a shadow in a queue or irritating beggars. They have a right to be informed, to be consulted, to participate in decisions affecting their lives, to raise concerns and complaints, and to get answers. Women and children should not be discriminated against, and, in particular, they should be protected against sexual violence.

To be accountable presupposes recognizing that individuals and populations affected by disasters have rights, including to information and participation in decisions and programmes that directly affect their lives, dignity and autonomy. But accountability requires more than participation, even though this is a step in the right direction. It also requires questioning one's own power and the exercise of it. It requires, in the case of humanitarian actors, moving away from the image and practice of the heroic Western intervener. Consequently, it demands consideration of crisis-affected populations as subjects of the humanitarian universe. Accountability also requires educating the public and donors about alternative approaches to humanitarian actions; heroism sells well.

The greatest challenge facing humanitarian actors resides in the operationalization of these requirements and principles. What does it mean to approach crisis-affected populations as subjects, rather than objects of our compassion? What are the implications in terms of programmes and policies? How do we deal with and address effectively the resulting principles of autonomy and informed consent? How do we address in a non-paternalistic fashion the evident imbalance of power, partly illustrated by and reflecting historical and global inequalities?

The attacks on September 11, the subsequent 'war on terror' and the interventions in Afghanistan and Iraq have exposed many of the ambiguities and contradictions of the humanitarian system and the role of international NGOs in shaping and participating in this system. By exposing the NGOs, it has also led to a crisis of large proportions for humanitarian agencies. HAP-I findings during the first three years of its existence have shown that civilian humanitarian agencies have the capacity to reclaim ownership over humanitarianism. This claim requires acknowledging and unpacking humanitarian power and locating humanitarian actions and functions within a historical context. Finally, and most importantly, the call for reclaiming humanitarianism must be associated with the beneficiaries of humanitarian assistance and the crisis-affected communities as subjects of the humanitarian universe.

Complex times may not always require complex solutions, but they do require engagement with their complexity. There is no single recipe or slogan that will do the trick. Instead, several models of engagement with this complex environment have to be tried out and assessed. Ultimately, success will depend on our capacity to address in full honesty the last frontier of accountability. This is also what will distinguish us from many competitors, present or future, whose motivations may have little to do with the humanitarian ethos: to safeguard and uphold the well-being and dignity of those who have been affected by disasters and armed conflicts.

NOTES

1   The following is based in part on previous overviews of HAP work, including Callamard and Van Brabant (2002) and Callamard (2003).
2   The United Nations Committee on the Elimination of Racial Discrimination, General Recommendation 20, 'Non-discriminatory Implementation of Rights and Freedoms', Geneva, 15 March 1996, article 5.
3   The United Nations Committee for the Rights of the Child, 'The Private Sector as Service Provider and Its Role in Implementing Child Rights', 31st session. Geneva, 20 September 2002.
4   There is also much we can learn from the disability sector, especially with regard to its approaches to, and understanding of, autonomy.
5   The HAP 2002 study into accountable organizations found a strong correlation between NGOs that had adopted a rights-based approach to their work and those that had set up accountability mechanisms (Davidson, 2002).

12

Addressing Accountability at the Global Level: The Challenges Facing International NGOs

Hetty Kovach

INTRODUCTION: TRADITIONAL VERSUS NEW APPROACHES TO ACCOUNTABILITY

This chapter seeks to explore the concept of NGO accountability from a global perspective, placing the accountability issues facing international NGOs within the broader context of how global organizations, be they from the corporate, intergovernmental or non-governmental sector connect with and are responsible to their stakeholders. Running throughout the chapter is the idea that there are universal core characteristics of accountability that are applicable to all types of global organizations and that vital lessons can and should be drawn from across organizations active in different sectors.

The chapter is divided into three sections. The first section sets out the global context and explores the accountability issues facing different types of organizations operating at this level. The section notes that all types of global organizations have woefully inadequate accountability mechanisms to enable citizens to hold them to account, largely the result of relying on outdated models of accountability. The section concludes that there are growing calls by the public for all types of organizations to be more accountable, including international NGOs. The second section explores the need for a new and dynamic approach to the issue of global accountability, highlighting the One World Trust's stakeholder-driven model of accountability.[1] This section goes on to explore the One World Trust's findings in relation to the transparency and governance of international NGOs. The third and final section looks to the future and identifies four key challenges facing the international NGO sector in the coming years: the need for more objective evaluations; the need for more stakeholder engagement; the need for more robust complaints and redress mechanisms; and the need for a far more proactive approach to the issue by the sector itself as perhaps the biggest challenge facing international NGOs.

It is important to note that this chapter focuses exclusively on international NGOs (INGOs). INGOs are NGOs who have national offices within multiple countries. They have evolved largely out of national NGOs and are often structured as federations or confederations, granting national offices various degrees of autonomy. Despite this chapter focusing exclusively on this set of NGOs and exploring unique aspects of their accountability, much of what is covered is equally applicable to NGOs operating at national and regional levels.

At its simplest, accountability refers to a process by which individuals or organizations are answerable for their actions and the consequences that follow from them. The concept becomes more complex when trying to unravel *who* has the right to hold whom to account and *how* one facilitates and delivers accountability.

Traditional approaches to accountability argue that organizations only have to be accountable to a small set of stakeholders (Kovach et al, 2003). These are normally individuals and groups who have a formal authority over an organization, primarily as a result of legal and financial powers. Within this approach, for example, a corporation is accountable to its directors, shareholders and the state, as each of these stakeholders has formal power over the corporation. In the case of international NGOs, accountability is often restricted to its national member organizations, its directors, its donors and again the state. Within the traditional approach, accountability is largely seen as an end stage process where judgement is passed on results or actions already taken. As such, the mechanisms adopted to facilitate accountability rely heavily on reporting actions already taken and the ability of internal stakeholders to impose sanctions if they are unhappy with the outcomes.

Over the last ten years, traditional approaches to accountability have been challenged by more dynamic conceptions that recognize the complexity and multiplicity of accountabilities existing within the modern world. New approaches to accountability cite a far wider group of stakeholders that organizations should be accountable to. It is not just those with the power to affect organizations, but also those affected by organizations' actions that should be able to hold those organizations to account. These stakeholders do not have any formal power within an organization, but are, nonetheless, impacted by its decisions. For example, in the case of international NGOs this could be their beneficiaries, the very communities and groups who are directly affected at the local level by an organization's project or advocacy work.

In newer and more dynamic approaches, accountability is also not confined to a retrospective activity of passing judgement on activities already undertaken. Rather, it is viewed as something dynamic and ongoing, which involves all stakeholders at all stages of an organization's decision-making, from formulation to evaluation. Not surprisingly, this approach stresses the need for engagement mechanisms throughout an organization, access to more information and ongoing, open evaluation procedures.

FAILINGS AT THE GLOBAL LEVEL

Despite a shift in the way accountability is perceived from a traditional to a more dynamic approach, there has been very little change in the practice of accountability, especially in the global arena. In fact, the practice of organizational accountability has remained worryingly static, with numerous organizations failing to adopt newer approaches. Most global organizations, including INGOs, are still reliant on traditional models of accountability, which not only privilege powerful stakeholders at the expense of others, but all too often rely on regulatory framework approaches that stop firmly at the national or regional border and fail to address the participatory and learning aspects of accountability.

Intergovernmental organizations' accountability

Intergovernmental organizations (IGOs) argue that they derive most of their accountability from the national governments that make up their membership.[2] Citizens (within democratically elected member nation states) elect their national governments, who in turn represent their interests within intergovernmental decision-making processes. The national electoral process is the key, enabling citizens to delegate decision-making to the global level, while retaining ultimate control.

However, even this limited form of accountability is extremely precarious when stretched to the global level. This is because, first, it relies on the caveat that all member states of IGOs are democratically elected, which is plainly not the case. Second, it ignores the differential degrees of power given to member nation states within the internal governance structures of IGOs. Very few IGOs are based on the principle of one member, one vote. Most privilege a minority of nation states, giving them far greater decision-making power at the expense of others. The result is that a small minority of citizens, by virtue of their national identity, have far greater access to accountability than others. Finally, it ignores the need for citizens to have access to information in order to exercise their accountability rights. Intergovernmental decision-making is often opaque and private, preventing citizens from ever finding out what position their governments have taken within a given IGO and hence holding them to account.[3]

IGOs, to be fair, have made significant attempts to try to adopt more dynamic approaches to accountability by trying to engage with a wider set of stakeholders. NGOs, business groups and parliamentarians are all encouraged to participate at both the project and policy level of IGO decision-making today. NGO participation in World Bank-financed projects, for example, increased from 6 per cent of all projects in 1973–1998 to 50 per cent in the late 1990s (Reimann, 2002). IGOs also have formal institutional links with other stakeholders, such as the World Bank's Committee for Non-governmental Organizations, or the World Trade Organization's NGO Forum to enable engagement around policy issues. However, there is often real concern over the degree of influence and meaningfulness of this type of engagement.

Transnational corporations' accountability

Corporations, on the other hand, argue that they derive all of their accountability from the market itself, either via the regulations imposed on the market by outside actors (the state), or via the financial choices of market actors like shareholders and consumers, whose choices can sanction or reward a corporation's behaviour. On the surface this appears a solid structural argument. However, delve deeper or place the argument within a global context and major weaknesses reveal themselves.

First, market regulation is still primarily the preserve of national governments, despite the fact that we clearly live in a global market place. The inability of governments from around the world to set globally binding social, environmental and financial laws has resulted in ineffective accountability mechanisms to protect less powerful stakeholders from the negative impacts of corporations' work. Global corporations are left to pick and choose between competing national regulations. A plethora of voluntary global initiatives and standards have sprung up to fill the vacuum, such as the Organization for Economic Cooperation and Development's Guidelines for Multinationals (OECD, 2000) and the Global Reporting Initiative (2002). However, without effective enforcement mechanisms it is highly unlikely that these initiatives will ever become the norm.

Second, consumer choice is not the effective accountability mechanism it is often made out to be. Consumers who are not happy with a transnational corporation (TNC) product or environmental record can indeed refuse to purchase its goods. Consumer boycotts, for example, have a long history and have resulted in companies changing their behaviour. However, the people who are most directly and negatively affected by the activities of a TNC are often not the same people who are able to exert their consumer power. Furthermore, employing exit strategies as a means of accountability relies on considerable consumer awareness and appealing alternative choices. Transparency in the sector is limited, and although moves for greater social and environmental disclosure are growing, consumers are still not fully aware of corporations' records and are definitely not able to compare data across companies. Alternative products are also surprisingly scarce as large TNCs take ever greater amounts of market share and dominate product lines. The result is that consumer choice in relation to accountability can be limited.

INGOs' accountability

International NGOs have structurally weaker accountability mechanisms than the other sectors in that there are less formal mechanisms imposing accountability from the outside. NGOs, for example, can not claim that they democratically represent the groups they advocate for, unlike democratic governments who can point to open electoral processes (Peruzzotti, Chapter 3). Nor can they claim their services are accountable as a result of market consumer choice, however weak this argument may be. Beneficiaries, NGOs' nearest equivalent to consumers, are often the most marginalized groups within a society and are not in a position to reject programmes and services if they are substandard. This leaves the sector highly open to criticism.

It would be wrong, however, to suggest that no structural mechanisms exist within the sector. State regulation and institutional donor-driven reporting, for example, provide mechanisms of accountability. Unfortunately, they do not translate up to the global level or ignore certain stakeholders, like NGOs' beneficiaries. States tend to regulate around disclosure of NGO financial information and governance structures. Like the corporate sector, this is limited to the national arena only. No international law exists for the regulation of INGOs and there are wide ranging debates as to whether such a law would be appropriate given the large diversity of organizations that fall under the non-governmental umbrella. A limited number of codes and standards are emerging at the global level. Interestingly, many of these draw on existing global accountability standards within the corporate and governmental sector, focusing primarily on reporting. For example, the Corporate Responsibility Campaign, which looks into social and environmental reporting, prides itself on applying its standards to corporations and NGOs alike.[4]

An absence of structural accountability mechanisms does not mean that NGOs are necessarily less accountable. For example, the NGO sector leads on consulting with less powerful stakeholders like its beneficiaries before, during and even after it has undertaken project work, even without formal mechanisms imposing such accountability (Neligan et al, 2003). The reason behind this is largely the sector's use of participatory development practices, which stress the need to empower beneficiaries to make their own choices and decide their own futures in order for effective development to take place. Engaging with beneficiaries is even becoming the case in the humanitarian emergency sector, despite the difficulties posed by the environment in undertaking this activity (Callamard, Chapter 11). Although INGOs lead in this area, it should be stressed that engagement is largely confined to the grassroots level in relation to projects and programmes, and is not replicated at the national, regional or international level of the organization. Nor is there much engagement around advocacy work.

Public awareness of accountability failings

The absence of effective accountability mechanisms at the global level has produced a worrying disconnection between global organizations and the individuals they impact. This has been cited by many academics, but also by numerous citizens, who increasingly feel the impact of global organizations in their daily lives, but have little ability to have their voices heard, much to their frustration (Held and Archibugi, 1995; Nye, 2001). More and more individuals around the world are calling for greater accountability at the global level, with a need for all organizations to listen and respond, including those once deemed immune from scrutiny.

Intergovernmental organizations are facing ever-increasing scrutiny from wide sections of the population. Organizations as diverse as the OECD, the World Bank and the WTO have all been targeted by highly vocal civil society campaigns over the last couple of years.[5] These campaigns often challenge not only the substance of the IGOs' policy decisions, but also the very processes by which IGO decisions are taken. Just as IGOs' accountability has been put under the spotlight, so has that of corporations. It is perhaps no wonder, given the extraordinary financial muscle of TNCs and their high visibility in terms of global branding. Until recently, calls for greater INGO accountability had been limited, with the sector viewed as essentially benign. Over the last couple of years this has changed, with a dramatic growth in the number of people voicing concerns. There is no single explanation for this growth in concern, but clearly it must be linked to the increasing financial and political impact of the sector. In 2002, NGOs turned over an estimated US$1 trillion globally, providing vital services to individuals and communities around the world (SustainAbility, 2003). INGOs also have an increasingly powerful voice, running campaigns on matters such as environmental degradation, workers' rights and trade rules, which corporations and governments ignore at their peril.

In addition, the nature of INGO work has also stimulated questions concerning their accountability. Many INGOs have taken on the role of monitoring the accountability of governments and corporations on behalf of citizens around the world. Recently, Christian Aid wrote a report on the 'real face' of corporate responsibility (Christian Aid, 2004). This level of critical review of the accountability of others has left INGOs exposed to questions surrounding their own accountability. This could be one of the biggest internal drivers for the sector to tackle this issue, as INGOs themselves realize that it is no longer tenable to demand accountability within other sectors without addressing it within their own. It is also, as noted later on in this chapter, one of the reasons why the issue of NGO accountability is so highly politicized.

NEW APPROACHES: THE ONE WORLD TRUST'S GLOBAL ACCOUNTABILITY PROJECT

A new approach to accountability is required that recognizes the complexity of accountability and the diversity of stakeholders' needs. In 2000, the One

World Trust (OWT) launched the Global Accountability Project (GAP). The project promotes greater accountability of global organizations. It does so by highlighting the key mechanisms that enhance the accountability of three main types of global organizations – intergovernmental, TNCs and INGOs, assessing the accountability of representative organizations within these three sectors, identifying accountability gaps and advocating for reforms on specific accountability issues. Through GAP, the OWT has developed a new model of accountability that identifies some core elements of accountability applicable to all types of global organizations. Before describing these elements in detail, it is important to explore how the Trust defines or perceives accountability.

Central to the Trust's model of accountability is the notion of the stakeholder whereby the right to hold an organization or individual to account is granted to 'any group or individuals who can affect or is affected by... an organization' (Freeman, 1984). The model, therefore, firmly places itself within the modern approaches to accountability, valuing a wide array of stakeholders. In fact, OWT employs a new categorization of stakeholders, employing the terms internal and external stakeholders. 'Internal stakeholders' refers to stakeholders who are directly linked to the organization and who often have formal powers to hold an organization to account. This group often has the power to impose accountability on an organization, although not always. 'External stakeholders' refers more to those stakeholders that are affected by an organization's work, but are not formally part of it, like the NGO's beneficiaries. External stakeholders tend to be less powerful and unable to exert their rights. The Trust's emphasis is on empowering those stakeholders that are less powerful and ensuring they have the ability to hold organizations to account. The categorization is not definitive and many stakeholders move from being external to internal and vice versa.

The Trust's definition of accountability also recognizes that accountability is not only a means through which individuals and organizations are held responsible for their actions, but it is also a means by which organizations can take internal responsibility for shaping their organizational mission and values, for opening themselves to external scrutiny and for assessing performance in relation to goals. It engages with both the sanctioning elements of accountability and the often negated learning and participatory aspects.

The GAP model recognizes that there are two complementary elements to accountability: on the one hand, international organizations have a responsibility to engage all their stakeholders in their decision-making and to be transparent about their actions; on the other hand, all stakeholders should also have the power to impose some sort of sanctions if organizations fail to comply with their stated objectives. Their notion of accountability extends beyond traditional mechanisms of oversight, monitoring or auditing by adding some element of control, exposure and potential redress.

The GAP Accountability Model

Dimension	Description of Dimension
Transparency	Transparency implies a free flow of information: processes are directly accessible to stakeholders and enough information is provided to understand and monitor them. This dimension covers the degree of information provided by organizations to the public, exploring access to internal decision-making through information on an organization's mission, activities and finances.
Participation	Participation refers to the degree to which organizations involve their stakeholders (internal and external) at all levels of decision-making within the organization. It covers not only internal governance issues, looking at, for example, the representativeness, transparency and degree of control governing and executive boards have over an organization, but also the extent to which an organization engages with external stakeholders via consultations and partnerships at both project and policy levels.
Evaluation	This dimension refers to the existence and effectiveness of tools and procedures that are in place to evaluate an organization's performance. It recognizes the need for two types of evaluations to help an organization increase its accountability – internal evaluations (carried out by staff assessing their own work) and external evaluations (where information is evaluated by a competent independent authority). Tools of evaluation can be combined with processes of participation to develop external downward accountability mechanisms through systematic involvement of stakeholders in evaluating organizations.
Complaints and Redress	This dimension refers to 'the mechanisms through which an organization enables its stakeholders (both internal and external) to address complaints against its decisions and actions, and through which it ensures that these complaints are properly reviewed and acted upon' (De Las Casas, 2005). Enabling stakeholders to bring complaints against an organization is a critical aspect of accountability.

Elaborating the GAP model of accountability

The GAP model of accountability identifies four core dimensions that make an organization more accountable to its stakeholders.[6] These must be integrated into an organization's policies, processes and practices at all levels and stages of decision-making and implementation, in relationships with both its internal and external stakeholders. These four dimensions are: transparency, participation, evaluation, and complaints and reddress. The higher the quality and level of embeddedness of these dimensions in all organizational policies, processes and practices, the more accountable the organization is. These four dimensions are connected with and impact on each other, thus highlighting how fundamental each and every single one of them is to the accountability of organizations. They are summarized in the table above.

Through participatory methods involving a wide range of academics, policy-makers and practitioners, One World Trust is undertaking research to identify the principles and guidelines of each of the dimensions. Quantitative and qualitative indicators have been developed for each of the dimensions, in order to offer users a more practical understanding of how accountability can be operationalized.

Findings from the first Global Accountability Report in relation to INGOs

In 2003, the Trust released its first report entitled *Power without Accountability?* (Kovach et al, 2003). The report assessed the accountability of 18 organizations from the intergovernmental, corporate and international non-governmental sector using an earlier version of its accountability model. It focused on two of the key dimensions identified in the model: participation and transparency. However, it only developed indicators for assessing and measuring partial aspects of these dimensions. In the case of participation, the report focused on examining the representativeness of internal governing structures and exploring the make-up of the governing and executive boards. In terms of transparency, the report assessed online information only, looking at the degree to which internal decision-making information was made available, as well as at the financial data and evaluation reports.

The report controversially ranked organizations according to the results it found. Overall, two clear conclusions emerged from the report. First, in terms of governance, the report found that INGOs had fairer and more representative governing structures at the board level than other global organizations, ensuring that a minority of stakeholders did not dominate decision-making. Second, in terms of transparency, the report showed that INGOs were not that transparent, especially in comparison to both the corporate and the intergovernmental sector. This finding was picked up by many in the media and some of the organizations assessed, especially those that had been subject to calls that they were not accountable.

The next sections will briefly summarize the findings of the report in relation to INGOs only, providing additional commentary and, at times, critical thoughts on the findings. Finally, it explores the impact of the report's findings in the media and policy-making circles, highlighting the highly political nature of NGO accountability.

INGO governance: Representative?

International NGOs, like all other organizations, have a governing[7] and an executive body.[8] The governing body is composed of representatives from all of the national member organizations who are part of the INGO's federal and con-federal structure. At the executive level, INGOs face the same tensions as IGOs as they try to ensure both efficiency (that is, small executives) and fair member representation. The report highlighted that most INGOs have resolved the dilemma successfully by appointing small executives and employing mechanisms to ensure fair representation of members within them. This is unlike IGOs, who have tended to let a small minority of members (in this case nation states) dominate. Five of the seven INGOs in the study opted for a smaller executive than their governing body and all but one of these ensured that a minority of members were not over-represented. The International Chamber of Commerce (ICC) was the exception. Most INGOs employed geographical formulas to ensure that different regions were fairly represented at the executive level and no one region could dominate (Amnesty International, International Confederation of Free Trade Unions (ICFTU)). Only CARE International and Oxfam International represented all national member organizations directly on the executive. The dilemma was reduced for them because they were small confederations, each made up of 12 members.

It also appeared that a minority of members did not dominate decision-making in any of the INGOs studied as a result of an unfair distribution of voting rights. Four of the INGOs distributed their votes equally among their members: CARE International, Oxfam International, the International Federation of the Red Cross and Red Crescent Societies (IFRC) and the World Wide Fund for Nature (WWF). Amnesty International, the ICC and the ICFTU distributed votes in relation to the size and financial contribution of members. However, a lack of transparency with the ICFTU and ICC over the distribution of votes to members made it difficult to tell whether a minority of members actually held a majority of votes. Only Amnesty International provided this information and it revealed that a minority did not dominate. For all of the INGOs, however, changes to the governing articles must be decided by a supermajority, preventing a small cabal of members from blocking change.

Despite these findings, it is important to note that the study did not look at the actual regional make-up of the member offices of INGOs, therefore avoiding asking just how international these INGOs really are. Many INGOs have grown out of Northern-based NGOs and therefore have a limited number of members from developing countries, reflecting their historical roots. What is problematic is that often many of these INGOs have numerous country offices within developing countries, but these country offices are not considered national members and are prevented from gaining access to governing and executive board decision-making processes. The weak financial muscle of developing country offices compounds this problem. INGOs that suffer from this problem should take into greater consideration how they can make their governance more international and truly representative of the places and people they purport to assist. Otherwise, they are liable to be open to criticism from the outside for not reflecting genuinely the international make-up of the organization within their governance and not learning from and listening to all their staff.

INGO transparency

Another finding of the Trust's report was that INGOs were the least transparent sector compared with IGOs and TNCs. Many INGOs did not provide access to even basic annual reports, let alone information on more in-depth evaluation material. INGOs, in particular, stood out from the other organizations because of a lack of consistency in publishing annual reports. Three of the INGOs did not provide an annual report online: CARE International, Amnesty International (which publishes only to members) and ICFTU (which publishes a report every four years). The failure to provide this important document makes scrutiny of an INGO's finances much more difficult. Even those INGOs that do produce an annual report varied substantially in their financial disclosure. Only the IFRC made its audited account available in its annual report.

Of concern was the use of the term 'annual report' itself by some INGOs. For example, both Amnesty International and ICFTU published reports labelled as such, but both documents were largely focused on human rights abuses or trade union issues, respectively, around the world in a given year. Confusingly, they both included a section on their activities but failed to provide financial information. Regulation at the national level could address this problem partially. One idea would be for a global standard to be created that clearly indicates what should be included in a basic annual report of an INGO.

INGOs were also not good at providing evaluation material to the public. There was generally limited disclosure of evaluation material relating to their activities. Publication of evaluations is important to enable stakeholders to assess the effectiveness of INGOs' work. Much work is being undertaken by INGOs to establish guidelines that enable effective evaluation, but this is not currently published online. Only IFRC systematically provided evaluation material online. CARE, Oxfam International and WWF provide material on an ad hoc basis, but Amnesty International, the ICC and ICFTU had none at all. The last three are all advocacy NGOs and face even greater problems in assessing the effectiveness of their campaigns due to the nature of their work. However, more could be done as they must certainly undertake internal evaluations of projects.

Finally, the report also found that INGOs were not very transparent when it came to issues surrounding their governance, although it should be pointed out that none of the sectors did very well in this area. Despite the majority of INGOs putting their governing articles online, governance information varied widely. IFRC, Amnesty International and the ICC provided good descriptions of governance structures. Both Oxfam International and WWF provided only brief descriptions of key decision-making bodies, and CARE International gave no description of its governance and even failed to identify the individuals on its executive body.

As a group, INGOs make limited disclosure of documentation from their governing bodies. Only the ICFTU and IFRC disclosed such documents. They provided summaries of their governing body meetings. However, none of the INGOs provided any documents relating to their executive bodies. In the case of some INGOs, Amnesty International, for example, security issues mean that disclosure may be difficult. However, to not have any information about what decisions are being taken and by which members reveals an accountability gap that should be plugged.

Although the Trust report does not draw this conclusion, it is highly likely that the INGO sector's lack of transparency is largely a result of a lack of demand from external actors for greater disclosure. This is clearly changing, as explained earlier in this chapter. It would also be reasonable to suggest that changes will occur quite quickly in this area in the near future, as has been the case with the other sectors. This is because providing greater access to information is often one of the easiest changes an organization can make if it wants to improve its accountability. Changing governance structures, for example, would require legal reform and fundamental organizational change, while improving transparency often only means making existing information available within a new domain. The presence of the internet has also reduced the costs of making information available within the public domain. It is important to highlight, however, that providing greater access to information by itself does not enhance accountability. The quality of the information and its relevance is crucial. Limited, but highly relevant information, is far more beneficial than excessive information of no real value.

How the report was received: The political nature of NGO accountability

Despite the report highlighting a number of interesting findings in relation to the accountability of different sectors working at the global level, it was the finding that INGOs were in many cases less transparent than IGOs and TNCs that was picked up most by the media and policy-making circles. What appeared irresistible to the outside world was the idea that the very sector that made its reputation on monitoring the accountability of other organizations had itself accountability failings or gaps. *The New York Times* ran an article entitled 'Holding Civil Groups Accountable' (21 July 2003), which noted that 'The WTO and the World Bank scored highly for online information disclosure, while NGO's like CARE, the World Wide Fund for Nature and the International Confederation of Free Trade Unions got much lower marks'. The WTO, subject to huge criticism by NGOs for its opaque and unrepresentative decision-making structures, shouted loudly about its relatively high ranking against other IGOs and INGOs, issuing its own press release, which sat on the front page of its media section for many weeks, 'WTO gets high marks for accountability and transparency' (11 February 2003). The press release noted that it was ranked above many NGOs, like Oxfam.

The experience showed the Trust the highly political nature of NGO accountability and the need to act cautiously, given this charged environment. One of the results of the experience was that the Trust set up an informal NGO

Accountability Forum for local, national and international non-governmental organizations based in the UK to understand and articulate better NGO accountability and to collectively strengthen it. The forum provides a safe space for NGOs to discuss critical opportunities and problems related to their accountability, away from those that wish to raise the issue for political point scoring.

CHALLENGES FOR THE FUTURE

The Trust's study highlighted both opportunities and dangers facing INGOs. However, it only provided a partial picture of the accountability of these organizations, given that it did not assess all aspects of their accountability. Through GAP, the Trust is currently working on developing indicators for all the dimensions in order to assess organizations against the whole model. This last section explores some of the other GAP dimensions that are likely to be highly relevant to INGOs in the near future, focusing on the need for more objective evaluations, greater engagement within the sector and the need for more robust complaints and redress mechanisms.

The lack of evaluation material in the INGO sector is extremely worrying. Also of concern is the content of INGOs evaluation reports. All too often, INGO evaluation material is largely positive, glossing over problems or failures and lacking in critical analysis. This is because there are fears within the sector that being honest and open about programme and project failings may jeopardize the ability to access funds. The concern is that greater honesty in evaluation could result in penalization by donors. This is the same argument that corporations make when they state that taking the lead in honest and objective social and environmental reporting may jeopardize their ability to retain shareholders and customers. The problem lies first with donors, who need to give more reassuring signals to INGOs that greater honesty in evaluations will not result in a withdrawal of funds. Second, it lies around collective action problems; no INGO wants to be the first organization to expose potential failings and be scrutinized. INGOs need to work collectively on this issue and move towards more frank disclosure in the future.

INGOs also need to expand on their engagement practices with internal and external stakeholders, as mentioned previously. This could happen in two ways. First, there is a need to engage more beneficiaries in the advocacy work of the organization. INGOs are particularly vulnerable to attack on this front and they need to have in place robust mechanisms to protect their right to speak on issues that affect marginalized groups. Critics, for example, argue that campaigns are being driven by what advocates and campaigners working in the international political sphere perceive to be the problem, and not what those in the developing countries actually want or need (Bello, 2003). Second, there is a need to scale up existing engagement practices from the local to the international level so that they influence all levels of decision-making within an organization (Neligan et al, 2003). Organizations are already beginning to move in this direction. Save the Children UK, for example, is undertaking a review of organizational procedure and performance with the view to strengthening its accountability to key stakeholders. ActionAid's Accountability, Learning and Planning System (ALPS) also seeks to improve interaction between staff, poor people and partners, and to bring the concerns and needs of ActionAid's beneficiaries to the centre of decision-making (Okwaare and Chapman, Chapter 10).

The One World Trust has produced a set of principles that it deems vital for ensuring the process of engagement, being worthwhile for both the organization and its stakeholders. These are: access to timely and accurate information; clear terms of engagement (that is, the parameters of what is subject to negotiation and what is not, clearly defined and understood); legitimate engagement procedures for selecting and working with stakeholders; and robust procedures for redress (Neligan et al, 2003).

Presently, very few mechanisms exist for stakeholders to voice their complaints within the sector. Complaints procedures for both internal and external stakeholders are of vital importance, ensuring that organizations gain an accurate picture of the impact of their work and are able to respond quickly to grievances and problems (De Las Casas, 2005). It is also a vital means through which to give power to stakeholders, giving them a unique opportunity to set the agenda and voice their concerns. The Humanitarian Accountability Project International (HAP-I), for example, has set up a Standing Complaints Committee for its members to deal with complaints by disaster-affected populations within the humanitarian sector (Callamard, Chapter 11). Another example is Save the Children UK's feedback committees in Zimbabwe. This involved establishing children feedback committees as a channel of communication independent from the agency to enable complaints from children, who were key beneficiaries of the projects, but whose views were previously little heard, to make complaints and have them responded to (McIvor, 2004). INGOs should work in collaboration on this issue, looking, perhaps, into an ombudsman for the sector that could be applicable to all types of INGOs, or developing different ombudsmen for different types of INGOs.

The most important challenge facing INGOs in the future is the need for a more proactive approach to the accountability issue by the sector itself. It is no longer tenable for an INGO to claim that their accountability rests on moral authority alone. Today, INGOs are required to be accountable to a wide number of stakeholders: trustees, staff, donors, governments and, most importantly, to their beneficiaries – the individuals and communities they serve. Calls for greater transparency, more constructive measurement and evaluation of NGO programmes and clearer and more robust governance structures are increasingly heard. These demands need to be viewed positively. They provide a welcome opportunity for the sector to not only strengthen its own internal learning mechanisms and to become more efficient and effective, but also to enhance and embed the legitimacy and standing of INGOs within society.

INGOs need to start taking the issue seriously and they need to work collaboratively to define the agenda and avoid having it shaped by those outside of the sector. Defensive posturing or putting one's head in the sand can be a disaster. As John Elkington notes citing the corporate sector's experience:

> *Shell, in 1995 was totally taken by surprise by what happened to them (Brent Spa), as was Anderson. People don't see stuff coming and I think it's the same with NGOs. There's a very real risk that one or more NGOs will be caught up in an accountability issue... But when the issue comes, the spikes come very, very fast, and the reaction time allowed by the media for companies or NGOs are [sic] precariously short. (Jepson, 2004)*

The corporations and intergovernmental organizations that have been successful in this area are those that have faced the challenge proactively, admitted weakness and mistakes and have in an open and transparent manner tried to rectify them. INGOs need to learn from the experience of other sectors and take action before an Enron-style scandal forces them to take it.

It is vital that the accountability mechanisms adopted by the INGO sector enhance rather than detract from the sector's work. It is crucial that the mechanisms adopted by INGOs contribute towards their dynamic and often fluid nature and add to their ability to be important critical voices on issues around the world. 'The challenge is to identify mechanisms that promote rights and accountability, by seeking ways to articulate NGO responsibilities that do not endanger the political space for the many positive roles that NGOs can play in securing rights' (Jordan, 2004).

All global organizations are facing questions regarding their accountability. This is part of a re-questioning by society of the rights, roles and responsibilities of all institutions in the light of globalization. INGOs have been drawn into this debate, and given their extremely important role within the world it is vital they take up this challenge.

NOTES

1 The One World Trust is a UK-based charity supporting and promoting work to establish democratic and accountable world governance through reform of the United Nations, global institutions and international law. For more information about the Trust go to www.oneworldtrust.org.

2 IGOs are defined by the International Year Book of Associations as organizations 'based on a formal instrument of agreement between the governments of nation states; including three or more nation states as parties to the agreement; and possessing a permanent secretariat performing an on-going task' (Union of International Associations, 2002).

3 The One World Trust's 'Global Accountability Report: Power without Accountability' concludes that only one of the five IGOs it assessed gave access to the minutes of executive board meetings.

4   For more information on the Corporate Responsibility Campaign see www.amnesty.org.uk/business/campaigns.
5   The OECD in 1998 faced civil protests around the introduction by member states of the Multilateral Agreement on Investment. The WTO faced violence and protest outside its Ministerial meeting in Seattle in 1999 and the World Bank has been subject to numerous protests and campaigns, predominately surrounding its environmental record.
6   The original GAP accountability model included eight dimensions of accountability. However, subsequent evaluation and reassessment of the framework by the GAP team reduced the number of dimensions to four. See Blagescu (2004) for further details.
7   An organization's governing body is its highest decision-making body. A governing body should bring together all members and is normally a large and inefficient decision-making instrument, meeting infrequently and only taking key policy decisions, which set the overall direction of the organization. Governing bodies delegate most of their decision-making power to an executive body.
8   The executive board acts on behalf of an organization's governing body by implementing and monitoring decisions on a more regular basis. The executive is normally smaller in size and can, in practical terms, have far more power than the governing body.

13

On Trying to Do Good Well: Practicing Participatory Democracy through International Advocacy Campaigns

Juliette Majot

INTRODUCTION

International advocacy campaigns exist in the realm of the possible and the probable. They are the inevitable offering of a responsible civil society as it attempts to meet the unrecognized, ignored or actively denied needs and desires of local communities. International advocacy campaigns are a specific response to the widespread reality that while local problems can be a direct result of actors on the international stage, this level of responsibility is not matched by an equal level of accountability. This chapter argues that international advocacy campaigns are a legitimate form of participatory democracy that addresses an international accountability deficit.

The chapter sets out to consider why, how and by whom legitimacy in international campaigning is both scrutinized and judged. I refer to the practice of legitimacy quite specifically, simply to make clear the ongoing nature of the effort. Far from something ultimately attainable, legitimacy is not as much a reachable destination as it is a road trip. This paper does not attempt to describe programme success or relevance based on an analysis of a data set. Rather, it is simply a brief reflection on years of advocacy campaigning. What follows are stories about two distinctly different types of international advocacy campaigns, and an analysis of how and why public scrutiny and self-scrutiny are important.

The first is a story about the Bujagali campaign, in which the wisdom of building a dam at Bujagali Falls in Uganda has been the central question. The second is a story of policy-focused work, that of the World Commission on Dams (WCD), an international multi-sectoral governance process compelled by a highly volatile debate about the contribution of large dams to development.

SEARCHING FOR ENERGY IN UGANDA

In 1994, the government of Uganda, The Mdhavani Group (a local company) and AES Corporation (a US-based energy corporation) signed a memorandum of agreement to build a hydropower dam in Uganda. Following recommendations from AES, a site was chosen near Bujagali Falls and designs followed for a US$582 million, 200 MW plant. Among the project's supporters was the World Bank.

The story of Uganda's Bujagali Dam is a story like many others, in which a country badly in need of energy development sees a rising public interest in determining how that development should proceed, who should pay for it and who should benefit. From the start, everyone agreed that Uganda needed more generating capacity and more Ugandans needed access to it. Less than 1 per cent of the country's rural population was connected to the national power grid, and in total less than 5 per cent of Ugandans had access to power. But everyone did not agree on what the best approach to providing and distributing electricity would be.

From their inception, plans for the Bujagali Dam faced questions from a skeptical public. Why was the project so expensive? Was the site the best possible choice? Was hydropower the best generating option? What about geothermal power? Why wasn't the government fixing the problems of electricity loss and poor maintenance on the existing system? How would the grid be expanded? And above all, how would the primarily poor population of Uganda ever be able to pay for the electricity the planned dam would generate? Together, the questions represented the desire of an interested public to participate in determining the development of their country. Their interest, in turn, gained international support when locally based NGOs reached out to a broader audience, among them the Berkeley-based NGO International Rivers Network (IRN).

Trust between IRN and Uganda-based NGOs had begun to build in 2000. IRN had been contacted by an American living in Uganda who suggested that IRN meet with Ugandan NGOs regarding a planned dam there. With another NGO campaigner, Graham Saul of the Washington DC-based Bank Information Center, Lori Pottinger accepted the invitation on behalf of IRN and embarked on a fact-finding trip. She met with representatives of two local NGOs who had been working on the issue: Save Bujagali Crusaders (SBC) and the National Association of Professional Environmentalists (NAPE).

The Ugandan groups hoped to convince their government to explore a number of options for energy development in hopes of minimizing economic and social costs, while maximizing benefits to Ugandans. This effort included their opposition to the Ugandan government's decision to proceed with the proposed Bujagali Dam before any other options had been adequately reviewed.

Both local organizations had been trying to persuade the World Bank to drop the project, insisting that poverty reduction in Uganda should be the Bank's primary interest. Because the market for high-priced hydroelectricity in Uganda was tiny, the project itself would not help alleviate Uganda's high level of poverty (SBC and NAPE, 2000). Instead, they suggested, electricity generating capacity should be increased through upgrading Uganda's distribution system, which was losing as much as 40 per cent of its power through faulty transmission lines (Basalirwa et al, 2000). They also voiced their concerns about the level of corruption in Uganda and pointed out that the Bujagali Dam project had been excluded from an open competitive bidding process (SBC and NAPE, 2000).

As an international NGO with some 15 years of experience working with local organizations around the world, IRN knew that its legitimacy in entering an advocacy campaign in Uganda would rest on whether the local organizations desired IRN's participation and on the legitimacy of the domestically based NGOs themselves. Ascertaining this required face-to-face conversation, initial steps of cooperation and a shared clarity of purpose.

It also required what can best be described as a shared set of values and commitments to basic human rights (not restricted to civil rights, but including the rights to food, water and shelter); to cultural integrity; to environmental integrity; to the need for responsibility and accountability in multilateral institutions and multinational corporations; to just law; and to the legitimate and necessary role of civil society in governance. All parties had to agree on the legitimacy of international advocacy campaigns as an expression of participatory democracy in a globalized world.

These values and commitments are not of the type that can be superficially surveyed, and in fact they are sometimes difficult to gauge accurately. An understanding of an organization's background, the insights of already trusted partners who are familiar with it and a reading of its integrity based on past actions are all starting points. Ultimately, however, commitment to shared principles plays out in practice, where trust continues to be earned or is lost.

While the above is not an exhaustive list, it does give an idea of the basic components necessary for a compact of trust to have been established between IRN and Ugandan NGOs. In the case of the Bujagali campaign shared commitments formed the foundation of an advocacy campaign aimed at encouraging the legitimate participation of civil society in determining the future of energy development in Uganda.

The following characteristics of the campaign help to illuminate how it worked:

1 The campaign was jointly undertaken by both international and local organizations. The work consisted of: analysing and publishing technical information; compiling information on how the Ugandan project

compared to other projects internationally; meeting with Ugandan and World Bank officials; and attempting to influence project related decisions made at the World Bank and AES. IRN worked jointly with local organizations to publicize their views internationally in an effort to strengthen the local campaign, as well as to contribute lessons from Bujagali to the broader international debate on the best approaches to energy development. This last point is of strategic importance to international advocacy campaigning generally, which aims to influence policy beyond the local to the global. The decision to build the Bujagali Dam followed a planning process similar in its shortcomings to many others worldwide. By pointing out these similarities, efforts to improve energy planning processes internationally ultimately benefited.

2   IRN and the other key international NGOs involved in the campaign understood that for IRN to have a legitimate role, it needed to bring added value to the campaign and to be fluid and responsive to local needs. When, what, how and by whom different tactics should be employed had been planned by the local organizations, IRN and other international NGOs together, and there was a shared understanding that changes in conditions inside Uganda, at AES or at the World Bank would lead to changes in tactics.

3   Daily or weekly communication between campaigners relied heavily on email and telephone. Face-to-face meetings between IRN and NAPE happened annually or more often in Uganda and in internationally relevant meetings.

4   Efforts were made on all sides to keep bureaucracy limited while keeping direct communication high. The need to move quickly, yet wisely, necessitated both of these conditions. There were no written agreements between IRN and NAPE about roles, deadlines, functions or responsibilities. The working relationship took the form of an informal contract, not a formal one. This required ongoing electronic communication. Accountability to each other was a matter of practice and integrity. As with most international advocacy campaigns, time considerations were notoriously prickly. While some decisions could be made with known and reliable timelines, others were time-pressured by the real need to respond to an unanticipated event.

5   Access to information, such as securing specific documents, their public dissemination, and analysis and evaluation by independent experts, was central to the overall goals of the campaign. This reflected the campaign's commitment to freedom of information as essential to civil society's ability to contribute intelligently to energy planning in Uganda. The public release of the stunningly complex power purchase agreement was a key point in the campaign because this document ultimately proved the poor economics of the project. That the public had a right to see this document and a right to be offered an explanation of its terms were both objectives in and of themselves.[1]

6   The strategy included the development of a discourse on energy conservation and on generating options other than the dam at Bujagali Falls.

Through national and regional education and debate, this aspect of the campaign fed directly into efforts to increase the influence of civil society in determining optimal energy development. For example, in 2003, a workshop organized by NAPE, the Joint Energy and Environment Project and the Uganda Wildlife Society drew participants from civil society organizations, government and geothermal energy experts from Uganda and other parts of the world. The workshop followed on the heels of a regional geothermal workshop held in Kenya the previous week (Muramuzi and Karnese, 2003).

7   As with other campaigns, neither IRN nor NAPE entered into each other's internal organizational decision-making processes or debates. This practice recognized the potential influence of INGOs in matters that should remain under the full purview of the local organizations with whom they work. In all international advocacy campaigning, the intent and extent of involvement of NGOs in each other's internal governance is an extremely sensitive matter, and one that is best approached openly and explicitly. Organizations working in coalitions and networks successfully interact when autonomy is respected, while at the same time standards of behaviour and ethical practices are upheld. Internal organizational conflicts are rarely appropriately addressed by even the best-intentioned outside NGOs.

8   The international NGOs and local organizations together developed and implemented media and public outreach strategies. This is another extremely sensitive area, in which the use of the wrong frame or even a single word can have negative or even dangerous consequences. One crucial element of these strategies was to refrain from spreading gossip or rumor, and to maintain and ensure accuracy in detail and analysis.[2]

The international advocacy campaign for optimal energy development in Uganda continues, even as Uganda's government moves forward with plans to dam Bujagali Falls.[3] The campaign's principal concern with participatory democracy was made clear in a statement dated 15 April 2005 and signed by 85 participants of a civil society workshop help in Kampala and organized by the NAPE: 'Civil society wishes to assure the public that we are interested in the promotion of public participation, accountability and transparency as a way [sic] of promoting the sustainable development of the energy sector in Uganda'.

Included in the statement was a list of demands consistent with this legitimate aim, including:

- that the government ensure civil society and other stakeholders participate fully in the planning process, and ensure the release of pertinent information;
- that the government organize a participatory consultative meeting where local communities, government and civil society be given equal opportunity to present their positions on the Bujagali Dam project;
- that the government consider the development of other, more cost effective, hydropower projects and invest in other energy sources;

- that thorough screening of engineering consultancies take place, that local engineering companies be attached to any foreign company considered and that approval be granted by the Uganda Institution of Professional Engineers in order to ensure that the country builds local capacity in the area of dam development;
- that the government publicly declare the losses incurred by Uganda as a result of the AES-Bujagali power deal before the project is revived; and
- that the parliament of Uganda be fully integrated and consulted in the planning process.

These final points go a long way towards illustrating the legitimacy and integrity of what has become known as the Bujagali Campaign.

ON POLICY, COALITIONS AND CRITICS: A STORY ABOUT THE WORLD COMMISSION ON DAMS

In November 2000, Nelson Mandela announced to a packed London ballroom the release of the findings and recommendations of the World Commission on Dams. Behind him sat the 12 commissioners who had spent the better part of 2 years hearing testimony, receiving submissions and finally evaluating the performance of large dams worldwide in an effort to address the conflicting points of view on the value of large-scale dams.

The commissioners were an unusually diverse group, including participants from the dam building industry, government ministries, academia and civil society. One of the commissioners, Medha Patkar, had spent most of her life working with indigenous people opposing dams in India's Narmada Valley.[4] Another, Goran Lindahl, was the Chief Executive Officer of Asea Brown Bovari Ltd, one of the world's largest engineering firms. Joining Mr Mandela on stage was James Wolfensohn, then President of the World Bank, and Kader Asmal, WCD Chairperson and South Africa's Minister of Water Affairs and Forestry.

Throughout the room were scattered representatives of CBOs, INGOs and social movements who had also spent the better part of the last two years doing WCD-related work. Their ideas had led to its establishment and their commitment and perseverance had helped ensure the quality of its production.

The WCD had been established in 1997 at a meeting convened by the World Conservation Union (IUCN) and the World Bank.[5] The meeting's 39 participants came from a wide variety of backgrounds, including dam-building companies, think tanks, NGOs and representatives of social movements opposed to specific dams. Frustrated by a weak attempt by the World Bank's Operations and Evaluations Department to assess the performance of World Bank-supported dams, the meeting's conveners and participants took a bold step: to establish an international and independent commission to move beyond the limitations of a World Bank study. Put simply, the WCD's mandate was to study the costs and benefits of large dams worldwide and to put forth a set of recommendations intended to increase benefits and diminish costs (of all kinds).

In the NGO community, there had been a well-documented history of calls for such a body, beginning in June 1994 and codified in the Manibeli Declaration (www.irn.org/basics/ard/manibeli). The call was reiterated in 1997, in the Curitiba Declaration, drafted at the First International Meeting of People Affected by Dams held in Curitiba, Brazil (www.irn.org/basics/ard/declarations/curitiba).

The nature and intent of the WCD process had been to include and encourage engagement between and among participants from the private and public sectors, experienced critics and defenders of large dams, industry representatives, project-affected people and independent experts.

NGOs of many kinds, including international NGOs and CBOs, as well as representatives from social movements were engaged extensively and in a variety of ways. NGOs submitted oral and written testimony, ranging from the anecdotal to the highly technical. Some NGOs, including the US-based Environmental Defense Fund, UK-based Oxfam International (a representative from Australia) and the Philippines-based Tebtebba Foundation actually had staff serving as commissioners, as did the Indian-based social movement Narmada Bachao Andolan.

There were two concentric layers of watchdog NGOs engaged in the process. Some NGOs monitored progress on case studies and other written documents generated by the Commission and attempted to influence the Commission.[6] In turn, these NGOs were themselves monitored by other NGOs, CBOs and social movements who were doubtful of the WCD process.

There were tenacious efforts by NGOs directly engaged to carry out work on the WCD in a transparent and accountable fashion, an effort not just supported, but also demanded by other NGOs. Similarly, participants close to and further away from the process were constantly on guard for signs of co-optation. Peter Bosshard, who participated in the International Committee on Dams, Rivers and Peoples (ICDRP) as director of the Switzerland-based NGO, the Berne Declaration, stressed that the watchdog role of NGOs on other NGOs made the entire process more transparent and accountable than it would have been without them.

The extent of NGO engagement in the WCD process is far too broad to cover with any depth in this chapter. I will remark on the role and practices of a coalition of international NGOs, local organizations, CBOs and social movements and the ICDRP.

Coordinated by Patrick McCully, campaigns director of IRN, ICDRP served as the primary strategic and tactical NGO alliance influencing the formation, process and product of the WCD, including ensuring the casting of a wide net for submissions. The coalition, and IRN's role in it, carried a high degree of risk, responsibility and accountability (McCully, 2003).

IRN's legitimacy to serve as a coordinator rested on its long record as an INGO chiefly concerned with human rights and environmental and cultural integrity as they relate to rivers and watersheds. The interest in the WCD was to ensure broad input from civil society, to make sure that the voices of those directly affected by dams were heard and that the final report of the WCD would both help bring an end to construction of environmentally and socially destructive dams, while at the same time mark a new beginning for more thorough consideration of energy and water supply options.

The ICDRP was self-selecting and evolutionary in nature, its structure that of concentric circles of people and groups whose level of involvement ebbed and flowed. While some participants were involved in WCD work on a daily basis, others were updated and consulted about new developments less frequently. Its legitimacy was anchored in the proven experience of individual members and a high degree of trust and reliability among them and further, among the larger group of NGOs, CBOs and social movements engaged in the WCD process but outside the active ICDRP core group. ICDRP participants brought a variety of perspectives grounded in a shared set of values and endeavoured to maintain consistency in both communication and decision-making processes. The number of active participants in the ICDRP core group varied between 10 and 18 international NGO, local organization, CBO and social movement representatives at any one time.

The ICDRP took on a number of activities, all of them directed at the goal of ensuring that the final report of the WCD would accurately reflect the actual performance, costs and benefits of large dams. Notable activities were as follows:

- Coordinating input from civil society by mobilizing submissions to the commission – because input in the form of formal submissions and hearing testimony was crucial for informing the WCD, this function was among the key activities of the ICDRP. Submissions were both written and oral. All told, 950 submissions were made from 79 countries and 4 regional consultations were held in Africa/Middle East, East and Southeast Asia, Latin America and South Asia (Imhof et al, 2002).
- Helping to define the Commission's mandate, work plan, methodology and the role of any potential follow-up bodies established for the purpose of forwarding WCD findings and recommendations – the ICDRP believed that the type of engagement called for in the WCD process needed to extend from the early foundational guiding principles, through application and implementation of the recommendations.
- Advocating for a balanced Commission. The ICDRP contributed more than theory to the make-up of the Commission, helping to screen nearly 100 candidates and also nominating candidates for consideration. The ICDRP also shared its insights on the selection of commissioners, Commission leadership and secretariat staffing.
- Monitoring and, when possible, influencing the role of the World Bank – the World Bank had been one of the Commission's midwives, calling for its formation, contributing to its funding and committing itself to withdrawing from the formal process once the Commission was up and running, which it did. Behind the scenes, the World Bank continued to

influence the working of the Commission. In this role, the World Bank was carefully monitored by NGOs, whose views were often at odds with those of the Bank.

- Informing and communicating directly with the WCD secretariat and commissioners throughout the process.
- Providing and soliciting information from other activists also monitoring the process – ICDRP members communicated information and sought direct input throughout their networks. This was highly successful in the area of mobilizing submissions to the Commission. Tactical and strategic planning on the day-to-day level was indirectly informed through this broader network, including media strategies. During much of the two-year Commission process, communication between ICDRP members took place on a daily basis. Phone and email were the primary means of communication, and face-to-face meetings took place three or more times per year.
- Participating in and influencing the thinking and actions of the WCD Forum, a 'multi-stakeholder' group that served to advise the Commission.

The ICDRP continues to serve as a coordinating body in the implementation phase of the WCD, which is ongoing in nature. Continued education at government levels, advocacy of adoption of WCD guidelines by private and public finance institutions and adoption of guidelines by the dam building industry are all programme priorities. Citizen's guides to the WCD have been written and translated into a number of languages. IRN has continued to coordinate ICDRP activities, and this has included responsibilities for raising and disbursing funds throughout the active network for follow-up work.

Among the many lessons and challenges presented by IRN's experience in the ICDRP have been the following:

- Work of this type on the policy level requires full-time, continuous commitment. The loose structure of ICDRP recognized and embraced the nature of activism and advocacy, allowing for times of greater or lesser interest and participation of individual members. This was possible only because a core group of five to six NGO and/or social movement representatives remained active on a day-to-day basis throughout the entire process;
- For strategic and tactical thinking to be truly informed by a coalition, highly detailed and ongoing communication must be consistent and continuous. This raises the always difficult challenge of the working language. Wanting and recognizing the need for as much ongoing translation as possible while pressed to move information quickly and accurately, ICDRP maintained English as the working language on the day-to-day operational level of the coalition. Hearings and submissions, however, took place in multiple languages. Still, the use of English as the working language necessarily contributed to the elite nature of the core group of the ICDRP.
- The conundrum of a coalition intended to be wide reaching and democratic, yet exhibiting elite qualities, was deepened by the primary means of communication – computer and telephone. Time pressures exacerbated

this. Members of the ICDRP were carrying a high level of responsibility, needing to rely heavily on their experience and understanding of the overall political implications of their actions.

• Among the risks of the WCD project was that of co-optation – either real or perceived. Knowledge and open discussion of this risk within and beyond the membership of the ICDRP were part of the informal account-ability process practiced by members of the ICDRP.

• One of the objectives of the process was to ensure that the so-called 'Knowledge Base' developed during the WCD process would become a usable and used resource.[7] This has not happened, nor has there been any significant strategy developed towards this objective.

The work of the ICDRP was not over when the report was successfully completed and the Commission disbanded. Rather, ongoing work to ensure the wide dissemination of the report's findings and implementation of its recommendations is necessary. Ongoing information collection from and reporting to the broader movement on effectiveness of the WCD report and the formation of new strategies that move the WCD experience from 'process' to 'campaign' are the current foci of the coalition. Monitoring the rather weak formal WCD follow-up body, the 'WCD Dams and Development Project', is also ongoing.

The ICDRP is an example of a type of coalition (and a risky one, at that) that operates and depends on high levels of understanding of NGO rights, responsibilities and accountability. The fluid and informal nature of the ICDRP meant that at any one time it would have been virtually impossible to have drawn up a definitive list of ICDRP members. By its nature and to ensure its success, ICDRP participants had to understand the foundation of ICDRP legit-imacy and to consciously attempt a practice of integrity.

While it is not possible here to provide an in-depth look at the Commission's impact,[8] the conclusions reached by an independent evaluation illuminate the relationship between the WCD and participatory democracy. An independent study, *A Watershed in Global Governance? An Independent Assessment of the World Commission on Dams*, concluded:

> *Multi-stakeholder processes typically have little formal decision-making authority, and the WCD was no exception. Instead, multi-stakeholder processes are designed to win consent for implementation through a process of inclusion, with a particular focus on civil society and the private sector. A process structured around representative stakeholders holds the potential for genuinely new and transformative formulations that can break policy deadlocks – a contribution that is less likely to be achieved through governmental processes alone...*
>
> *[Although] democratization of decision-making at the global level can bring significant advantages, ultimately advances in principles and practices must be translated to and implemented*

> *at the national level and below. However, as the experience of the WCD suggests, efforts at global and national democratization are mutually reinforcing. In the WCD process civil society organizing at the national level served as the catalyst for creating the Commission and the seedbed for a transnational civil society alliance on dams. Conversely, the WCD process provided an avenue for greater expression at the national level and stimulated further dialogue across sectors at that level. The full potential of the WCD – and other multi-stakeholders processes – lies in this promise of democratization, at both the national and global levels.* (Dubash et al, 2001)

The WCD process was and continues to be an excellent case study of the interplay between NGO rights, responsibilities and accountability within a broad international coalition. It is also an excellent example of participatory democracy.

The exercise, widely considered successful to date, is not without its significant challenges and shortcomings. The success of the WCD process and the ongoing campaign to include civil society in the development of optimal energy production and use remains to be seen, and will be measured over time. As a model, the WCD process has very high value, bringing critics and defenders of large dams together and asking them to unanimously put forth findings and recommendations that should, in the long run, help protect indigenous rights, the environment and human rights – as long as, and this is key, the individual and joint efforts of NGOs of all kinds, including social movements, are considered integral to the WCD process.

ON SCRUTINY: ITS ROLE AND IMPORTANCE IN INTERNATIONAL ADVOCACY CAMPAIGNS

The legitimacy of all manner of actors participating in democracy is a matter of ongoing consideration. The question of legitimacy benefits from both inwardly and outwardly directed scrutiny. Civil society calls for and assesses it in public officials, in corporations, in agencies ranging from the local to the multilateral and vice versa. Importantly, NGOs can and do demand it of each other.

The presence, absence or extent of legitimacy is judged, fairly and unfairly, for reasons both transparent and covert, for points of principle and for points of political gain. When present, legitimacy can be used as a shield, and its absence can lead to deserved vulnerability.

The media, for better and for worse, provides its own form of scrutiny. Media coverage of the ongoing debate in Uganda included coverage of the advocacy campaign itself, in particular scrutiny of NAPE and IRN. For example, NAPE was pressured by Ugandan President Museveni, who had denounced opponents to the Bujagali Dam as 'economic saboteurs' and 'enemies'. In the 26 January 2002 issue of the state-owned newspaper, *New Vision*, Museveni expanded on the theme, saying, 'Those who delay industrial projects are enemies and... I am going to open war on them' (Okello, 2002).

Some of the coverage provides a clear picture of how the mischaracterization of a campaign and its participants can erroneously suggest that the campaign is, in fact, not legitimate. A case in point is coverage provided by British journalist Sebastian Mallaby, who is unimpressed with NAPE and IRN and questions the legitimacy of international advocacy campaigns generally: 'Uganda's National Association of Professional Environmentalists had all of 25 members – not exactly a broad platform from which to oppose electricity for millions', Mallaby wrote (Mallaby, 2004). Mallaby failed to place NAPE in the broader context in which it is seen as a responsible, credible and accountable leader in the region and assigned its opposition to 'electricity for millions', rather than to a large dam that they believed would most certainly fail at just that.

Finding information to support NAPE's credibility in the region would not have been difficult. NAPE served as the Ugandan chair of ECOVIC, a regional environmental network of more than 100 organizations working on Lake Victoria resources in Tanzania, Kenya and Uganda, and it was a member of the Uganda NGO Forum, which has more than 700 members. NAPE also chaired the Committee on Integrated Fresh Water and Ugandan Energy for Sustainable Development, which included more than 100 organizations. NAPE sat on the Council of the Nile Basin Discourse, and its Secretary, F. C. Afunaduula, served as vice chair of the Ugandan Discourse on the Nile. NAPE also sat alongside the Minister of Energy as one of only two Ugandan entities on the Dams and Development Project under the United Nations Environment Programme (UNEP).

What Mallaby's coverage lacks is consideration of the history of cooperation between the many actors in the campaign. That he simply saw NAPE as what he described as 'a grouplet' implies more about his view of international advocacy campaigning than it does about his reporting skills. Had he believed in even the possibility that NAPE gives legitimate voice to public concerns, he could have learned much more about NAPE's standing in the region and internationally.[9]

A lack of investigation into the relationship between INGOs and national, regional, indigenous or community-based NGOs with whom they work implies a lack of recognition of international advocacy campaigns as legitimate actors in participatory democracy. It can also imply actual opposition to them as such, or opposition to participatory democracy itself. In the absence of sound analysis of who is involved in a given advocacy campaign, why and how that work is carried out, criticism intended to imply that a campaign lacks legitimacy can easily be perceived as ideologically motivated. Ultimately, it can be read as questioning the legitimacy of participatory democracy itself, not those attempting to practice it.

The ideologically-based targeting of INGOs is the first step in a kind of sequential discrediting that leads directly to local organizations, CBOs and social movements. It is particularly effective at harming the reputations and therefore perceived legitimacy of organizations who build international support and who are problematic for governments and corporations that do not wish to face local opposition to their plans. Accusations of being unduly influenced by INGOs, who are in turn labeled illegitimate and unaccountable, need not be true to cause serious problems for many organizations, both personally and in terms of overall campaign progress, while in most instances leaving unscathed the INGOs who are ostensibly the target of those who oppose their position and/or influence.

In practice, the complex and interwoven relationships between INGOs, professional associations, CBOs and social movements are perhaps more immediately vulnerable to ideologically driven attacks when these relationships can be interpreted as existing for the primary purpose of stopping a specific project. The intimidation that can and often does accompany such attacks on the local level helps ensure this. When based on a high level of trust and strength of experience, international campaigns are perhaps less vulnerable, but they are even more likely to be subjected to ideologically driven attacks when the campaigns are aimed at creating global policy. It's a matter of power. The logic here is simple. Changes in – or the creation of new policy – can have far reaching consequences, hence a stronger backlash.

Consider the language and intended message of a book review that appeared in the 23 September 2004 print edition of the highly respected UK-based magazine, *The Economist*:

> [The World Bank]... is besieged by single-issue fanatics in the West who condemn it whenever it fails to make their issue a top priority. James Wolfensohn, the World Bank's president since 1995, has made strenuous efforts to accommodate the NGO swarm. Every infrastructure project the Bank funds must meet rich-world standards; nothing pretty may be bulldozed unless strictly necessary, and no worker may be asked to do anything that a Californian might find demeaning. As a result, fewer dams, roads, and flood barriers are built in poor countries. More poor people stay poor, live in darkness and die younger.[10]

There is the nub. An international 'NGO swarm' is actively ensuring that poor people stay poor, live in darkness and die younger. President Museveni says it one way, *The Economist* says it another.

Contrast the above views expressed by *The Economist* to those of Jim MacNeill, chairperson of the World Bank's inspection panel (March 1999–December 2001):

> NGO's have strengthened the fabric of democracy in many fragile states, as I have witnessed personally in parts of Africa, Asia and, more recently, the Caucasus. They are indispensable agents of broader public participation and greater openness in private

sector and government decision-making. In many countries they deliver essential services that weak governments will not or can no longer manage. And, yes, thanks to the computer, they are now able to network across borders and sometimes exert enormous influence. In the case of the bank, local NGOs can enable the poorest and weakest of those affected by a Bank-funded project to voice their concerns and, through the [World Bank] Panel, the Bank's Board has provided a vehicle to investigate their claims while respecting the rights of all parties involved. International NGOs can augment local voices, strengthen local NGOs, and provide the sometimes much needed protection of a global spotlight. (MacNeill, 2004)

MacNeill later adds:

The development of a vigorous civil society, interconnected through the web, does raise novel questions of governance that merit serious study. It is conceivable, for example, that a multiplicity of single purpose groups in a given jurisdiction could so fragment the public will that democratic governance is threatened. A rigorously balanced analysis is needed. (MacNeill, 2004)

There is a clear difference between the principled scrutiny of NGOs legitimacy and the targeting of that legitimacy as a means to undermine them; a difference between the principled demand for integrity in NGOs and their work, and targeting them precisely because they effectively participate in governance.

One critique that did attempt to gauge the legitimacy and integrity of a given international advocacy campaign was undertaken at Harvard University. When Harvard Business School chose IRN and the Bujagali Dam Project as the subject for a full case study, Professor Ben Esty and Research Associate Ado Sesia Jr, took the time to consider the legitimacy not just of arguments against the dam and for a broader energy options assessment, but also of the international and community-based NGOs who held these views (Esty and Sesia, 2004).

Based on fact-checked research that included lengthy interviews and written correspondence, the Harvard case study attempted to chart the mission of both IRN and NAPE, the history of their working relationship and the evolution of their advocacy campaign. In short, the case study attempted to consider the integrity of the campaign. Harvard also attempted to consider the integrity of the Ugandan government, the World Bank and AES. In other words, the Harvard study ultimately challenged business students to consider the legitimacy of international advocacy campaigns and their role in participatory democracy.

Self-policing – the practice of NGOs of all types scrutinizing each other in the many and varied campaigns in which they participate – has a long and unfortunately mostly undocumented history. (I am talking here of evaluations of how work is undertaken, not the more common and certainly more documented area of what issues are highlighted.) Scrutiny of *how* campaigns work – the deconstruction of an international campaign, of questioning its assumptions and processes, strategic relevance, recognition and discussion of mistakes, failures and successes – while widely practiced, is rarely shared with the broader public outside the campaign. While some reasons for this are compelling, most are not.

For example, when individuals in CBOs are closely watched and threatened by powerful interests, broad public disclosure of internal debate within an international campaign is, usually wisely, actively and consciously discouraged. This limitation on outside scrutiny is a hallmark of responsible campaigning, and not the brunt of concerns regarding the legitimacy, accountability or transparency of international campaigns and NGOs.

Less compelling reasons for limiting scrutiny to internal participants abound, often falling under the rubric of weak thinking, characterized by the saying 'Don't air your dirty laundry in public'. This is a silly yet sadly played out dictum, created to ease embarrassment, put on a false front or maintain self-denial.

Avoiding embarrassment by putting on a false front ('I must always appear to know what I'm doing, and appear to be right about it') and maintaining self-denial ('I *do* always know what I'm doing, and I *am* always right about it') are among the two most deadly toxins in international campaigning. They are forgivable only very briefly and only because of the universality of their affliction.

In settings where repression is less of a problem, open and rigorous scrutiny of international campaigns and the role of international NGOs in them is automatic among CBOs, social movements and the communities they serve, because the campaign and its consequences can directly influence day-to-day living. If, for example, an INGO as a lone wolf campaigns for the designation of restricted park status for a piece of land in contravention of traditional land rights, indigenous peoples and CBOs will object not just to the outcome, but to why and how the campaign is being carried out. The integrity of the campaign and those involved in it will be legitimately condemned.

While the findings of self-policing often do remain outside of the public sphere, some are finally seeing the light. One example is the recent public debate on the roles and campaign practices of some of the largest, richest and most powerful international conservation NGOs.

In *A Challenge to Conservationists*, Mac Chapin chronicles complaints against the campaign practices of WWF, Conservation International and the Nature Conservancy, among others (Chapin, 2004). The complaints, which focus on a lack of legitimacy and accountability, are certainly not news to the CBOs or other international NGOs who work through a social justice framework. Indigenous organizations have long identified fundamental problems with the way in which these organizations work and have explicitly and repeatedly made these feelings known. What is news to CBOs and INGOs is that the debate is finally a public one and, more importantly, it extends beyond narrow definitions of legitimacy and accountability (including lack of financial transparency, potential conflict of interest among board and/or staff members, or the over-reporting of programme success) to include consideration of whether the manner in which these organizations work reinforces or diminishes the underpinnings of participatory democracy. International campaigns in which local and indigenous rights and responsibilities are ignored or actively denied are particularly destructive to participatory democracy.

CONCLUSIONS

Without well-executed international advocacy campaigns, critics of participatory democracy get what they want, which is, as IRN executive director Patrick McCully recently put so succinctly, 'to get international advocacy NGOs to shut up' (McCully, 2004).

Of course, critics of participatory democracy would equally hope to silence the voices of local and regional organizations, indigenous organizations and social movements too. This will not happen for a variety of reasons, chief among them, the diversity and commitment of civil society organizations worldwide and the legitimacy of their standing.

In a globalized world, local, regional and international campaigns succeed through deep respect for societal governance and strategic organization, and a clear understanding that global policies influence our lives every bit as much, perhaps more, than nationally developed law. Representative democracy does not, on its own, provide an answer to this challenge, nor do established multilateral and bilateral institutions.

Both the Bujagali Campaign and the NGO work surrounding the WCD are aimed not at limiting development or stopping particular projects; rather, they are aimed at expanding the role of civil society in determining how best to provide for basic needs. In Uganda, local organizations were as interested in contributing to the policy discussion presented by the WCD as they were in questioning the wisdom of one particular dam at Bujagali Falls. Members of the ICDRP, in turn, were as interested in the specifics of the Bujagali controversy as they were in the broadest policy implications of the findings and recommendations of the WCD. This is why project and policy work are so clearly related, why they are strategically mutually reliant and why local organizations and international NGOs thrive together.

Ultimately, legitimate international advocacy campaigns are not about the dam or the oil pipeline or the strip mine. They are about the rights of individuals to hold an opinion, to put that opinion forward in an organized and strategic campaign at home and abroad in a globalized world. How better to question the wisdom of governments ostensibly working in the interests of the governed, multinational corporations serving their own interests, or multilateral and bilateral development institutions whose declared interests are often at odds with their actions? How better for a responsible, rights-based civil society to act with integrity?

Responsible governance in a globalized world does not merely accept an active civil society organized across borders of nations, class, race and gender, it actually requires it. This is the role that NGOs of all sizes and shapes willfully play, confident in their *raison d'être*, visionary in their thinking and legitimate in their practice.

NOTES

1   IRN had hoped that the World Bank inspection panel would require the Bank to disclose the Power Purchase Agreement. This did not occur. Following the petition of the Ugandan NGO, Greenwatch, the Ugandan High Court asked the Ugandan government to release the Agreement. The government responded to the request, insisting that such a document did not exist. The High Court eventually received a leaked copy from a local NGO (name not released to the public), and subsequently ordered the report's public release. The report was analysed by the India-based Prayas Energy Group. For more information see: www.irn.org/programs/bujagali/pdf/bujagalippa-review.pdf.

2   While rumors of corruption associated with the case had existed for some time, the campaign did not forward them to the media. Eventually, corruption investigations were launched by the World Bank, the government of Norway, the government of Uganda and the governments of Sweden and the United States. In its own internal investigation, AES uncovered one US$10,000 bribe paid in 1999 by an employee of the Norwegian subcontracting firm Veidekke to the Ugandan energy minister Richard Kaijuka.

3   The plans do not include AES, which withdrew from the project in August 2003. The withdrawal was announced in AES's quarterly report to the US Security and Exchange Commission: www.sec.gov/archives/edgar/data/874761/000110465903017847/a03-1517_110Q.

4   WCD Commissioners and their affiliations: Kader Asmal, WCD Chairperson, Ministry of Water Affairs and Forestry, South Africa; Lakshmi Chand Jain, WCD Vice-Chairperson, High Commissioner to South Africa, India; Judy Henderson, Oxfam International, Australia; Goran Lindahl, Asea Brown Bovari Ltd., Sweden; Thayer Scudder, California Institute of Technology, US; Joji Carino, Tebrebba Foundation, Philippines; Donald Blackmore, Murray-Darling Basin Commission, Australia; Medha Patkar, Struggle to Save the Narmada River, India; Jose Goldemberg, University of Sao Paolo, Brazil; Deborah Moore, Environmental Defense, US; Shen Guoyi, Ministry of Water Resources, China (later resigned); Jan Veltrop, Honorary President, International Commission on Large Dams, US; and Achim Steiner, WCD Secretary General.

5   While the decision to establish the Commission was made in 1997, the Commission itself was not formed until 1998.

6   Case studies were intended to evaluate actual against projected performance, including: costs and impacts; unanticipated benefits; the distribution of benefits and costs; how planning and operations decisions were made; whether the project complied with criteria and guidelines of the day; and what lessons were learned from the project.

7   The formal Knowledge Base consists of 11 case studies in 5 regions, 17 thematic reviews on social, environmental and economic impacts and other issues, a cross-

check survey of 125 dams in 56 countries and the proceedings of 4 regional consultations in Africa/Middle East, East and Southeast Asia, Latin America and South Asia, and 950 submissions from 79 countries.

8   While the findings of the WCD are widely respected at government levels, actual implementation of WCD guidelines has been sluggish. Germany and South Africa remain the only governments who have officially adopted the report or parts of it. Other countries claim to use it as a guide or have rejected it outright. Multilateral and regional development banks have all rejected the report's recommendations. Among the multilaterals and regional banks, the World Bank has led the opposition to adherence to WCD guidelines.

9   IRN's policy director Peter Bosshard makes a different point about equating the integrity of a CBO with the size of its membership, saying, 'Uganda's NGO networks and parliamentarians opposed the project primarily because of the high cost, corruption, political arm-twisting and secrecy that are associated with it. In this context, the membership base of the NGO that coordinates this effort is irrelevant' (Bosshard, 2004).

10 In this attack on international NGOs, the insights, experience, knowledge and legitimacy – the integrity – of local organizations and social movements have deftly been denied and replaced with 'anything a Californian might find demeaning'. CBOs and social movements are not even considered part of the 'international NGO swarm'.

References

Abidin, H. and Rukmini, M. (2004) *Kritik dan Otokritik LSM. Membongkar Kejujuran dan Keterbukaan Lembaga Swadaya Masyarakat Indonesia* ('Critique and Self-Critique of NGOs, Unpacking the Integrity and Openness of Indonesian NGOs') YAPPIKA, Jakarta

Ackerman, J. (2004) 'Co-governance: Beyond "Exit" and "Voice"', *World Development*, vol 32, no 3, pp447–463

ActionAid (1999) 'Fighting Poverty Together, ActionAid's Strategy 1999–2005', ActionAid, London

ActionAid (2000) 'Accountability Learning and Planning System', ActionAid, London

ActionAid (2005) *Real Aid: An Agenda for Making Aid Work*, www.actionaid.org

ActionAid Uganda (1999) 'Organization Development Process Workshop Report', ActionAid Uganda, Mbarara, Uganda

ActionAid Uganda (2002a) 'Kanambut: Learning and Planning and Reporting Guidelines for ActionAid Uganda', ActionAid Uganda, Kampala, Uganda

ActionAid Uganda (2002b) 'Northern Region PRRP Report 2002', ActionAid Uganda, Kampala, Uganda

ActionAid Uganda (2004) 'Partner Review Forum', ActionAid Uganda, Kampala, Uganda

ALTERLAW (undated) 'Primer on BIR Regulation No. 12-98: Accreditation of NGOs for Tax Purposes', ALTERLAW, Manila, The Philippines

Amnesty International (2000) *Respect, Protect, Fulfil*, Amnesty International, London

Amnesty International (2001) *Broken Bodies, Shattered Minds: Torture and Ill-treatment of Women*, Amnesty International, London

Anderson, K. (2000) 'The Ottawa Convention Banning Landmines: The Role of International Non-governmental Organizations and the Idea of International Civil Society', *European Journal of International Law*, vol 11, pp91–120

Anderson, K. (2001) 'The Limits of Pragmatism in American Foreign Policy: Unsolicited Advice to the Bush Administration on Relations with International Non-governmental Organizations', *Chicago Journal of International Law*, vol 2, pp371–388

Anderson, K. and Rieff, D. (2004) 'Global Civil Society: A Skeptical View', in H. Anheier, M. Glasius and M. Kaldor (eds) *Global Civil Society 2004/5*, Sage Publications, London

Archibugi, D. (2000) 'Cosmopolitical Democracy', *New Left Review*, July/August, pp137–144

Arrangements (1996) 'Arrangements for Consultation with Non-Governmental Organizations', UN Economic and Social Council Res. 1996/31, para.9, UN, New York

Aspen Institute (1997) *Competing Vision: The Nonprofit Sector in the Twenty-First Century: Perspectives from A Conference Convened By the Non-Profit Sector*

Research Fund 1995, Nonprofit Sector Research Fund Dialogue Series, Aspen Institute, Washington DC,

Atack, I. (1999) 'Four Criteria of Development NGO Legitimacy', *World Development*, vol 27, no 5, pp855–864

Austin Hu (2003) 'Zai kuaguo gongsi yu gongyi shiye gaoji luntan shang de jianghua' ('Speech at the Senior Forum on Multinational Corporations and Welfare Undertakings'), World Bank, Beijing, 9 November

Bakker, I. (2002) 'Fiscal Policy, Accountability and Voice: The Example of Gender Responsive budget Initiatives', UNDP Human Development Report Office Occasional Paper, UNDP, New York

Baron, B. F. (2003) 'Deterring Donors: Anti-terrorist Financing Rules and American Philanthropy', www.allavida.org/alliance/articles/DeterringDonors.pdf

Baron, B. F (2004) 'US Charities Propose Alternatives to Treasury Guidelines', *Alliance Extra*, www.allavida.org/alliance/axdec04c.html

Basalirwa, A., Babirye, Y. and Kidega, F. (2000) 'Concerns about the Bujugali Dam Project', paper sent to the World Bank group and the International Financial Corporation, August, www.irn.org

Bello, W. (2000) 'From Melbourne to Prague: The Struggle for a Deglobalized World', in *ZMag*, September 6–10, www.zmag.org/melbourne_to_prague.htm

Bello, W. (2003) 'What's Wrong with Oxfam Trade Campaign?', www.context.nz:8080/stories

Bendell, J. (2004) 'Barricades and Boardrooms: A Contemporary History of the Corporate Accountability Movement', Programme Paper 13, United Nations Research Institute for Social Development (UNRISD), Geneva

Bendell, J. (2005) 'In Whose Name? The Accountability of Corporate Social Responsibility', *Development in Practice*, vol 15, nos 3 & 4, June, pp362–374

Berresford, S. (2004) 'Foundations Must Play a Role in Policing Themselves', paper presented as part of the Philanthropy Discussion Series, Stanford Graduate School of Business, www.gsb.stanford.edu/news/headlines/csi_phil_disc_series_berresford.shtml

Bissio, R. (2003) 'Civil Society and the MDGs', *UNDP Development Policy Journal*, vol 3, April, www.undp.org/dpa/publications/DPJ3Final1.pdf

Blagescu, M. (2004) *What Makes Global Organizations Accountable? Reassessing the Global Accountability Framework*, One World Trust, London

Blitt, R. C. (2004) 'Who Will Watch the Watchdogs? Human Rights Non-governmental Organizations and the Case for Regulation', *Buffalo Human Rights Law Review*, vol 10, pp261–398

Boisson de Chazournes, L. (2005) 'The World Bank Inspection Panel: About Public Participation and Dispute Settlement', in T. Treves, M. F. Di Rattalma, A. Tanzi, A. Fodella and R. Pitea (eds) *Civil Society, International Courts and Compliance Bodies*, T. M. C. Asser Press, The Hague

Bolton, J. R. (2000) 'Should We Take Global Governance Seriously?', *Chicago Journal of International Law*, vol 1, pp205–216

Bosshard, P. (2004) 'IRN Response to Foreign Policy', www.irn.org/programs/finance/index?id=sebastianmallaby/040927mallaby.html

Broadhead, T (1987) 'NGOs: In One Year, Out the Other?', *World Development*, vol 15, supplement, Fall, pp1–6

Bucholtz, B. (1998) 'Reflections on the Role of Nonprofit Associations in a Representative Democracy', *Cornell Journal of Law & Public Policy*, vol 7, pp555, 579–583

Callamard, A. (2001) *Humanitarian Accountability: Key Elements and Operational Framework*, HAP, Geneva

Callamard, A. (2003) 'The HAP and humanitarian accountability', *Humanitarian Exchange*, March, Overseas Development Institute, London, pp35–37

Callamard, A. and Van Brabant, K. (2002) 'Accountability: A Question of Rights and Duties', in IFRC, *World Disaster Report*, International Federation of Red Cross, Geneva, pp148–169

Centre for Science in the Public Interest (2003) 'Lifting the Veil of Secrecy: Corporate Support for Health and Environmental Professional Associations, Charities and Industry Front Groups', http://cspinet.org/integrity/liftingtheveil.html

Centre on Philanthropy (2005) (first quarter) 'Million Dollar List: Executive Summary', www.philanthropy.iupui.edu/Million

CEP (Centre for Effective Philanthropy) (2004) 'Listening to Grantees: What Nonprofits Value in Their Foundation Funders', April, www.effectivephilanthropy.com/publications

Centre for Reproductive Rights (2003) 'Expanded Global Gag Rule Limits Women's Rights and Endangers Their Well-being', www.crlp.org/hill_int_ggr_hiv.html

Chapin, M. (2004) 'A Challenge to Conservationists', *World Watch*, Worldwatch Institute, Washington, DC

Chapman, J. (2003) 'ActionAid's Accountability Learning and Planning System: Challenges of Implementing Downward Accountability in an International Organization', paper presented at Intract 5th Evaluation Conference, The Netherlands

Chapman, J. and Wameyo, A. (2001) *Monitoring and Evaluating Advocacy: A Scoping Study*, ActionAid UK, London

Chapman, J., Rosalind D. and Mancini A. (2004) 'Transforming Practice in ActionAid: Experiences and Challenges in Rethinking Learning, Monitoring and Accountability Systems', in Earle L. (ed) *Creativity and Constraint: Grassroots Monitoring and Evaluation and the International Aid Arena*, INTRAC, Oxford

Charnovitz, S. (1997) 'Two Centuries of Participation: NGOs and International Governance', *Michigan Journal of International Law*, vol 18, pp183–286

Christian Aid (2004) 'Behind the Mask: The Real Face of Corporate Social Responsibility', Christian Aid, London

Christoplos, I. (2002a) *The Humanitarian Accountability Project: First Trial in Sierra Leone*, HAP, Geneva

Christoplos, I. (2002b) *The Humanitarian Accountability Project: Field Trial in Afghanistan*, HAP, Geneva

Chronicle of Philanthropy (2005) 'The Giving Spree', March 3, http://philanthropy.com/free/articles

Cidse (International Cooperation for Development and Solidarity) (2005) 'Europe: A True Global Partner for Development', Shadow Report on European Progress Towards MDG Goal 8, International Cooperation for Development and Solidarity, www.cidse.org/docs/200505201324183260.pdf

Civil Society Forum (2004) 'Declaration to UNCTAD XI São Paolo', June, available at www.forumsociedadecivil.org.br/dspMostraBiblioteca.asp?idBib=62

Clark, J. (1991) *Democratizing Development: The Role of Voluntary Organizations*, Earthscan, London

Clegg, S. (1989) *Frameworks of Power*, Sage, London

Coalition for Freedom of Information (2004) 'Guiding Principles for an Access to Information Legislation in Uganda', Coalition for Freedom of Information, Kampala, Uganda

Cohen, J. and Arato, A. (1992) *Civil Society and Political Theory*, The MIT Press, Cambridge, MA

Cohen, J. and Rogers, J. (eds) (1995) *Associations and Democracy*, Verso, London

Common Cause (2005) 'Mutual protection: Why mutual funds should embrace disclosure of corporate political contributions', Common Cause, Washington, DC, www.commoncause.org

Common Dreams (2003) 'Corporate Money Co-opts Nonprofit Groups: Critics Silenced & Friends Won Through Corporate Donations', 9 July, www.global policy.org/ngos

Crimm, N. J. (2004) 'High Alert: The Government's War on the Financing of Terrorism and its Implications for Donors, Domestic Charitable Organizations, and Global Philanthropy', *William & Mary Law Review*, vol 45, pp1341–1451

CRM (Civil Rights Movement of Sri Lanka) (1996) 'Some Comments on the World Bank's Draft Handbook "Global Standards and Best Practices for Laws Governing Non-Governmental Organizations"', August 6 (using an early title of the Draft Handbook), Civil Rights Movement of Sri Lanka, Colombo

Dahl, R. A. (1961) *Who Governs? Democracy and Power in an American City*, Yale University Press, New Haven

Dalton, R. J. and Kuechler, M. (eds) (1990) *Challenging the Political Order: New Social and Political Movements in Western Democracies*, Oxford University Press, New York

Damayanti, R. A. (2002) 'Membangun NGO yang Sehat dan Kuat, Transparan dan Akuntabel: Perspektif Donor' ('To Develop Strong and Healthy NGOs, Democratic, Transparent and Accountable: A Donor Perspective'), paper presented during the Seminar on the Development of Strong and Healthy NGOs, Democratic, Transparent and Accountable, Palembang, South Sumatra, 9 July

Davidson, S. (2002) *The Accountable Organization*, HAP, Geneva

De Coninck, J. (2005) 'Voluntary Certification for NGOs in Uganda: What Way Forward?', a discussion document produced for the NGO Forum, MS Uganda, The Development Network of Indigenous Voluntary Associations, Kampala, Uganda

De la Torre, C. (2000) *The Populist Seduction in Latin America: The Ecuadorian Experience*, Ohio University Center for International Studies, Athens, OH

De Las Casas, L. (2005) *Complaint and Redress Mechanisms in International Organizations: Background Research for the Complaint and Redress Dimension*, One World Trust, London

De Tocqueville, A. (1988) 'Democracy in America', in Mayer J. P. (ed), *Harper Perennial*, New York

Don Xueqing (2002) 'Dong Yuge xianxiang tan xi' ('Analysis of the Dong Yuge Phenomenon'), www.xinhua.sd.cn, 31 May

Dubash, N.K., Dupar, M., Kothari, S. and Lissu T.(2001) *A Watershed in Global Governance? An Independent Assessment of the World Commission on Dams*, World Resources Institute, Washington, DC, Lokayan, Delhi and Lawyer's Environmental Action Team, Dar Es Salaam

Ebrahim, A. (2003) 'Accountability in Practice: Mechanisms for NGOs', *World Development*, vol 31, issue 5, pp813–829

Eckstein, H. (1960) *Pressure Groups Politics*, Stanford University Press, alo Alto, CA

Edelman, R. (2005) 'Edelman Trust Barometer 2005: The Sixth Global Opinion Leaders Study', Edelman Public Relations, Brussels

Edwards, M. (1999) *Future Positive: International Co-operation in the 21st Century*, Earthscan, London

Edwards, M. (2000) *NGO Rights and Responsibilities: A New Deal for Global Governance*, Foreign Policy Centre, London

Edwards, M. (2004) *Civil Society*, Polity Press, Cambridge

Edwards, M. and Fowler, A. (2002) *The Earthscan Reader on NGO Management*, Earthscan, London

Edwards, M. and Hulme, D. (eds) (1995) *Beyond the Magic Bullet: NGO Performance and Accountability in the Post-Cold War World*, Kumarian Press, New York

Ehrenberg, J. (1999) *Civil Society: The Critical History of an Idea*, New York University Press, New York

Eldridge, P. J. (1995) *Non-Government Organizations and Democratic Participation in Indonesia*, Oxford University Press, Kuala Lumpur

Esty, B. C. and Sesia Jr, A. (2004) *International Rivers Network and the Bujagali Dam Project (A) and (B)*, President and Fellows of Harvard College, Harvard Business School Publishing, Boston, MA

Esty, D. C. (1998) 'Non-governmental Organizations at the World Trade Organization: Cooperation, Competition, or Exclusion', *Journal of International Economic Law*, vol 1, pp123,135–137

European Foundation Center (2004a) 'Chart: Number of Public Purpose Foundations in EU Countries', www.efc.be/projects/eu/research/num

European Foundation Center (2004b) 'Creation of New Foundations Over the Last Decade', www.efc.be/projects/eu/research/num

European Foundation Center (2005) 'The Joint Working Group on Accountability in International Giving', ww.efc.be/projects/ic/account.htm

Fakih, M. (1991) *Non Governmental Organizations in Indonesia*, Center for International Education, University of Massachusetts, Amherst, MA

Featherstone, A. and Routley, S. (2002) *Facilitating and Monitoring Accountability: HAP Field Trial in Afghanistan*, HAP, Geneva

Feulner, F. (2001) *Consolidating Democracy in Indonesia: Contributions of Civil Society and State. Part One: Civil Society*, United Nations Support Facility for Indonesian Recovery (UNSFIR), Jakarta, Indonesia

Forsythe, D. P. (1996–97) 'International Humanitarian Assistance: The Role of the Red Cross', *Buffalo Journal of International Law*, vol 3, pp235–260

Foundation Centre (2002) 'EFC–COF Joint Working Group on Accountability in International Giving', www.efc.be/projects/ic/account.htm

Fowler, A. (1997) *Striking a Balance: A Guide to Enhancing the Effectiveness of Non-governmental Organizations in International Development*, Earthscan, London

Fox, J. A. and Brown, L. D. (eds) (1998) *The Struggle for Accountability: The World Bank, NGOs, and Grassroots Movements*, The MIT Press, Cambridge, MA

Freeman, R. (1984) *Strategic Management: A Stakeholders Approach*, Pitman, Boston, MA

Friedrich, C. J. (1963) *Man and His Government*, McGraw Hill, New York

Ganie-Rochman, M. (2000) *Needs Assessment of Advocacy NGOs in a New Indonesia*, Unpublished report to the Ford Foundation, Jakarta

Gao Bingzhong (2001) 'Shehui tuanti de xingqi ji qi hefaxing wenti' ('The Rise of Social Organizations and Their Legitimacy'), in Kang Xiaoguang (ed.) *Zhongguo Disan Bumen Yanjiu Nianjian 2000 Nian: Chu Yu Shizi Lukou de Zhongguo Shetuan* (*The Research Yearbook on the Third Sector in 2000, Chinese Social Organizations at the Crossroads*), Tianjin People's Press, Beijing

Gerber, E. R. (1999) *The Populist Paradox: Interest Group Influence and the Promise of Direct Legislation*, Princeton University Press, Princeton, NJ

German, T. and Randell, J. (2004) 'World Aid Trends', *The Reality of Aid 2004: Focus on Governance and Human Rights*, www.realityofaid.org/roa.php

Gibelman, M. and Gelman, S. (2001) 'Very Public Scandals: Nongovernmental Organizations in Trouble', *Voluntas: International Journal of Voluntary and Nonprofit Organizations*, vol 12, no 1, pp49–66

Glidden, J. A. (2001) 'Election Monitoring, Technology and the Promotion of Democracy: A Case for International Standards', *Wisconsin International Law Journal*, vol 19, pp353–367

Global Reporting Initiative (2002) *Sustainability Reporting Guidelines 2002*, Global Reporting Initiative, Amsterdam

Goetz, A. M. and Jenkins, J. (2001) 'Hybrid Forms of Accountability: Citizen Engagement in Institutions of Public Sector Oversight in India', *Public Management Review*, vol 3, no 3, pp363–383

Goetz, A. M. and Jenkins, R. (2002) 'Voice, Accountability and Human Development, The Emergence of a New Agenda', UNDP Human Development Report Office, Occasional Paper, http://hdr.undp.org/docs/publications/background_papers/2002/Goetz-Jenkins_2002.pdf

Gordon Drabek, A. (ed) (1987) 'Development Alternatives: The Challenge for NGOs', Special issue of *World Development*, vol 15, supplement, Fall

Greaves, H. R. G. (1931) *The League Committees and World Order: A Study of the Permanent Expert Committees of the League of Nations as an Instrument of International Governance*, Oxford University Press, London

Gutman, A. (1998) *Membership and Morals*, Princeton University Press, Princeton, NJ

Hadiwinata, B. S. (2003) *The Politics of NGOs in Indonesia. Developing Democracy and Managing a Movement*, Routledge Curzon, London

Hadiz, V. R. (2003) 'Power and Politics in North Sumatra: The Uncompleted Reformasi', in Aspinall, E. and Fealy G. (eds) *Local Power and Politics in Indonesia*, Institute of Southeast Asian Studies, Singapore

HAP-I (Humanitarian Accountability Partnership International) (2003a) *Constitution*, HAP, Geneva

HAP-I (2003b) *Complaints Against Member Agencies: Procedures*, HAP, Geneva, December

HAP-I and WHO (2003) *Medical Ethics and Humanitarian Work, Report of a Round-table Discussion*, HAP, Geneva, October

Harmer, A. and Cotterrell, L. (2004) 'From Stockholm to Ottawa, a Progress Review of the Good Humanitarian Donorship Initiative', Humanitarian Policy Group, Overseas Development Institute, London

Held, D. and Archibugi, D. (1995) *Cosmopolitan Democracy: An Agenda for a New World Order*, Polity Press, Cambridge

Hidayat, H. (2003) *The Roles of NGOs in Decentralized Indonesian Development*, MA thesis, University of Hull, UK

Hirst, P. and Bader, V. (2001) *Associative Democracy: The Real Third Way*, Frank Cass, London & Portland, OR

Holloway, R. and Anggoro, K. (2000) *Civil Society, Citizens Organizations and the Transition to Democratic Governance in Indonesia*, Civil Society Support and Strengthening Program, USAID, Jakarta

Hufbauer, G. C. and Oegg, B. (2003) 'Beyond the Nation-State: Privatization of Economic Sanctions', *Middle East Policy*, vol 10, no 2, pp126–134

Human Rights in China (1998) *Bound and Gagged: Freedom of Association in China Further Curtailed under New Regulations*, Human Rights in China, Hong Kong and New York

Human Rights Watch (2000) 'An Unwarranted Role: State Control of Nongovernmental Organisations in Egypt', Briefing Paper prepared for Novib, Egypt Experts Meeting, Human Rights Watch, New York

Ibrahim, R. (2002) 'Mengapa NGO Membutuhkan Kode Etik' ('Why NGOs Need a Code of Ethics'), position paper prepared for the Program for the Formulation and Implementation of an NGO Code of Ethics and the Formation of NGOs Umbrella Organization, Jakarta, LP3ES

ICCR (Interfaith Center on Corporate Responsibility) (2005) 'Johnson & Johnson and Schering-Plough to Publicly Disclose All Political Contributions: Religious Investors Score Two Victories in Reform Effort as Four Other Pharmas Face Shareholder Resolutions Demanding Transparency', 7 April, www.iccr.org/news/press_releases/pr

ILO (1919) *Treaty of Versailles*, June 28, 1919, 225 Consol. T.S. 188, art. 389; Constitution of the International Labour Organization, www.ilo.org/public/english/about/iloconst

Imhof, A., Wong, S. and Bosshard, P. (2002) *Citizen's Guide to the World Commission on Dams*, International Rivers Network, Berkeley, CA

InterAction (2003) 'Natsios: NGOs Must Show Results; Promote Ties to U.S. Or We Will Find New Partners', *Monday Developments*, May 21, InterAction, Washington, DC,

International Council on Human Rights Policy (2002) *Beyond Voluntarism: Human Rights and the Developing International Legal Obligations of Companies*, ICHRP, Geneva

Irvin, R. (2005) 'State Regulation of Nonprofits: Accountability Regardless of Outcome', *Nonprofit and Voluntary Sector Quarterly* 34, vol 2, pp161–178

Isbister, J. (2001) *Capitalism and Justice: Envisioning Social and Economic Fairness*, Kumarian Press, Bloomfield, IN

Jepson, D. (2004) 'Review of a Lecture "The 21st Century NGO" given by John Elklington on February12, 2004 as part of the Green Power: Green Responsibility Lincare Lectures at Oxford University', Oxford University Press, Oxford

John Hopkins (John Hopkins University Institute for Policy Studies (1999) 'Definitions and Classifications of Non Profit Organizations: Uganda Memo', The Comparative Nonprofit Sector Project, www.jhu.edu/%7Ecnp/pdf/uganda.pdf

Johns, G. (2000) *NGO Way to Go: Political Accountability of Non-government Organizations in a Democratic Society*, www.ipa.org.au/publications

Johnson, M. (1990) 'Non-Governmental Organisations at the Crossroads in Indonesia', in Rice, R. C. (ed) *Indonesian Economic Development: Approaches, Technology, Small-Scale Textiles, Urban Infrastructure and NGOs*, Center for Southeast Asian Studies, Monash University, Melbourne, Australia

Jordan, L. (2004) 'The Importance of Rights to NGO Accountability', unpublished paper

Jordan, L. (2005) *Mechanisms for NGO Accountability*, GPPI Research Paper Series No. 3, Global Public Policy Institute, Berlin

Jordan, L. and van Tuijl, P. (2000) 'Political Responsibility in Transnational NGO Advocacy', *World Development*, vol 28, no 12, pp2051–2065

Kahn, P. L. (2003) *Evaluation Report: The Humanitarian Accountability Project Field Trial in Cambodia*, HAP, Geneva

Kaldor, M. (2003) *Global Civil Society: An Answer to War*, Polity Press, Cambridge

Kaplan, A. (2001) 'ActionAid Uganda Organizational Development Report', ActionAid Uganda, Kampala, Uganda

Kaufmann, D. and Kraay, D. (2002) *Growth without Governance*, World Bank, Washington, DC

Keane, J. (2003) *Global Civil Society?*, Cambridge University Press, Cambridge

Keck, M. and Sikkink, K. (1998) *Activists Beyond Borders*, Cornell University Press, New York

Khagram, S., Sikkink, K. and Riker, J. (eds) (2002) *Restructuring World Politics: Transnational Social Movements, Networks, and Norms*, University of Minnesota Press, Minneapolis, MN

King, L. A. (2003) 'Deliberation, Legitimacy, and Multilateral Democracy', *Governance*, vol 16, pp23–50

Kingsbury, B. (2002) 'First Amendment Liberalism as Global Legal Architecture: Ascriptive Groups and the Problems of the Liberal NGO Model of International Civil Society', *Chicago Journal of International Law*, vol 3, pp183–195

Klein, N. (2004) 'Democracy and Robbery', *The Guardian*, 10 February

Kovach, H., Neligan, C. and Burall, S. (2003) *The Global Accountability Report: Power without Accountability?*, One World Trust, London

Lasswell, H. D. and McDougal, M. S. (1997) *Jurisprudence for a Free Society*, New Haven Press, New Haven, CT

Latham, E. (1952) *The Groups Basis of Politics*, Cornell University Press, Ithaca, NY

Lawyers Committee for Human Rights (1997a) *The World Bank, NGOs and Freedom of Association: A Critique of the World Bank's Draft Handbook on Good Practices for Laws Relating to Non-Governmental Organizations*, Lawyers Committee for Human Rights, New York

Lawyers Committee for Human Rights (1997b) *The Neglected Right: Freedom of Association in International Human Rights Law*, Lawyers Committee for Human Rights, New York

Lister, S. (2003) 'NGO Legitimacy: Technical Issue or Social Construct?', *Critique of Anthropology*, vol 23, no 2, pp175–92

MacNeill, J. (2004) Correspondence to the editor of *Foreign Policy*, www.irn.org/programs/finance/index?id=sebastianmallaby/041013formerwb.html

Mallaby, S. (2004) *The World's Banker: A Story of Failed States, Financial Crises, and the Wealth and Poverty of Nations*, Penguin, New York

Manheim, G. B. (2003) 'Biz-War: Origins, Structure and Strategy of Foundation-NGO Network Warfare on Corporations in the United States', unpublished paper presented at the American Enterprise Institute Workshop, June, www.aei.org

Manin, B. (1997) *The Principles of Representative Government*, Cambridge University Press, Cambridge

Marks, S. (2001) 'Democracy and International Governance', in Coicaud, J. and Heiskanen, V. (eds) *The Legitimacy of International Organizations*, United Nations University Press, Tokyo, pp47–68

McAdam, D., McCarthy, J. D. and Zald, M. N. (eds) (1996) *Comparative Perspectives on Social Movements*, Cambridge University Press, Cambridge

McBride, J. (2003) 'International Law and Jurisprudence in Support of Civil Society', in *Enabling Civil Society: Practical Aspects of Freedom of Association*, Public Interest Law Initiative, New York and Budapest, pp22–81

McCarthy, P. (2002) 'A Thousand Flowers Blooming: Indonesian Civil Society in the Post-New Order Era', unpublished paper prepared for the World Bank Office in Indonesia, Ottawa/Jakarta, March

McCully, P. (2003) 'The Use of a Trilateral Network: An Activist's Perspective on the Formation of the World Commission on Dams', *American University International Law Review*, vol 16, no 6, pp1453–1475

McCully, P. (2004) 'Should International Advocacy NGOs Shut Up?', Twelfth Annual Hopper Lecture, University of Guelph, Ontario

McDougal, M. S. and Lasswell, H. D. (1959) 'The Identification and Appraisal of Diverse Systems of Public Order', *American Journal of International Law*, vol 53, pp1–29

McIvor, C. (2004) *Children's Feedback Committees in Zimbabwe: An Experiment in Accountability*, Save the Children, London

Melucci, A. (1996) *Challenging Codes*, Cambridge University Press, Cambridge

Mertus, J. (1995) 'From Legal Transplants to Transformative Justice: Human Rights and the Promise of Transnational Civil Society', *American University International Law Review*, vol 14, pp1335–1372

Meyer, C. (1992) 'A Step Back as Donors Shift Institution Building from the Public to the Private Sector', *World Development*, vol 20, no 8, pp1115–1126

Ministry of Finance, Planning and Economic Development (2004) 'Poverty Eradication Action Plan 2004/5–2007/8', Ministry of Finance, Planning and Economic Development, Kampala, Uganda

Minor, D. M. (2005) 'Dying While Waiting for the FDA to Act', *Wall Street Journal*, 15 April

Montúfar, C. (2005) 'Antipolítica, Representación y Participación Ciudadana', in *Ecuador/Debate*, vol 62, pp83–102

Mufti, I. (2000) 'Policy and Legal Framework for NGOs in Pakistan', paper prepared on behalf of the Pakistan NGO Forum for the Enabling Environment Seminar Legal Dimensions, The Hague, October 2–3

Mulgan, R. (2000) 'Accountability: An Ever-Expanding Concept?', *Public Administration*, vol 78, no 3, pp555–573

Muramuze, F. and Karnese, G. (2003) 'Geothermal Energy: A Hot Option for Uganda', *World Rivers Review*, vol 18, no 3, pp14–15

Murphy, S. D. (2005) 'Taking Multinational Corporate Codes of Conduct to the Next Level', *Columbia Journal of Transnational Law*, vol 43, pp389, 431–32

National Council on Responsive Philanthropy (2005) 'Reforming The United States Philanthropic Sector', www.ncrpl.mediastudio.tv/downloads/STATEMENT-04-05-StatementtoHouseWaysandMeans.pdf

Neligan, C., Blagescu, M. and Kovach, H. (2003) *An Overview of International Organizations and Their External Stakeholder Engagement*, One World Trust, London

Nyamugasira, W. (1998) 'NGOs and Advocacy: How Well Are the Poor Represented?', *Development in Practice*, vol 8, no 3, pp297–308

Nye, J. (2001) 'Globalization's Democratic Deficit: How to Make International Institutions More Accountable', *Foreign Affairs*, July/August, no 5, pp2–6

O'Connell, M. E. (2005) 'Enhancing the Status of Non-State Actors through a Global War on Terror', *Columbia Journal of Transnational Law*, vol 43, pp435–440

O'Donnell, G. (1994) 'Delegative Democracy', *Journal of Democracy*, vol 5, no 1, pp55–69

Ocaya, J. and Roden R. (2004) 'Re-thinking Participation: Poverty Reduction Strategy Paper', discussion paper shared within ActionAid International and wider civil society

OECD (Organisation for Economic Co-operation and Development) (2000) *OECD Guidelines for Multilateral Enterprises*, OECD, Paris

OECD (2003) 'Philanthropic Foundations and Development', *DAC Journal*, vol 4, no 3

Offe, C. (1985) 'The Attribution of Public Status to Interest Groups', in Offe, C. (ed) *Disorganized Capitalism*, MIT Press, Cambridge, MA, pp221–258

Offe, C. (1987) 'Challenging the Boundaries of Institutional Politics: Social Movements since the 1960s', in Charles S. Maier (ed) *Changing Boundaries of the Political: Essays on the Evolving Balance between the State and Society, Public and Private in Europe*, Cambridge, Massachusetts, Cambridge University Press, pp63–105

Okello, J. (2002) 'Museveni Warns Economic Saboteurs', *New Vision*, Kampala, Uganda, January 26

Oldfield, S. (2004) 'Sophy Sanger (1881–1950)', in Matthew, H. C. G. and Harrison B. (eds) *Oxford Dictionary of National Biography*, Oxford University Press, New York, p942

Ovsiovitch, J. O. (1998) 'Feeding the Watchdogs: Philanthropic Support for Human Rights NGOs', *Buffalo Human Rights Law Review*, vol 4, pp341–363

Pérez-Díaz, V. (1999) *Spain at the Crossroads: Civil Society, Politics and the Rule of Law*, Harvard University Press, Cambridge, MA

Perry, G. E., Arias, O. S., Lopez, J. H., Maloney, W. F. and Serven, L. (2006) *Poverty Reduction and Growth: Virtuous and Vicious Circles*, World Bank, Washington, DC

Peruzzotti, E. (2002) 'Toward a New Politics: Citizenship and Rights in Contemporary Argentina', *Citizenship Studies*, vol 6, no 1, pp77–93

Peruzzotti, E. and Smulovitz, C. (2002) 'Accountability Social, la otra cara del control', in Peruzzotti, E. and Smulovitz, C. (eds) *Controlando la política. Ciudadanos y Medios en las Nuevas Democracias Latinoamericanas*, Editorial Temas, Buenos Aires, pp23–52

Pettit, P. (forthcoming) 'Two-Dimensional Democracy, National and International', *The Monist*, www.iilj.org/papers/2005.8Pettit.htm

Pianta, M. (2001) 'Parallel Summits of Global Civil Society', in H. Anheier, M. Glasius and M. Kaldor (eds) *Global Civil Society*, Oxford University Press, Oxford

PIRAC (2002) *Investing in Ourselves: Giving and Fund Raising in Indonesia*, PIRAC, Jakarta

Pitkin, H. F. (1978) *The Concept of Representation*, University of California Press, Berkeley, CA

PIW (Public Interest Watch) (2004) 'Grabbing Huge Amounts of Public Money that Doesn't Belong to Them', www.publicinterestwatch.org

Pope Leo XII (1891) *Rerum Novarum* (On the Condition of Workers), www.vatican.va/holy_father

Przeworski, A., Stokes, S. C. and Manin, B. (eds) (1999) *Democracy, Accountability and Representation*, Cambridge University Press, Cambridge

Public Trust Standards for Chinese NPOs (2003) 'Zhongguo feiyingli zuzhi gongxin li biaozhun' ('Public Trust Standards for Chinese NPOs'), *NPO Tansuo* (*NPO Exploration*), December, back cover

Reimann, K. (2002) *International Politics, Norms and the Worldwide Growth of NGOs*, Harvard University Press, Boston, MA

Reinisch, A. (2001) 'Developing Human Rights and Humanitarian Law Accountability of the Security Council for the Imposition of Economic Sanctions', *American Journal of International Law*, vol 95, pp851–872

Rieff, D. (1999) 'The False Dawn of Civil Society', *The Nation*, February 2

Robert, E. (1999) 'A Social Watch Report on the Copenhagen Summit', The Development Network of Indigenous Voluntary Associations, Kampala

Robison, R. and Hadiz, V. (2004) *Reorganizing Power in Indonesia: The Politics of Oligarchy in an Age of Markets*, Routledge Curzon, London

Rutherford, K. R. (2000) 'A Theoretical Examination of Disarming States: NGOs and Anti-Personnel Landmines', *Journal of International Politics*, vol 37, pp457–477

Salamon, L. with Toepler, S. and Associates (1997) *The International Guide to Nonprofit Law*, John Wiley, New York

Sanger, S. (1920) 'Practical Problems of International Labour Legislation', in Solano, E. J. (ed) *Labour as an International Problem*, Macmillan, London

Satunama Foundation (2002) *Report of the Workshop on Increasing Quality of NGOs with Accreditation and Certification*, 4–6 November, Satunama Foundation, Yogyakarta

SBC and NAPE (2000) 'Memorandum to the World Bank', February 22, www.irn.org

Schattschneider, E. E. (1960) *The Semisovereign People: A Realist's View of Democracy in America*, Holt, Rinehart and Winston, New York

Schmitter, P. (2001) 'Parties Are Not What They Once Were', in Diamond, L. and Gunther, R. (eds) *Political Parties and Democracy*, Johns Hopkins University Press Baltimore and London, pp67–89

Schmitter, P. and Lehmbruch, G. (eds) (1979) *Trends Toward Corporatist Intermediation*, Sage Publications, London

Scholte, J. A. (2000) 'Global Civil Society', in Woods, N. (ed) *The Political Economy of Globalization*, Palgrave Macmillan, Basingstoke, pp173–201

Scholte, J. A. (2004) 'Civil Society and Democratically Accountable Global Governance', *Government and Opposition*, vol 39, pp211–230

Schweitz, M. L. (1995) 'NGO Participation in International Governance: The Question of Legitimacy', in *The Growing Role of Non-governmental Organizations*, Proceedings of the American Society of International Law, vol 89, pp413–415

Scott-Joynt, J. (2003) 'Charities in Terror Fund Spotlight', Global Policy Forum, 15 October, www.globalpolicy.org/ngos/credib/2003/1015terror.htm

Scott-Villiers, P. (2002) 'How the ActionAid Accountability, Learning and Planning System Emerged – The Struggle for Organizational Change', *Development in Practice*, vol 12, nos 3&4, pp424–435

Sebtongo, P. (2004) 'Workshop Report on the Stakeholders' Meeting on the Government of Uganda/Civil Society Organizations Partnership Policy', International Conference Centre, Kampala

Shang Yusheng and Cui Yu (2003) 'Zhongguo NPO Chengxin Fazhan Baogao' ('On Accountability Building of Chinese NPOs'), *NPO Tansuo (NPO Exploration)*, December, pp17–21

Shelton, D. (1994) 'The Participation of Non-governmental Organizations in International Judicial Proceedings', *American Journal of International Law*, vol 88, pp611–624

Sidel, J. (2004) *Watering the Flowers, Killing the Weeds: The Promotion of Local Democratization and Good Governance in Indonesia*, unpublished report to the Ford Foundation, Jakarta

Slim, H. (1997) 'Doing the Right Thing', *Studies on Emergencies and Disaster Relief*, no 6, Nordiska Afrika Institutet, Oslo

Slim, H. (2002) 'By What Authority? The Legitimacy and Accountability of Non-governmental Organisations', *Journal of Humanitarian Assistance*, www.jha.ac/articles

Spiro, P. J. (2002) 'Accounting for NGOs', *Chicago Journal of International Law*, vol 3, pp161–169

Stanley, A. P., Priyono, A. E. and Törnquist, O. (eds) (2003) *Indonesia's Post-Soeharto Democracy Movement*, DEMOS, Jakarta

Steering Committee of the Joint Evaluation of Emergency Assistance to Rwanda (1996) *Joint Evaluation of Emergency Assistance to Rwanda*, Copenhagen, March

Streetnet International (2006) 'Informal Economy Organizer Deported From Zimbabwe', Press Statement, 2 March, info@zctu.co.zw

Sudarbo, Y. O. (2002) *Performance Management of Non-Governmental Organizations: Case Study of NGOs in Indonesia*, MBA thesis, School of Public Policy, University of Birmingham, UK

Suryaningati, A. (2003) 'Tingkat "Kesehatan" Masyarakat Sipil: Petunjuk Penggunaan Indeks Masyarakat Sipil Civicus' ('The Level of "Health" of Civil Society, Guidelines for the Use of the Civicus Civil Society Index'), YAPPIKA, Jakarta

SustainAbility (2003) *The 21st Century NGO In the Market for Change*, SustainAbility, London

Tan Ailing (2003) 'Xiuding san da tiaoli banfa guifan wo guo NGOs de weilai, fang Minzheng Bu Minjian Zuzhi Guanliju Fu Juzhang Li Yong' ('Amending the Three Regulations and Measures to Regulate the Future of NGOs in China'), interview with Li Yong, Deputy Director General, Bureau of Civil Organizations, Ministry of Civil Affairs, *Ershiyi Shiji Jingji Baodao (21st Century Economic Reports)*, Beijing, 21 May

Tandon, R. (1989) *NGO-Government Relations: A Source of Life or a Kiss of Death?*, Society for Participatory Research in Asia, New Delhi

Tannenbaum, E. R. (1969) 'The Goals of Italian Fascism', *American Historical Review*, vol 74, pp1183, 1995–1201

Tarrow, S. (1994) *Power in Movement: Social Movements, Collective Action and Mass Politics in the Modern State*, Cambridge University Press, Cambridge

Tasch, E. and Viederman, S. (1995) 'New Concepts of Fiduciary Responsibility', in F. Capra and G. Pauli (eds) *Steering Business Toward Sustainability*, United Nations University Press, Tokyo, p125

Thompson, J. B. (2002) *Political Scandals: Media and Visibility in the Media Age*, Polity Press, Cambridge

Three Freedoms Project (1997) 'Why the World Bank's Handbook on Good Practices for Laws Related to Non-Governmental Organizations Should Not Be Released', Statement at World Bank/IMF Annual Meetings in Hong Kong, September 23

Three Freedoms Project (1998) 'Letter to James D. Wolfensohn', President of the World Bank, 1 October

Tulung, F. H. (2002) 'Membangun NGO yang Kuat, Demokratis dan Transparan: Perspektif Pemerintah' ('To Develop Strong, Democratic, and Transparent NGOs: A Government Perspective'), paper presented for the 'Seminar on the Development of Strong and Healthy NGOs, Democratic, Transparent and Accountable', Jakarta, 17 July

Uhlin, A. (1997) *Indonesia and the 'Third Wave' of Democratization: The Indonesian Pro-Democracy Movement in a Changing World*, Surrey, Curzon Press

Union of International Associations (2002) *The Year Book of International Organizations 2001/2002*, Saur, London

UN (United Nations) (1999) 'Declaration on the Right and Responsibility of Individuals, Groups and Organs of Society to Promote and Protect Universally Recognized Human Rights and Fundamental Freedoms', A. Res. 53/144, 8 March, United Nations, New York

UN (2002) *UN Handbook on Non-Profit Institutions in the System of National Accounts*, United Nations, New York

UN (2004) *We the Peoples: Civil Society, the United Nations and Global Governance*, Report of the Panel of Eminent Persons on United Nations–Civil Society Relations (known as the Cardoso Report), United Nations, New York

(UNDP) United Nations Development Programme (2003) *Millennium Development Goals: A Compact Among Nations to End Human Poverty, Human Development Report 2003*, UNDP, New York, http://hdr.undp.org/reports/global/2003

Vakil, A. (1997) 'Confronting the Classification Problem: Toward a Taxonomy of NGOs', *World Development*, vol 25, no 12, pp 2057–2070

Van Brabant, K. (2002) *Promoting Transparency and Accountability: Field Trial in Sierra Leone*, HAP, Geneva

Verweij, M. and Josling, T. E. (2003) 'Deliberately Democratizing Multilateral Organization', *Governance (special issue)*, vol 16, pp1–12

Vibert, F. (2003) *NGOs, Democratisation and the Regulatory State*, European Policy Forum, London

Viederman, S. (2002) 'Community Organizing and Shareholder Activity', www.foundationpartnership.org/articles/stevev4

Volker, T. and Timmer, K. (2002) 'Innovative Forms for Foundations: Investments in the Common Good' (Draft), International Network on Strategic Philanthropy, www.insp.efc.be/show.php

Wacana (1999) 'Masyarakat Sipil' ('Civil Society'), Wacana, Edisi 1, vol 1, Institute for Social Transformation (INSIST), Yogyakarta

Wallace, T. (2001) 'ActionAid Uganda Ten Year Country Review Report', ActionAid Uganda, Kampala, Uganda

Wallace, T. and Kaplan A. (2003) The Taking of the Horizon: Lessons from ActionAid Uganda's Experience of Changes in Development Practice, ActionAid, London

War on Want (2003) 'Mayday Colombia, British Education Workers Witness the Horror Faced by Colombian Teachers', www.waronwant.org

Watson, A. (2002) ' Jiaru WTO zhihou, Zhongguo de NPO ruhe shiying guoji guize?' ('How Can Chinese NPOs Adapt to International Standards upon China's Entry into the WTO?'), *Yanjiu Baogao Zhuankan (Journal of Research Reports)*, China NPO Network, no 14, March, pp11–13

WDM (World Development Movement) (2005) 'Past Campaigns, Tied Aid and Development', www.wdm.org.uk/campaigns/past/pergau

World Bank (1994) 'Republic of Uganda: The Role of Non-governmental Organizations and Community-Based Groups in Poverty Alleviation', Report No. 12262-UG, Eastern Africa Department, World Bank, Washington, DC

World Bank (1997) Handbook on Good Practices for Laws Relating to Non-Governmental Organizations – Discussion Draft, International Center for Not-for-Profit Law for the World Bank, Washington, DC

World Bank (2000/2001) 'World Bank–Civil Society Collaboration – Progress Report for Fiscal Years 2000 and 2001', http://siteresources.worldbank.org/CSO/Resources

World Bank (2006) World Bank Civil Society Engagement: Review of Fiscal Years 2002–2004, World Bank, Washington DC

WTO (World Trade Organization) (1994) 'Agreement on Technical Barriers to Trade, Annex 3: Code of Good Practice for the Preparation, Adoption and Application of Standards', WTO, Geneva, available at www.wto.org

WTO (World Trade Organization) (2005) *The Future of the WTO*, Report of the Consultative Board to the Director-General Supachai Panitchpakdi (known as the Sutherland Report), WTO, Geneva, www.wto.org/english/thewto_e/10anniv_e/10anniv_e.htm#future

Wu Zhongze and Chen Jinluo (eds) (1996) *Shetuan Guanli Gongzuo* (*Administration of Social Organizations*), Beijing, China Social Press

Xie Lihua (2002) 'Gongshang zhuce NGO mianlin de kunjing, cong Nong Jia Nü Wenhua Fazhan Zhongxin tanqi' ('The Dilemma of NGOs Registered at the Industrial and Commercial Bureau, a Case Study of Rural Women Knowing All Cultural Development Center'), *Yanjiu Baogao Zhuankan* (*Special Journal of Research Reports*), China NPO Network, no 16, pp14–16

Yan Mingfu with other signatories (2003) 'Zhongguo feiyingli zuzhi chengxin he hangye zilu huyushu' ('Letter of Appeal for Accountability and Self-Discipline Among Chinese NPOs'), NPO Tansuo (NPO Exploration), December, p54

YAPPIKA (Civil Society Alliance for Democracy) (2002) *Report of the Civil Society Assessment Program: Implementing the Index on Civil Society*, Civil Society Alliance for Democracy, Jakarta

Zailani, L. (2003) 'Membangun Perjuangan Terorganisir, Keadilan untuk Semua. Pengalaman Membangun Proses Kolektif Perempuan Pedesaan' ('The Development of Organized Efforts: Justice for All. The Experience of Developing a Collective Process of Rural Women'), paper presented at the National Workshop on Advocacy, People Empowerment and Accountability: Between Rights and Responsibilities of NGOs, Jakarta, 9–11 January

Zia, S. (1996) 'A Policy and Legal Framework for Non-Governmental Organizations', report prepared for UNDP, Islamabad, Aurat Publication and Information Service Foundation

Zullo, C. (2003) 'NGOs – Unlikely Targets of Azerbaijan's and Georgia's Wars on Terrorism', Central Asia-Caucasus Institute, Johns Hopkins University, www.cacianalyst.org

Acronyms and Abbreviations

AAIU	ActionAid International Uganda
ALNAP	Active Learning Network for Accountability and Performance in Humanitarian Action
ALPS	Accountability, Learning and Planning System
ALTERLAW	Alternative Law Research and Development Center, Inc.
APPC	Asia Pacific Philanthropic Consortium
BIR	Bureau of Internal Revenue
CBO	community-based organization
CIVICUS	World Alliance for Citizen Participation
CODE-NGO	The Caucus of Development NGO Networks
CRM	Civil Rights Movement
CSR	corporate social responsibility
CSO	civil society organization
CYDF	China Youth Development Foundation
DAC	Development Assistance Committee
DANIDA	Danish International Development Agency
DENIVA	Development Network of Indigenous Organizations
DFA	donor advised fund
DFID	Department for International Development
DOF	Department of Finance
ECOSOC	Economic and Social Council
EU	European Union
GAP	Global Accountability Project
GDP	gross domestic product
GONGO	government-organized non-governmental organization
HANet	Humanitarian Accountability Network
HAP-I	Humanitarian Accountability Project International
HRO	human rights organization
HRT	hormone replacement therapy
ICC	International Chamber of Commerce
ICCR	Interfaith Center on Corporate Responsibility
ICDRP	International Committee on Dams, Rivers and Peoples
ICFTU	International Confederation of Free Trade Unions
ICJ	International Court of Justice
ICNL	International Center for Not-for-Profit Law
IDP	internally displaced people
IFRC	International Federation of the Red Cross and Red Crescent Societies
IGO	intergovernmental organization
ILO	International Labour Organization
IMF	International Monetary Fund

INGO	international non-governmental organization
IRN	International Rivers Network
ISS	International Institute of Social Studies
IUCN	The World Conservation Union
JICA	Japan International Co-operation Agency
KPMM	Consortium for the Development of Civil Society
MBO	mutual benefit organization
MDG	Millennium Development Goal
NAPE	National Association of Professional Environmentalists
NAS	Neak Akphihat Sahakum
NGO	non-governmental organization
NPO	not-for-profit organization
NRM	National Resistance Movement
OECD	Organisation for Economic Co-operation and Development
OWT	One World Trust
PBO	public benefit organization
PCIJ	Permanent Court of International Justice
PCNC	Philippine Council for NGO Certification
PIW	Public Interest Watch
PRRP	Participatory Review and Reflection Process
PRSP	Poverty Reduction Strategy Paper
RTI	Research Triangle Institute
SAI	Social Accountability International
SBC	Save Bujagali Crusaders
SIDA	Swedish International Development Cooperation Agency
SWHR	Society for Women's Health Research
TBT	Technical Barriers to Trade
TNC	transnational corporation
TRIPS	Trade-Related Aspects of Intellectual Property Rights
ULA	Ugandan Land Alliance
UN	United Nations
UNDP	United Nations Development Programme
UNEP	United Nations Environment Programme
UNICEF	United Nations Children's Fund
UNSFIR	United Nations Support Facility for Indonesian Recovery
USAID	United States Agency for International Development
UWI	United Way International
WCD	World Commission on Dams
WDM	World Development Movement
WTO	World Trade Organization
WWF	World Wide Fund for Nature
YLBHI	Indonesian Legal Aid Foundation

Contributors

Dr Hans Antlöv has published several books on Indonesia and Southeast Asia. His most recent volume is *The Java that Never Was: Academic Theories and Political Practices*, edited with Jorgen Hellman and published by Lit Verlag in 2005. Antlöv was director of the Centre for East and Southeast Asian Studies at Göteborg University until January 1998, when he joined the Ford Foundation in Jakarta to develop a programme on governance and civil society. In 2005, he moved to the USAID-funded Local Governance Support Program in Jakarta.

Patricia Armstrong is an independent legal consultant specializing in international human rights and a part-time member of the staff of New York University's Center for Human Rights and Global Justice. After practicing law in New York City for 14 years, in 1988 she joined the staff of the Lawyers Committee for Human Rights (now Human Rights First), and from 1993 to 1999 headed its International Financial Institutions Program, focusing on the World Bank. She has degrees from the University of Nebraska and Washington University School of Law.

Dr Jem Bendell is a researcher, writer, educator and advisor on organizational strategy and relations for sustainable development. An Adjunct Professor of Management, and leading commentator on organizational responsibility, he has written over 40 publications. Director of the progressive professional services firm Lifeworth, Dr Bendell has worked with non-governmental organizations, intergovernmental organizations and international companies from 14 countries. His report *Debating NGO Accountability* is published by the United Nations Non-Governmental Liaison service in 2006.

Dr Agnès Callamard is the Executive Director of Article XIX, an international human rights organization working on freedom of expression. She has founded and led the Humanitarian Accountability Partnership International, the first international self-regulatory body for humanitarian agencies committed to strengthening accountability to disaster-affected populations. She is a former Chef de Cabinet for the Secretary General and Research Policy Coordinator for Amnesty International, and has conducted human rights investigations in a large number of countries in Africa, Asia and the Middle East. She has published broadly in the field of human rights, women's rights, refugee movements and accountability and holds a PhD in Political Science from the New School for Social Research in New York City.

Jennifer Chapman is a consultant and researcher with over 20 years experience in the development sector. She recently left the Impact Assessment Unit of ActionAid International, where, among other things, she coordinated an action research initiative with country programmes and partners in Brazil, Ghana, Nepal and Uganda on planning, learning and assessing advocacy work, on which the chapter in this book is based. The resulting manual, *Critical Webs of Power and Change*, has been published by ActionAid International. She is now working as a freelance consultant with a particular interest in deepening and supporting learning processes around North–South relationships, partnership and advocacy, including issues of power and gender.

Steve Charnovitz is Associate Professor of Law at George Washington University Law School. Before joining the Faculty, he practiced law at the firm now known as Wilmer Hale. Prior to that, he was Director of the Global Environment & Trade Study (GETS), which he helped to establish in 1994. In his earlier career, he was Policy Director of the US Competitiveness Policy Council and a Legislative Assistant to the Speaker of the US House of Representatives. Mr Charnovitz serves on the board of editors of several academic journals.

Phyllida Cox is an activist and researcher specializing in gender. She recently spent two years working in South America as an advocate on gender and trade issues. She is currently a post-graduate student at The African Gender Institute, University of Cape Town. She is undertaking anthropological fieldwork in urban townships on the cultural processes that inform both individual decision-making and government accountability with respect to reproductive health policy.

Dr Feng Li is Project Officer with the China Not-for-Profit Organizations Network.

Stephen Golub teaches International Development and Law at Boalt Hall Law School of the University of California at Berkeley, writes about development issues, and consults and conducts research for such organizations as the Ford Foundation, the Open Society Justice Initiative, the Carnegie Endowment for International Peace, the UK Department for International Development, the World Bank, the Asian Development Bank and UNDP. His professional foci include civil society, governance, social development, the rule of law, legal empowerment, legal services for the poor, non-state justice systems, gender, human rights, post-conflict situations, and monitoring and evaluation. Mr Golub's work in recent years spans 30 countries and all major regions.

Rustam Ibrahim has worked since 1976 with the *Lembaga Penelitian, Pendidikan dan Penerangan Ekonomi dan Sosial* (LP3ES – The Institute for Economic and Social Research, Education and Information), a national Indonesian NGO in Jakarta. He held various positions in the organization, including Executive Director (1993–1999), Senior Advisor (1999–2000) and Senior Research Associate, and is currently a member of the Board of Directors. He is one of the founders and members of the Advisory Board of the Indonesian Foundation to Strengthen Civil Society Participation (YAPPIKA). Since 2002, Mr Ibrahim has played a leading role in facilitating the formulation and implementation of a code of ethics/conduct for Indonesian NGOs.

Lisa Jordan is based in New York and serves as the Deputy Director of the Governance and Civil Society Unit at the Ford Foundation. Previous positions included serving as the Director for the Bank Information Center, a non-profit in Washington DC; directing the US component of the Global Legislators Organization for a Balanced Environment (GLOBE); acting as a legislative assistant to Congressman Jim Scheuer; and directing the multilateral development bank programme of BothEnds, a non-profit organization in The Netherlands. Ms Jordan graduated cum laude in 1992 with a Master's Degree in Development Studies from the Institute of Social Studies in The

Hague, The Netherlands. She has published articles on development, NGOs, the rise of global civil society, NGO accountability and the multilateral development banks.

Professor Kang Xiaoguang received his Master's Degree in Ecology from the Chinese Academy of Sciences in 1993. He is currently teaching at the School of Agricultural Economics and Rural Development, Renmin University of China (RUC). His main research areas are: poverty issues, state–society relations and the development of NGOs in contemporary China. He is the author of many books and articles, including *Benevolent Government (Ren Zheng): The Third Path of China's Political Development* (2005) and *A Study of Poverty Reduction Activities of NGOs* (2001).

Hetty Kovach is the Policy and Advocacy Officer for the European Network for Debt and Development (Eurodad). Prior to this she helped to devise and manage the One World Trust's Global Accountability Project, which assessed the accountability of international NGOs, intergovernmental organizations and multinational corporations. She has a BSc in Politics from Bristol University and a Master's Degree in Development Studies from the London School of Economics.

Professor Jassy B. Kwesiga is the Executive Secretary of the Development Network of Indigenous Voluntary Associations (DENIVA), a platform of Ugandan NGOs and CBOs to discuss development concerns and how to engage with the institutions and powers that impact on them. He holds a BSc (Economics) and a Masters of Education, both from London University. Prior to his current work, he taught at Makerere University's Institute of Adult and Continuing Education. He left at the rank of Associate Professor. Professor Kwesiga has written extensively on governance and civil society issues and held a number of positions in different organizations working on literacy and adult education, rural development, and advocacy and capacity building for civil society.

Juliette Majot became an activist during her teens as part of a successful grassroots effort to halt construction of a Westinghouse nuclear reactor along the shore of Lake Michigan, Indiana. She later served as Deputy Director of Friends of the Earth US, and Executive Director of the Berkeley-based International Rivers Network. She was a co-founding editor of *BankCheck Quarterly*, dedicated to reporting the policies and practices of the World Bank and the International Monetary Fund. She has written and spoken extensively on the role of international financial institutions in perpetuating poverty, poor governance, environmental destruction and human rights violations.

Harriet Namisi holds a BA (Social Sciences) from Makarere University in Kampala, Uganda, and an MA in Rural Sociology and Community Development from the University of Nairobi, Kenya. She is the Program Coordinator for Communications and Advocacy in the Development Network of Indigenous Voluntary Associations (DENIVA). Previously, she worked as a manager of community-based training for a private company and as a project coordinator for the National Association for Women Organizations in Uganda (NAWOU).

Sarah Okwaare is an activist and researcher with a longstanding interest in participatory research, evaluation and learning. Currently she is the Impact Assessment and Shared Learning Manager for ActionAid International Uganda. Previously, she was Manager of Action Research, a project that pioneered the development of methodologies and frameworks for assessing policy and advocacy work in Africa for ActionAid International, and co-authored the resulting manual, *Critical Webs of Power and Change* (2006). She has an MA in Gender and Development Studies and a BA in Political Science.

Enrique Peruzzotti is a professor of Political Science at Di Tella University in Buenos Aires. He has co-edited *Enforcing the Rule of Law: Social Accountability in Latin America* (2006) and published numerous articles on democratization, civil society and accountability. He is a former resident fellow at the Woodrow Wilson Center and has held visiting positions at the American University of Paris, FLACSO Ecuador, Columbia University, Cornell University, University of New Mexico, the Federal University of Minas Gerais and the University of London.

Peter van Tuijl has over twenty years of experience working on NGO capacity-building, governance and accountability issues. He has been employed by Novib (now Oxfam Netherlands) and UNDP. He is based in Jakarta and works as Senior Technical Advisor for a project to combat corruption in the Indonesian National Police, supported by the US Department of Justice. He has a Master's Degree in Modern Asian History from the University of Amsterdam and has published a number of articles on the role of NGOs, transnational civil society, accountability and human rights, as well as on social and political developments in Indonesia.

Index

Join our
online community
and help us save paper and postage!

www.earthscan.co.uk

By joining the Earthscan website, our readers can benefit from a range of exciting new services and exclusive offers. You can also receive e-alerts and e-newsletters packed with information about our new books, forthcoming events, special offers, invitations to book launches, discussion forums and membership news. Help us to reduce our environmental impact by joining the Earthscan online community!

How? – Become a member in seconds!

>> Simply visit **www.earthscan.co.uk** and add your name and email address to the sign-up box in the top left of the screen – You're now a member!

>> With your new member's page, you can subscribe to our monthly **e-newsletter** and/or choose **e-alerts** in your chosen subjects of interest – you control the amount of mail you receive and can unsubscribe yourself

Why? – Membership benefits

✔ Membership is free!

✔ 10% discount on all books online

✔ Receive invitations to high-profile book launch events at the BT Tower, London Review of Books Bookshop, the Africa Centre and other exciting venues

✔ Receive e-newsletters and e-alerts delivered directly to your inbox, keeping you informed but not costing the Earth – you can also forward to friends and colleagues

✔ Create your own discussion topics and get engaged in online debates taking place in our new online Forum

✔ Receive special offers on our books as well as on products and services from our partners such as *The Ecologist, The Civic Trust* and more

✔ Academics – request inspection copies

✔ Journalists – subscribe to advance information e-alerts on upcoming titles and reply to receive a press copy upon publication – write to info@earthscan.co.uk for more information about this service

✔ Authors – keep up to date with the latest publications in your field

✔ NGOs – open an NGO Account with us and qualify for special discounts

Join now?
Join Earthscan now!
name
surname
email address

Earthscan Member
[Your name]

Click to Change

My profile
My forum
My bookmarks
All my pages

www.earthscan.co.uk

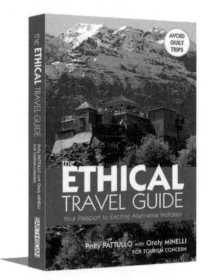